## *About the Author*

AUSTIN MURPHY is a senior writer at *Sports Illustrated*. He has been on staff there since 1984. Murphy lives in northern California with his wife and their two young children.

## ALSO BY AUSTIN MURPHY

Nonfiction

*How Tough Could It Be?*
*The Sweet Season*

# SATURDAY RULES

## Why College Football Outpasses, Outclasses, and Flat-Out Surpasses the NFL

# AUSTIN MURPHY

HARPER

NEW YORK • LONDON • TORONTO • SYDNEY

HARPER

Portions of this book have originally appeared in different form in *Sports Illustrated.*

A hardcover edition of this book was published in 2007 by Harper, an imprint of HarperCollins Publishers.

FIRST HARPER PAPERBACK PUBLISHED 2008.

*Designed by Renato Stanisic*

The Library of Congress has catalogued the hardcover edition as follows:

Murphy, Austin.
   Saturday rules : a season with Trojans and Domers (and Gators and Buckeyes and Wolverines) / Austin Murphy.—1st ed.
     p.  cm.
  ISBN: 978-0-06-137577-4
  ISBN-10: 0-06-137577-2
  1. Football—United States.  2. University of Notre Dame—Football.
3. University of Southern California—Football.  I. Title.
  GV940.M87  2007
  796.332'63—dc22                    2007021365

ISBN 978-0-06-137579-8 (pbk.)

08  09  10  11  12  DIX/RRD  10  9  8  7  6  5  4  3  2  1

To my father, J. Austin Murphy Jr.: former Colgate "end" who also sang in the Thirteen; who never made a bad snap as a single-wing center at St. Joe's Prep in Buffalo, New York, nor missed an opportunity to remind us of that fact. Rex, you rule.

# CONTENTS

# Prologue

I come not to praise Pete Carroll, but to bury him.

What else is there to do, really? It's halftime of the 2007 Rose Bowl, and I am marshaling synonyms for "decline." I am casting about for different ways to say that the Carroll Era at the University of Southern California is over, finito, kaput, deceased. It was fun while it lasted.

On New Year's Day, 2007, I am one of 94,000 souls at the Rose Bowl, a venue the Trojans had transformed, under their manic, mop-topped head coach, into a kind of home away from home, an annex to the L.A. Coliseum. Over the past year, however, this grand and glamorous old showground has become an open-air sepulcher for USC's national championship hopes.

The once-dynastic Trojans, winners of 52 of their last 57 games, owners of two national championships, plodded through much of the 2006 season on clay feet. Bereft of quarterback Matt Leinart and his Mercury-and-Mars tailback tandem of Reggie Bush and LenDale White, hobbled by injuries to key players—including the first-, second- and third-string fullbacks—the USC offense in 2006 was a halting, hiccuping, sclerotic shell of its former self. The periodic scoring binges orchestrated by first-year quarterback

John David Booty proved the exception, rather than the rule. With every false start, each three-and-out, Southern California squandered a little more of the mystique that in the not-so-distant past had some teams beaten before they stepped off the bus.

Coming off a game in which they put up all of seven points, a loss to UCLA that knocked them out of the national title game and flung open the door for Florida, the Trojans are proving to a national TV audience that there's plenty more offensive slapstick where that came from. They've mustered all of three points in the first half against the Wolverines, who have mirrored their struggles on offense. The halftime score is 3-all.

After winning 44 of 45 games between October 12, 2002, and December 3, 2005—a span that included two national championships—the Trojans have now dropped three of their last 13, and are staring down the possibility of a fourth defeat. If 'SC were a stock, it would be past time to sell. That would have been my rundown on this once-great outfit, if not for one minor occurrence.

They played the second half.


DURING A TENSE halftime exchange, we will later learn, Lane Kiffin and Steve Sarkisian pleaded with Carroll to allow them to throw the running game overboard. Offensive coordinator Kiffin and assistant head coach Sarkisian—SarKiffian, as they are known—share play-calling duties. The head man comes around to their way of thinking on 'SC's first drive of the second half, as the Trojans gain zero yards on consecutive rushes, forcing a punt. Fine, he tells SarKiffian. Air it out. Do what you need to do.

Like Julia Roberts dumping Lyle Lovett, the Trojans abandon the run, and discover something about themselves. They learn that when the offensive line gives quarterback John David Booty time, when the fullback figures out whom he is supposed to block, and when Booty refrains from throwing the ball into the outstretched palms of opposing defensive linemen, this offense is capable of engineering the sort of serial big plays that hold their own beside the pyrotechnics engineered by Leinart, or Carson Palmer before him.

One of the more irresistible songs played by the Spirit of Troy marching band throughout the 2006 season was a drum-heavy number that would read, if anyone wrote the lyrics:

*BOOTYbootybootybootybootybootybooty,*
*Rockin' everywhere! Rockin' everywhere!*

(Repeat until TV time-out ends.)

The song is catchy and welcome for several reasons: (1) It's eminently danceable; (2) It is relatively fresh, for the simple reason that the Trojan marching band has not played it roughly one hundred times every autumn Saturday for the last century; (3) It is, in the second half against Michigan, highly relevant. Booty is rockin' everywhere, gouging the Wolverines for big chunks of yardage almost every time he cocks his arm to throw. The redshirt junior shreds Michigan for four touchdowns and 289 yards in the second half, while the Trojans defense continues to treat Wolverines quarterback Chad Henne like its own personal piñata (Henne will be sacked six times). By the time the game is over—a 32–18 Trojans win—Southern California has announced to the college football cosmos that reports of its demise have been greatly exaggerated.

The 2007 Rose Bowl has been entertaining and revealing— seeming to suggest that the lords of the Big Ten remain unable to match the speed of the teams from warmer climes. (More light will be shed on this trend a week later, when the Gators take on highly favored Ohio State in the national title game.)

But the Rose Bowl is not the best game of college football's postseason. Indeed, it is not even the best game of the day.

A time zone away, in the Phoenix suburb of Glendale, in a newly minted domed stadium that calls to mind nothing quite so much as an almost-ready batch of Jiffy Pop popcorn, a mismatch is brewing.

. . . .

THE OKLAHOMA SOONERS ached to prove that they were a Top 5 team, never mind their two losses. They'd weathered multiple tempests: the preseason banishment of their starting quarterback; a screw-job from Pac-10 officials that cost them a victory at Oregon; the loss of the nation's top running back, Adrian Peterson, who'd snapped his collarbone in mid-October. But the Sooners had regrouped and rallied to win the Big Twelve. With Peterson finally recovered, Oklahoma intended to remind the Republic that they were not so far removed from the mighty Sooner squads that reached three national title games between 2000 and '03. They could make their point in the Fiesta Bowl by blowing out the poor, overmatched Broncos of Boise State.

As widely predicted, the score got lopsided in a hurry. Sick and tired of hearing how they had no business in one of these top-shelf BCS bowls, the Broncos mugged the Big Twelve champions the moment they stepped out of the tunnel. Boise State led 14–0 early, 21–10 at the half, and 28–10 with just over five minutes to play in the third quarter, when the equilibrium in big-time college football seemed to reestablish itself. A Broncos turnover led to 25 unanswered points, resulting in a 35–28 Oklahoma lead with 17 seconds left in regulation. And this is where the 2006 college football season stepped through the looking glass. This is where Broncos quarterback Jared Zabransky, ignoring torn rib cartilage he incurred while being sacked two plays earlier, looked to the sideline on fourth and forever. There was his backup, Taylor Tharp, pantomiming the act of juggling. Why juggling? I would ask Zabransky after the season.

"You know, like in a circus," he replied. "The play is called Circus."

That description understates the implausibility, the outrageousness, of the action that unspooled as I navigated my way from the Rose Bowl back to my hotel in West L.A. While I focused on not missing any turnoffs—merging from the 134 to the 2 to the 5 to

110 to the 10—ESPN Radio's Ron Franklin did his damnedest to keep listeners abreast of the increasingly surreal goings-on in what was shaping up to be one of the greatest games in the history of what is, to my mind, our nation's greatest sport.

FROM 1994 THROUGH '98, I covered the NFL for *SI*. "Yeah, I know who you are," Cowboys guard Nate Newton informed me one afternoon, when I reintroduced myself. "You're that preppy motherf____r from *Sports Illustrated*."

I made plenty of friends in the league, including Nate, who became one of my go-to guys, and to whom my heart went out when they sent him away to federal prison in 2001 for dealing massive amounts of marijuana. Nate might empathize when I describe my NFL tenure as a block of hard time.

My NFL period has been book-ended by four- and six-year stints covering the college game. I've made multiple pilgrimages to South Bend and Ann Arbor; East Lansing and Columbus; Coral Gables and Tallahassee; Tuscaloosa, Auburn, and Oxford; Norman and Lincoln; Corvallis and Eugene. I've been to 'SC so many times that I can tell you the names of the original Wild Bunch, the members of the late-1960s defensive line immortalized by a bronze statue outside Heritage Hall. (One of them is Al Cowlings, who played in the NFL, but achieved greater fame years later as a chauffeur.)

I've been to State College, College Station (where I attended Texas A&M's midnight yell practice), and Collegeville, Minnesota. There, in a setting suspiciously similar to Lake Wobegon, I've chronicled the feats of the incomparable John Gagliardi, head coach at Division III powerhouse St. John's. While smaller than D-III by two thirds, Division I remains sprawling and unwieldy: 118 programs employing a casserole of different schemes, from the triple-option favored by the service academies to the flexbone-based orbit sweeps of Wake Forest to the spread option Urban Meyer was criticized for bringing to Florida. ("We don't hear that [criticism] much anymore," he noted toward the end of last season.) It is a cornucopia of singular traditions, a menagerie of living, breathing animal mascots; an arm-long list of ancient blood grudges. It is, in all its variegated splendor, the antidote to the corporate, clinical NFL, where the grail is parity, and a head coach needs a special waiver from the league to wear a suit on the sideline. Indeed, college football is the opposite of the pinched, unsmiling bureaucratic No Fun League, which last January put the kibosh on a church's plans to use a wall projector to show the Colts-Bears Super Bowl game, tut-tutting that it would violate copyright laws. This after announcing that, for security reasons, there would be no tailgating within a mile of Dolphin Stadium on Super Sunday. (Because, really, how do we *know* those are charcoal briquettes?) In the weeks after the big game, it came to light that the NFL was seeking to trademark the phrase "the Big Game." By using the phrase to attract patrons to their establishments for the Super Bowl, a league spokesman complained, these scofflaws were diluting "the value of the Super Bowl and our ability to sell those rights to our partners."

Oh yeah. I want to party with these guys.

WHERE THE NFL is corporate and inconstant—with players and, every so often, *entire franchises* skipping town—college football is steeped as deeply in tradition as the "corny dogs" (and Snickers bars and cheese curds and alligator cubes) are immersed in cooking oil at the Texas State Fair, site of the Cotton Bowl and the Texas-Oklahoma game (a.k.a. Red River Rivalry, née Red River Shootout), a game first played in 1900, when Oklahoma was still a territory, not a state.

If, like me, you've ever sat down to interview such mirthless droids as Tom Coughlin or Marty Schottenheimer; if you've ever been chewed out by such monomaniacs as Bill Parcells, Mike Shanahan, and Don Shula (I know he's a legend, but he was a cranky old SOB to me); if you've ever glanced despairingly at your watch, wondering why time has slowed to a crawl during one of Paul Tagliabue's beyond-arid Super Bowl–week State of the League addresses, you'd know that something happens to these guys when they get to the NFL. The joy is sucked out of the game for them as if by Dementors.

For sports columnists, one of the gifts that kept on giving in 2006 was the story of malfeasant Bengals. Nine Cincinnati players were arrested for a medley of misdeeds: burglary, spousal abuse, resisting arrest, operating motor vehicles—cars *and* boats—under the influence.

Nor could journalists ignore the travails of misunderstood leviathan Tank Johnson, the Chicago Bears defensive tackle and stalwart champion of the Second Amendment. Not quite six weeks after playing in the 41st Super Bowl (feel free to join me in a boycott of the League's self-important use of Roman numerals), Johnson began serving a 120-day sentence for a probation violation. Earlier in the season, police had raided his home and found six firearms, including two assault rifles. (He'd pled guilty to a misdemeanor gun charge earlier in his career, making this latest arrest a probie violation.)

And then there was Pacman Jones, the exceptionally gifted, exceptionally dimwitted Tennessee Titans cornerback whose apparent ambition it was to single-handedly break the Bengals record for arrests. In less than three years with the Titans, he'd been interviewed ten times by police, who saw fit to arrest him on five of those occasions.

The most recent of those was the most serious. During the NBA's All-Star Weekend in Las Vegas, Jones and his retinue arrived at a gentlemen's club with a trash bag filled with $81,000. They proceeded to shower the dancers with dollar bills, a pastime known to strip joint connoisseurs as "making it rain."

The flurry of legal tender led to a free-for-all that ended in the shooting of three people: one patron and two security guards, one of whom suffered a severed spinal cord.

Following the League, I am depressed by the malfeasance off

the field ("Altercation with bouncers" . . . "Police found an unregistered handgun in the glove compartment" . . . "his second strike in the NFL's substance abuse policy") and the lack of creativity on it. Have you noticed how similar NFL offenses are?

"They could change uniforms at halftime," says Chester Caddas, a retired college coach we will meet in chapter 5, "and you wouldn't know the difference. I just don't enjoy it. Unless a really good friend is coaching, I don't watch [the NFL]. I'd rather watch replays of SEC games. Or the Food Channel."

The two most breathtaking offensive performances of the last college football season took place one week apart in January. What did they have in common? They featured coaches unafraid to go against the grain. The stunning upsets of Boise State over Oklahoma and Florida over Ohio State resulted from the application of what football coach and prolific author John T. Reed calls the "principles of contrarianism."

Contrarianism requires originality of thought, and freedom from fear of being criticized, should the scheme not work. It was manifest in Boise State's ballsalicious (coinage: Jon Stewart) use of legerdemain in the Fiesta Bowl, and Florida's dizzying array of motions, unbalanced lines, and the option in the national title game. As Reed observes, the higher up football's food chain you go, the less of this courage you see. The result: a homogeneity and poverty of imagination that neither the bluster of John Madden nor the logorrhea of Joe Theismann can conceal.

"I'm all for giving each team an equal chance to win with regard to spending limits and the draft," Reed writes. "However, when parity takes the form of uniformity of offensive tactics and strategy, it is not entertaining at all. It is boring."

DIVISION I COLLEGE football can be a cold business in its own right. Still, for all its pathologies and imbalances—the embarrassing graduation rates of players at certain schools; the lack of black men in head coaching positions; the inequitable loot-grab that is the Bowl Championship Series—there is an undeniable beauty to its landscape, and I'm not just talking about the USC Song Girls, or the chaps worn by the gifted young women comprising the Texas Pom Squad. This sport, more than a century old, comes with a pageantry and passion that is simply not found in other games. It is talismans and rituals: Clemson players touching Howard's Rock before descending into Death Valley, 'SC players tapping "Goux's Gate" before each practice, Notre Dame's fans lighting candles in the Grotto.

College football tradition is the undergraduates at Ole Miss donning evening wear to tailgate in The Grove, those ancient oaks throwing shade outside Vaught-Hemingway Stadium. (To embark on a stroll through The Grove before kickoff is to be reminded that not all the talent is on the field. Of course college football is selling sex; it just goes about it with more subtlety than the NFL, many of whose cheerleaders look like they should be pole-dancing at Scores.)

College football tradition is the slightly less genteel atmosphere of the Red River Shootout, where I once spotted a woman in the crimson T-shirt bearing the legend, You Can't Spell Slut Without U-T. It is the coaches at Hawaii wearing leis on the sideline, the students at Missouri toppling the uprights after a big win and bearing them to a Columbia watering hole named Harpo's. It's the Volunteer Navy, a flotilla of boats up to 90 feet long that dock on the Tennessee River, a mile or so from Neyland Stadium. It's a set of rites and customs so disparate that they could not be contained, you would think, by a single sport.

While the NFL has its share of rivalries, they have been sapped of vitality by conference realignment and free agency. (While providing a windfall for the athletes, the movement of players from team to team has reduced today's fans, in the words of one NFL writer I know, to "rooting for laundry." It has also compelled them to create their own teams, in "fantasy" leagues whose toll on the American economy, in terms of lost productivity, is incalculable.) Sunday's rivalries lack the pedigree and passion of Saturday's historic feuds. College football features showdowns predating World War I—teams clashing for such whimsically named trophies as the Old Oaken Bucket and Floyd of Rosedale, a bronzed swine that goes to the winner of the Wisconsin-Minnesota tilt. College football features long-simmering feuds that are border disputes and culture clashes, all at once. Two of those—Florida-Georgia and Texas-Oklahoma—engender so much hostility that they must be played in neutral settings. When Gerald Ford emerged from the Cotton Bowl tunnel for the coin flip before the 1976 Red River Shootout, he was accompanied by Oklahoma head coach Barry Switzer and his Longhorns counterpart, Darrell Royal. As the former later recalled, "Some redneck from Oklahoma stands up and shouts, 'Who are those two assholes with Switzer?' "

Such coarseness is considered beneath the principles of the nation's oldest, coolest intersectional rivalry. When you get past the O.J. references on the one side and the prophylactic jokes on the other (TROJANS BREAK, reminds the perennial Domer T-shirt), Notre Dame–USC is as much long-distance mutual admiration society as it is a rivalry.

There are few better marquee matchups than the battle for the Shillelagh, the jeweled Gaelic war club at stake when Notre Dame and Southern California knock heads. College football, always interesting, is more compelling by a degree of magnitude when the Irish are relevant. Under Charlie Weis, the Falstaffian, flat-topped second-year head coach, their mojo is back in a big way. Weis may look like a guy who just took off his tool belt, but the truth is, he is scary smart. He and Bill Belichick were the big brains behind the New England Patriots' three Super Bowl victories. The Irish last won a national title in 1988 under the lisping autocrat Lou Holtz. While the program had flashes of glory under Bob Davie (1997–2001) and Ty Willingham (2002–2004), the failure of the Fighting Irish to seriously contend for a national championship since the days of Holtz seemed to signal a decline, an entropy, which, on account of the university's stringent admissions standards, appeared irreversible.

Bull*shit*, said Weis, who took the same players Willingham went 6-6 with in 2004 and coached them to a 9-2 record and a $14.5 million Fiesta Bowl payday in his first season as a head coach. He followed that up by signing a Top 10 recruiting class—this after the Irish had repeatedly finished outside the Top 20. Notre Dame would enter the 2006 season with an explosive offense and a No. 2 AP ranking.

The Trojans, meanwhile, had worked their way to the cusp of college football history at the end of the 2005 season. They were 17 seconds from becoming the first team ever to finish atop the AP poll for three years running. But a force of nature named Vince Young single-handedly redirected that history, giving the Longhorns their first national title in 35 years.

Carroll responded to the most gut-wrenching loss of his career by reeling in the nation's top recruiting class (for the third time in four years), after which adversity began raining down: Bush's parents stood accused of living for a year, rent-free, in a $775,000 home, on the dime of a character trying to steer them to a San Diego–based agent. The *L.A. Times* reported that the Leinart family subsidized the rent of Matt's apartment-mate, All-American receiver Dwayne Jarrett. Eleven USC players were taken in the 2006 NFL draft, including Bush and fellow tailback LenDale White. Leinart's heir, John David Booty, underwent back surgery and missed spring practice.

As always Carroll played alchemist, transforming adversity into opportunity; convincing his players that they could play loose, because they had nothing *to* lose; that they were being written off, counted out, disrespected. The truth is, they remained the most talented team in the Pac-10 and one of the three best in the country.

Truths that seemed unassailable at the start of the 2006 season—*Rutgers will never win big; Ohio State is in a class by itself*—would prove as leaky as the Notre Dame secondary. Little wonder that college football delivers more upsets than the pro game. It is wilder and woollier; more passionate, less predictable—like young love. Even if collegians are fed at training tables and nudged to do their homework by tutors provided by the athletic department, even if it strains credulity to call many of them "student athletes," they are, at the end of the week, still muscle-bound postadolescents who do not, technically, do this for a living. The NCAA limits the amount of time they can spend on football to 20 hours a week. Football may be their job, but it's not their only job. They are between 18 and 22 years old. They've got classes, they've got girlfriends, they've got brains that are not yet fully formed. I am thinking, in this case, of the star wide receiver at Utah who—speaking of young love—was suspended a few years ago for shoplifting condoms. Hey, the guy meant well.

Like Reggie Bush in the 2006 Rose Bowl.

I was sitting at a bar in Boulder with first-year Colorado coach Dan Hawkins a month after that game. (I was drinking alone: The Hawk does not imbibe in public, although he may have revisited that policy after winning two games the following season.) I mentioned Bush's most memorable play in it. With his team ahead of Texas by a touchdown, the Trojans' All-Cosmos tailback capped off a long run with a bonehead play that will rank right up there with Bill Buckner's boot. As a pair of tacklers converged, Bush lateraled to a walk-on teammate who, not surprisingly, could not keep up with him. The ball ended up on the ground, and Texas recovered. The Trojans lost momentum, and, eventually, the national title.

Bush had been pilloried for that gaffe, so I felt safe piling on. But Hawkins wrongfooted me. "You know what?" he said. "I *liked* that he did that. He's out there cutting it loose. I tell my guys: We're not on this earth for very long. You've got to get out there and sing your song. Do your dance."

Bush had famously shoved Leinart through the plane of the goal line at Notre Dame on October 15, 2005, a day in college football featuring more dramatic endings than the *Riverside Shakespeare.* You had Michigan's Chad Henne (a native Pennsylvanian) ruining Penn State's undefeated season with a last-second touch-

down pass to Mario Manningham. There was Louisville, cough-
ing up a 17-point third-quarter lead, only to lose to West Virginia
in triple overtime, 46–44. And that was the afternoon Minnesota
punter Justin Kucek endured the lowest moment of his career.
With the Gophers ahead by four points in the final minute against
Wisconsin, Kucek fumbled a snap. Rather than calmly take a
safety, which would've sealed the win, he tried to get the kick off.
It was blocked; the Badgers recovered the ball in the end zone,
winning the game and retaining a certain bronzed swine.

I come not to bury Kucek, but to embrace him, to elevate him
as an example of why fall Saturdays pack more wackiness and
drama than the 14 or so games they play the next day. These guys
don't fully realize they are cogs in a multibillion-dollar business.
They still think they're playing a game. They're still singing their
song, still "trailing clouds of glory." That, at least, is how Hawkins's
fellow romantic, William Wordsworth, once described the innocence that attends youth—an innocence that we lose by adulthood,
provoking the poet to ask:

> *Wither is fled the visionary gleam?*
> *Where is it now, the glory and the dream?*

Hint: you won't find it at the Meadowlands.

# CHAPTER 1

# Irish Eyes

ugust 11, South Bend, Ind. —I feel His gaze. I feel those granite eyes on me before I turn to meet them. Making my unhurried way across the Notre Dame campus on a still August evening, heading east on a thoroughfare named for one Moose Krauss, I am captivated, as usual, by the monument to my right, the tan-bricked colossus that is Notre Dame Stadium. I've covered huge games in this old bowl: Notre Dame's upset of top-ranked, Charlie Ward–led Florida State in 1992; its near misses against Nebraska in 2000 and 'SC last season—the Bush Push game. But my most vivid memories tend to be small-bore and personal. Playing catch with Raghib Ismail during a 1990 photo shoot. Chatting on the grass with Bobby Bowden on the eve of that upset in 1992. Seeing the

**AP PRESEASON TOP 10***

1. *Ohio State*
2. *Notre Dame*
3. *Texas*
4. *Auburn*
5. *West Virginia*
6. *USC*
7. *Florida*
8. *LSU*
9. *California*
10. *Oklahoma*

---

* Note to readers: Each chapter will begin with a list of that week's Top 10 teams, as ranked by the Associated Press. Starting in mid-October, with the release of the first BCS rankings, we will switch to that poll.

Trojans react to the savannah-length grass the groundskeeper prepared for the visitors in 2005. ("Do you think they might be trying to slow us down?" inquired Frostee Rucker, feigning shock.)

And I remember Notre Dame's comeback win over Boston College 20 years ago. Fueled by flanker Tim Brown's 294 all-purpose yards, the Irish rallied from a 25–12 second-half deficit. What success Notre Dame had running the ball that day, according to the lore of my family, it earned by attacking the *left* side of the Eagles' line, away from starting defensive tackle Mark Murphy. (I have since told Brown, who won the 1987 Heisman Trophy, that he owes my brother at least a thank-you note.)

Less than a year after that 32–25 Irish victory, I was back on campus, reporting a preseason cover story on the resurgent Fighting Irish, when my mother phoned with news that Mark had been cut by the Detroit Lions.

"That's a shame," sympathized Lou Holtz, with whom I shared the news, and who graciously feigned a recollection of No. 67 of the BC Eagles. "Your brother's a fine football player."

This being Holtz, the word "brother's" came out "brutherth." As well documented as the coach's lisp is the fact that he could be a son-of-a-bitch on the practice field, a saliva-spritzing martinet whose players referred to him as "Lou-cifer." His sideline histrionics used to get on my nerves, as did his compulsion to inflate the upcoming opponent into the second coming of the 1985 Chicago Bears—"They've got a lot of great athletes at Navy; they do some things very well"—while reflexively poor-mouthing his own more talented outfit.

These quibbles amount to a modest pile beside the mountain of reasons to admire and respect the man who may have been the most charisimatic coach of his generation. Certainly none of his peers was handier with the one-liner. (When an apoplectic Woody Hayes shouted at the 1969 Rose Bowl, *Why did O.J. go 80 yards?* it was his young assistant Holtz who replied, "Coach, that's all he needed.") And he was a hell of a game coach.

. . . .

Maybe I am thinking about Holtz when I come upon a familiar commons. Despite having been to this campus a dozen times, I have yet to gain such a firm handle on it that I am not taken by surprise, just a bit, each time I come upon this green rectangle, which pulls the eye to the north. There above the reflecting pool is a massive, vibrantly colored mural called *The Word of Life*, a 163-foot rendering of the resurrected Christ better known by its more populist handle, "Touchdown Jesus."

In no particular hurry, I walk toward the pool and the Theodore Hesburgh Library, whose south-facing façade is brought to life by the most famous mosaic in sports. What's the deal with this haloed, Fu Manchu–ed, vaguely cubist Christ? Who are these smaller figures milling about beneath him? A plaque by the reflecting pool identifies apostles, just beneath "Christians of the early church," who reside on the mural above the guys representing for the "age of Science," whose bookishness is thrown into sharper relief by their proximity to the manly "explorers," whom the artist has blessed with better muscle tone and whose loins are girded with armor. Below them stand envoys from the "medieval era" and "ancient classic cultures." The scene is not static. Some heads are turned toward the Wonder Counselor, others are talking, gesticulating, arguing their positions, possibly discussing grant applications. Diagonal shafts of light further animate the tableau.

Later, I will learn that the mural has been rendered in granite to better withstand the Michiana elements. The artist, Millard Sheets, used 140 different colors. In a terrific little video clip on the university's Web site, Notre Dame architecture professor John W. Stamper explains that Sheets "visited 16 foreign countries and 11 different states" to find the granites he needed. Says Stamper, "The theme of the mural, Christ the Teacher, was based upon a biblical passage" from the first chapter of John. After sketching out the figure of Christ, Sheets drew in a cross (one of the last things you notice about the mural), then sketched in a kind of who's-who of Christianity. After the classical scholars and Old Testament prophets, he "moved upward on the mural, to the Byzantine, the medieval, the Renaissance."

"It's like a kaleidoscope of personalities making up the history of Christianity, and pre-Christianity as well," adds Father Hesburgh, who gets in the best line of the clip. "We knew that if we didn't do something with this building," he explains, when asked why the library needed a mural in the first place, "it could be mistaken for a grain elevator."

WALKING BACK TO the car I smile at a guy roughly my age—a dad playing Wiffle ball with his three sun-kissed daughters. They look to be around 14, 12, and 10. The youngest is at bat, rifling her old man's underhanded pitches past his head, despite the fact that she is confined to a wheelchair.

Covering the Tour de France for *SI*, I've stayed several times in Lourdes, in southwest France, always reminding myself not to stare at the cripples and infirm with whom I am sharing the town. This once-sleepy Pyrennean village was transformed into a mecca for Catholic pilgrims in the years after 1858, when a peasant girl named Bernadette Soubirous witnessed a series of apparitions: a white-clothed woman, radiant beyond description, who identified herself as "the Immaculate Conception." I wasn't surprised to learn that the Grotto at Notre Dame was patterned after Bernadette's Grotto at the caves of Massabielle.

The sidewalks of Lourdes teem with the halt and the lame, the stooped and wheelchair-bound. From all over the world they arrive by vast air-conditioned coaches that occlude the city's narrow lanes. So do their occupants crowd the public spaces of the city's hotels, the lobbies and buffet lines, all the while daring you to begrudge them anything—you with your erect spine and smoothly functioning limbs. There are, of course, marked differences between Notre Dame and Lourdes: While visiting Notre Dame, for instance, the word "cheesy" is not at the tip of one's tongue.

But there are similarities: There seem to be more physically challenged people at Notre Dame, per capita, than at any other campus I've visited, particularly on football weekends. They are drawn by faith and hope—by what is often described as the Notre Dame "mystique," an ineffable quality upon which Lou Holtz cannot quite put his finger. Asked to explain the mystique, the coach replies with the rhetorical equivalent of a punt: "If you were there," he says, "no explanation is necessary. If you weren't, no explanation is satisfactory."

I would describe the mystique as an inner calm that descends on visitors, if they are receptive. There is something about Notre Dame that soothes the psyche; that provides, if not outright physical healing, a balm for the spirit.

IT HELPS TO have the Grotto and the *Word of Life* mural and the hauntingly beautiful Basilica of the Sacred Heart. But the mystique, in my experience, is less about architecture than it is about people. The morning after my face-to-face with "Touchdown Jesus," I find myself sharing a golf cart with the mayor of South Bend. Steve Luecke, a former student at Notre Dame (who graduated from Fordham), is a tall, friendly, gracious man whose takeaway and backswing are a train wreck. His divots eclipse the sun. But as the good alcalde points out, there's something a little unseemly about a mayor with a miniscule handicap.

Chatting with Luecke, I learn that, before he was the mayor he was . . . a carpenter. Then he took a job with a local foundation whose mission it is to develop affordable housing, and to organize citizens to address such issues as public safety and crime deterrence.

Steve makes the point, while we wait to tee off on 16, that when the football team is doing well it gives South Bend a certain lift.

"And when it isn't doing well," he says, with a smile, "the letters to the editor tend to complain about the coach, and not the mayor."

This gets a big yuk from Dick Nussbaum, a free-swinging lefty who in the early 1970s played centerfield for Jake Kline, the legendary Fighting Irish baseball coach who'd been a student during the Rockne days. Nussbaum is a Double Domer—he majored in English before earning his juris doctorate at the university's law school in 1977. He spent six years in Cavanaugh Hall, whose corridors in those days were ably—indeed, zealously—patrolled by the legendary Father Matt (Black Mac) Miceli, a grim-visaged rector with "a machine-gun laugh," Nussbaum recalls. "It sent chills up and down my spine." Black Mac took Notre Dame rigid parietals very seriously. "Women visitors had to be out of the dorm at midnight on weekdays and 2:00 a.m. on weekends," says Nussbaum. Before making his rounds, Black Mac would lace up a tennis shoe on one foot and his regular, hard-soled oxford on the other. "That way," says Nussbaum, "when he broke into a run, in pursuit of curfew-breakers, it would sound like he was walking."

Father Miceli's diligence did not go unnoticed in the athletic department. Many star athletes—Adrian Dantley, Gary Brokaw, Dwight Clay, Eric Pennick, Ross Browner, Art Best, and Gene Smith (now athletic director at Ohio State)—were steered to Cavanaugh, where they could be assured a studious, sober, and, once curfew had passed, *all-male* environment.

To voice the opinion that these parietals are silly and archaic is to stand accused by Notre Dame's true believers (the expression may be redundant) of indulging in the moral relativism the Vatican is so often warning us against. If it was a sin when Father Sorin and the Seven Brothers founded this place 164 years ago, it's no less a sin today, dammit.

A generalization about Domers: The strength of will to overcome earthly appetites is of a piece with an overarching determination to do the right thing in all walks of life. The most obvious example is community service. Once enrolled here, there is an expectation that you will do your part, as it says in the New Testament, for the least among us. "Something like 86 percent of our students do some sort of service work while they're here," says Heather Tonk, '98. "Plus our alumni clubs throughout the country are very active." When the Irish accepted a bid to the Sugar Bowl, it was Tonk, director of service programs for the school's alumni association, who put together a project that enabled 400 or so students, alumni, faculty, and staff to pitch in when they got to New Orleans. Before the game, they teamed up with Catholic Charities of New Orleans to restore a ruined park in the Gentilly neighborhood—there was my pal, Dick Nussbaum, scraping paint off a swingset—and restore a facility for at-risk youth called Hope Haven.

Nussbaum and his wife put in four hours; his wife went back the next day, with their two sons, and put in four more. "The goal," Dick told me, "was just to get things so people would want to come back. What struck me most was how the people who'd stuck it out just needed to tell their stories."

More impressive than the fact that this was how some people chose to spend their Christmas vacations was how *routine* such decisions are in the extended Notre Dame family. A hundred students, including 30 athletes—and athletic director Kevin White—spent their fall break in New Orleans. As Tonk notes, "It's just part of the culture here."

Resent them for having their own private network; excoriate them for getting an annual shortcut to a BCS bowl. Exult in their postseason floundering: the Irish have lost eight straight bowl games. Roll your eyes at their love of institution, which absolutely crosses the line, oftentimes, into smugness. But give the Domers their due. They aren't just a bunch of young swells taking communion on Sunday, bowing their heads and looking the part. These people walk the walk.


IT CARRIES OVER to the football team. After Friday afternoon's full-pads practice, I sit at a round table with Ambrose Wooden, the corner who'd lined up opposite Dwayne Jarrett on that critical fourth-and-nine the previous October. Wooden had tight coverage, but Leinart parachuted in a perfect pass. Jarrett went 61 yards on that play, setting up the Bush Push, and the Trojans escaped with their 28-game winning streak. Wooden talked about how he'd improved since the previous season: "I'm working on the little things, fundamentals, techniques . . . I'm just trying to contribute to the team. We're building our confidence. That's what camp is about."

Camp is also about rinsing away the sour taste of an ugly number.

Six-one-four is the area code of Columbus, Ohio. It was also the number of total yards an overmatched Notre Dame defense surrendered in a 34–20 loss to Ohio State in the Fiesta Bowl. So, while the Irish return nine starters on defense this season—including the entire secondary—that Fiesta Bowl performance begs the question: Is that a good thing?

Tom Zbikowski, the Mohawk-sporting strong safety, tells me it is. Several of the Buckeyes' big plays in that game were the result of "mental breakdowns," he says—miscues that were addressed during spring drills, when the defense "got back to basics." This is the new party line coming out of the football offices: It's not that we're not fast. It's that we didn't *play* fast against the Buckeyes.

Further steps have been taken to correct this deficiency. In his most intriguing gamble of the off-season, Weis moved Travis Thomas, a hardnosed running back, to linebacker. Recognizing that he needed more speed on defense, mindful of Thomas's superb tackling on special teams (and the fact that he had starred as a strong safety in high school), Weis popped the question last spring. Thomas accepted. Included in Notre Dame's 2006 recruiting class are two of the nation's top lockdown corners, Raeshon McNeil and Darrin Walls. "I don't care if the guy playing is a freshman or a senior," says Weis. "I just want the best guys out there."

A year ago, the Fighting Irish had to keep it pretty vanilla on defense. So far this August, they've been fielding five-, six-, and seven-defensive back packages. "I mean, we wouldn't play seven dbs in an entire game last year," said Weis. "I really like the speed of our defense. And I'm much more encouraged about the depth of our defense than I was at any time last year."

Let's talk about the new wrinkles, I suggest to Wooden. Tell me about those six- and seven-defensive back packages.

He looks at me as if I've asked for his ATM card and PIN number. "I'm not at liberty to talk about that right now," he replies. "That's for you to see in the first game. Right now we're working on fundamentals."

Somber and serious, Wooden strikes me as an old soul, mature beyond his years. He's had to become so. When Wooden was a freshman at the Gilman School in Baltimore, his older brother was struck by a hit-and-run driver while crossing the street. "His head was the size of a balloon," Wooden recalls. "He suffered brain damage, and he's partially blind now. He's 31 or 32. When my mom passes away—knock wood—he's going to be be my responsibility."

He isn't looking for sympathy. It's clear, talking to him, that Wooden sees his brother as a blessing, not a burden. "He is my inspiration," he says. "He keeps me going."

While he was devastated by that near-miss loss to the Trojans, Wooden was also able to put it in perspective. Even before he became a Division I cornerback, he knew, as he said, "Life can change in seconds."

SATURDAY, AUGUST 12, is a special day. Not just because it's the first day of double-sessions. I arrive at the Notre Dame practice field, duck under the yellow tape while waving gaily to a security guard, and stride right up to the sideline. Weis has opened practice to the media. While reporters are routinely allowed to look on during the first 20 minutes of practice, this is the first and only time the coach gives us access to an entire session.

At 'SC, Carroll virtually never closes practice to the media. Weis never opens it. (On the one day he does, he apparently wants a medal, opening the ensuing press conference by saying, "Let me hear it from just one of you." Meekly, obediently, several of us reply, like schoolchildren, "Thank you.")

We are in something called "pre-period," an easy-tempo run-through of what Weis will emphasize later, after stretch and individual drills and other violent and profanity-laced exercises. The offense is installing its "Multiple Tight End, Pound It" package, which sounds vaguely like a DVD that would arrive in your mailbox in a plain brown wrapper, but is in fact a short-yardage offense.

Offense is in white jerseys, dee in blue. Brady Quinn, on whose shoulders the season rides, sports a red Jersey, which fairly shouts to defenders, *Nobody so much as breathes heavily in this guy's direction.*

Weis shuttles between offense and scout team defense, covering a surprising amount of ground with his distinctive, flatfooted mince. "Bottom line," he is telling offensive line coach John Latina, "if he's really, really wide, that guy won't be in a seven technique."

"Slide over a little this way, 36," he tells a scout teamer.

To right guard Dan Santucci: "This is a heavy left flip, not a heavy right flip."

Seeing the defense lined up a certain way, he sighs. "Ahh. Pray they line up like that. I could get five yards every time, if they line up like that."

The idea of Weis's tucking the ball and chugging for the first down strikes several linemen as amusing.

"What are you laughing at?" he asks them, smiling himself.

There is an air horn, and the players form what are known as stretch lines, obeying instructions such as "Okay, work it down! Try to get your chest down to your thigh—work the hamstring!"

Many of the coaches issuing the instructions are not exactly paragons of flexibility and cardiovascular efficiency. The unspoken command behind their orders: *Do as I say, not as I do.*

I conclude, after watching the defensive linemen assault one another after a particularly fierce drill, that Jappy Oliver is the most animated coach on the field, if not all of Division I.

Aside from his dissatisfaction with the attitude of the players and the tempo and execution of the drill, Oliver couldn't be happier with how the morning is unfolding.

"I got three helmets off, and it's all three freshmen." If they didn't know it before, they'll know it now: You don't take your hat off in the office. Too late: Oliver has one of the frosh doing push-ups ("GIVE ME TWENTY!") while he serves as a belated alarm clock to another ("WAKE YOUR ASS UP!").

Like a Zen master, kind of, Oliver seeks to bring his pupils into the moment: "You are not in high school anymore! This is a contact sport. Make the collisions more violent!" I lament the air horn signaling the end of this period. The defensive linemen, I am guessing, do not.

Taking a counterclockwise loop of the practice fields, I next drop in on the linebackers, in time to see Travis Thomas wrap up a ballcarrier and drive him 15 feet into the backfield.

THE NEXT PERIOD brings all the big bodies together for "Irish Eyes," a drill whose titanic collisions can be heard across campus. An offensive lineman and a defensive lineman go nose to nose between two tackling dummies. The running back is allowed a single cut. The defender's job: shed blocker, make tackle.

There is Travis Leitko, a senior who took the 2005 season off, catching up on schoolwork and ministering to his parents, both of whom were battling cancer. Weis has invited Leitko back as a walk-on, and the Texan is having a strong camp. "I keep noticing you, Leitko!" roars Weis, who will later make the defensive tackle one of four walk-ons awarded scholarships.

There is Victor Abiamiri, a sculpted, glowering end, goat-roping some poor running back—driving the crook of a muscular arm into the poor fellow's Adam's apple in what is more commonly known as a "clothesline."

During kickoff drills, Weis is riding Toryan Smith, a freshman from Rome, Georgia, who has been slow to grasp "the tempo [at which] we do these things," according to Weis.

"All right, Toryan, I'm watchin' you!" shouts the coach as the unit takes off in pursuit of the kick. Thus goaded, Smith roars down upon the returner, who, as a member of the scout return team, has been required to stretch a dignity-stripping orange beanie over his helmet. Smith hits the ballcarrier so hard that the poor fellow hits the ground shoulder blades first. The beanie wafts to earth like a falling leaf. Smith's kickoff team compadres go apeshit. "That's what I'm talking about!" shouts Weis. We have our defensive highlight of the day.

THE OFFENSIVE HIGHLIGHT is easy to pick out, too. During seven-on-seven drills, I am admiring the athleticism of No. 2 on defense—no one on the team has quicker feet. This is Walls, the freshman corner, who promptly bites, then is spun 360 degrees by a double-move from Jeff Samardzija, the accidental All-American. Bursting onto the scene in 2005, the beneficiary of a season-ending injury to Rhema McKnight, the lanky wide receiver set school records for receiving yards (1,576) and touchdown catches (15) in a season.

Quinn hits him with a bomb that travels 70 yards in the air. It is a throw that leaves me slack-jawed, a reminder that the best player on the field is also the one Weis can't resist riding.

Quinn wasn't just the team's most valuable player in 2005. He was also its most improved: transformed by Weis from a 6' 4", 227-pound tower of mediocrity to a Heisman candidate and certain first-round pick in the 2007 NFL draft. In addition to presenting Quinn with a playbook the approximate thickness of the

*Oxford English Dictionary,* Weis immediately set about tinkering with his new pupil's mechanics. When I asked Weis for examples, he ticked off several. "Well, we noticed right away that he was having problems simply taking the snap." Center John Sullivan was so low in his stance that it forced the quarterback to begin each play in an ungainly squat. That was an easy fix: Sullivan was instructed to get his ass up in the air. Peter Vaas, whom Weis brought in as quarterbacks coach, worked with Quinn on everything from drops, to hand placement on ball fakes, to keeping his hips open when he throws to the left. Also pitching in was New England Patriots quarterback Tom Brady.

Not in person. But Weis brought with him from New England four years' worth of video of Brady running the same offense he has installed at Notre Dame. "The ability to watch a Pro Bowl quarterback run the same plays you're running," Weis told me, "that's an advantage not many people have at the college level."

It all sounds so clinical and painless. It wasn't. In the preseason, Quinn said, "He would ride you and ride you and ride you and ride you. He'd take you to the point where you're thinking, man, I just want to go to sleep. I just want it to be tomorrow."

The end result was a 9-2 regular season that pumped new life into a moribund program and had some Notre Dame fans fretting that Quinn's stock had shot up so dramatically that he might enter the draft after his junior season. The quarterback scotched those rumors shortly after the season, allaying the fears of ND Nation by confirming that yes, he would be returning in 2006 to get his PhD in quarterbacking from Weis.

One of the interesting questions going into the 2006 season is: What will be the new dynamic between teacher and pupil? Will Weis lighten up on Quinn? Treat him more like a peer than a subject?

For me, that question is answered early in that Saturday practice. During the pre-period, Quinn has been deficient in his presnap read—failed to acknowledge the overly generous cushion that a scout-team corner was giving Samardzija.

Quietly, but with a decided edge in his voice, Weis asks the quarterback, "Is that part of that play?"

"I think so," replies a chastened Quinn.

"Then why don't you look at it?"

"Yes, sir."

A FEW DAYS earlier, Weis had promised to use his "New Jersey rhetoric" to keep uber-talented teen idol Quinn from falling victim to the vast hype surrounding this team, and quarterback. "I just rag them all the time," the coach admitted. "Every time Quinn throws an incomplete pass, he already knows it's coming. I'll say, 'Yeah, there's my Heisman Trophy winner.' "

Quinn, said Weis, is "miserable, because he knows he's going to be the public sacrifical lamb." When I ask Quinn how his relationship with Weis has evolved over the previous year, he tells me that the coach's putdowns from early 2005 ("This is why, for your entire frikkin' life, you're going to be a 50-percent passer! Your ENTIRE FRIKKIN' LIFE!") have given way to subtler, but no less effective, admonitions. "It's evolved now to where, when he's not talking to you, that's when you know he's pretty upset with you. When he's quiet, that's when he's mad."

Weis had confirmed this after the Saturday practice. I told him that I'd expected more verbal pyrotechnics. I suggested that, having allowed reporters inside the ropes, he'd treated us to a sanitized version of practice. "I wasn't doing that because the press was there," he said, smiling like a capo on *The Sopranos*. "I was doing that because I wasn't very nice yesterday." He lets that sink in, then elaborates. "My not nice was a quiet not nice. Where they expected me to kill 'em [verbally], I did it in a quiet, go-for-the-throat kind of way."

To everything, in both Ecclesiastes and the World According to Weis, there is a season. A time to build up, a time to tear down. After Quinn beats Walls on that gorgeous rainbow of a throw, he goes deep again, this time incomplete. "I'd take that one every time," says Weis, approvingly. Going into this season, the coach has given his quarterback much more latitude to check out of plays, to take shots down the field if the signs are favorable. Whereas Quinn merely "grasped" the offense in 2005, this year, according to the coach, he's been able "to take it mentally to another level."

If the offense is improved, and the defense is improved, the record will improve, right?

"We're better on both sides of the ball" than in 2005, says Weis, a week before the opener. "On the flip side of that, no one we were playing [in 2005] thought we were gonna be any good." In '05, "it was 'Oh, it's Notre Dame,' " he said, affecting a blasé tone. "Now it's 'Oh! It's Notre Dame!' There's a big difference."

How big? We'll find out in eight days.

# CHAPTER 2

# Here We Come Again!

**A**ugust 18, Los Angeles —With six minutes and change left in the 2006 Rose Bowl, I stood in the press box and headed for the elevator. Dwayne Jarrett had just gone skywalking over a pair of Texas defensive backs, speared a 22-yard pass for a touchdown, and put the game on ice.

By God, it *looked* that way. The Longhorn defenders didn't just fail to break up that pass—they collided, knocking heads like Curly and Moe, then lying woozily on the turf before being helped off the field. Texas had put up a spirited fight—had even led 17–7 at one point—but now the natural order had been restored. USC's fifth score in five second-half possessions (a field goal, followed by four TDs) gave the defending national champions a 38–26 lead with 8:46 to play. Yes, Texas quarterback Vince Young had been brilliant much of the night. But the Longhorns needed two touchdowns, and had less than nine minutes to get them. What it boiled down to was that

**AP PRESEASON TOP 10**

1. *Ohio State*
2. *Notre Dame*
3. *Texas*
4. *Auburn*
5. *West Virginia*
6. *USC*
7. *Florida*
8. *LSU*
9. *California*
10. *Oklahoma*

'SC needed one stop—one measly hold—to secure their third straight national championship.

*Sports Illustrated* usually closes tight on Monday night; it was now two hours shy of Thursday. To squeeze the Rose Bowl into that week's issue, the magazine had been left open two extra days. Where I normally have all night to write, on this occasion I would have roughly 90 minutes after the game ended. Downside: I would spend that time feeling what F. Scott Fitzgerald described as "the hot whips of panic." Upside: I would be drinking by midnight.

With 'SC up by a dozen, I felt I could cheat a little. When I stood to catch that elevator, I had half the story already written, including this Dewey-Defeats-Truman excerpt:

*Thus did the Trojans secure their 35th consecutive victory and their place in college football's annals. No team, not the Blanchard & Davis-powered Army clubs of the '40s, not the dynastic Oklahoma Sooners of the mid-'50s, had ever finished the season No. 1 in the AP poll three years running.*

*If they weren't the best that ever was, these Trojans were a link in the chain of the most impressive dynasty this sport has seen in half a century. Bud Wilkinson's Sooners rang up 47 straight wins between 1953 and 1957, a record long regarded as unassailable—and one which Southern California could break—by going undefeated next season. The Trojans have pieced their streak together in an era of reduced scholarships and increased parity; of underclassmen bolting for the NFL; of stringent NCAA regulations that would have complicated the efforts of the Oklahoma boosters who routinely bought players during Wilkinson's day. For a 21st century team to be within a single season of that DiMaggio-like mark borders on unbelievable.*

Having reread that passage, I closed my laptop and descended to field level, where Vince Young proceeded to redefine unbelievable.

Looking back on that surreal evening of stellar play and whip-sawed emotions—the two teams combined for 53 second-half points—I'd forgotten what a beast White had been (124 yards on 20 carries, three TDs); how masterful was Leinart, throwing for 365 yards and one touchdown. Their heroics were crowded from memory's slate by the superhuman performance of VY, who outplayed a pair of Heisman Trophy winners, running and passing for 467 yards. Young completed 30 of 40 passes, ran for 200 yards on 19 attempts, and ran for three touchdowns. The last of those, on fourth-and-five from the eight-yard line with 19 seconds left in the game, clinched the Longhorns' first national championship in 35 years.

Shortly before midnight, Carroll had made his way out of the media tent where he'd spent the previous 20 minutes trying to disguise the devastation he felt, and giving it up for Young, for whom he made no effort to disguise his admiration. "He just ran all over the place on us. We couldn't stop him."

I'd caught him on his way out of the tent. "Well, Austin," he said with a rueful smile. "Where do we go from here?"


THE TROJANS WENT to work. Carroll and his staff lured another five-star recruiting class to Troy. The returning players busted their behinds in winter workouts, went into spring drills feeling at once pissed off and hopeful. Going into fall camp, morale is superb, despite (or, more likely, because of) significant losses from last year's team. Half the starters from 2005—including Leinart, Bush, and White—have moved on.

The exodus of that touchdown-making trinity makes for a much more proletarian vibe at Trojans practices. There are fewer TV trucks, fewer luminaries from the L.A. demimonde lining the fence at Howard Jones Field. It is, as 'SC's sports information director Tim Tessalone observes, "as if the Beatles broke up." Bush, Leinart, and White were the second, tenth, and forty-fifth picks in the draft. After going through spring football with zero scholarship tailbacks (Chauncey Washington remained locked in his annual death struggle with his grade-point average;

Desmond Reed hadn't recovered from reconstructive knee surgery), the Trojans now have seven. Five of them come from a bumper crop of freshmen, including Emmanuel Moody, a slashing runner with great burst; inside-outside threats C. J. Gable and Stafon Johnson; and the beastly converted linebacker Allen Bradford.

At no position has the celebrity wattage been ratcheted down more drastically than at quarterback. Once a pudgy, cross-eyed boy, now a dashing, gunslinging millionaire, Leinart appeared to be fueled by twin quests: to start for the Arizona Cardinals, and to snog as many starlets and bimbos as humanly possible. The NFL's 2006 Playboy of the Year has been succeeded, in Troy, by longtime understudy John David Booty, a fourth-year junior and native Louisianan who has as much use for the L.A. club scene as Leinart does for duck calls and blaze orange camo.

Booty is not off to a blazing start. Having missed virtually all of spring ball—he underwent surgery to repair a bulging disc in his back—his timing is off with his primary receivers, wide outs Jarrett and Steve Smith, both of whom have missed significant stretches of two-a-days with nagging injuries of their own. Jarrett's strained quad is the least of his problems: The NCAA had declared him ineligible earlier in the season. As the *L.A. Times* first reported, he'd been living with Leinart for more than a year in an apartment that cost $3,866 a month. While Jarrett kicked in $650 a month, Bob Leinart, Matt's father, picked up the balance of the rent. That's an NCAA no-no. Finally, on August 10, the NCAA ruled that if Jarrett paid $5,352 to a charity of his choice (the Reggie Bush Legal Defense Fund?), he will be reinstated. Done and done.

It doesn't help Booty that in practices and scrimmages, he's going up against a vastly improved 'SC defense, a unit which, despite the loss of six starters, somehow looks better—I mean, a lot better—than the gang Vince Young fricasseed in Pasadena.

Carroll, for whom the glass is perpetually half-full, attributes the hiccups in 'SC's aerial assault to the superb play he's getting from the defensive backs, which he describes as "the best we've had since I've been here—the most athletic, the fastest."

And if Booty hasn't played lights out, big deal. He's done an overall "nice job running the offense, making the checks, handling the adjustments, getting guys lined up right when they're in the wrong place. He's been real sharp in all that stuff."

Booty, for his part, channels—and, in his new crewcut, vaguely resembles—Alfred E. Neuman. Interceptions? Passes batted down at the line of scrimmage? He leaves all that stuff on the field. *What, me worry?* The passing game? It'll come around. The exodus of top playmakers from last year's squad? You can't swing a dead cat without hitting a future star, Booty insists. "It's just that nobody's seen 'em yet." Today's relatively anonymous freshmen—with such unfamiliar names as Moody, Gable, Vidal Hazelton, Travon Patterson, and David Ausberry—are tomorrow's All-Americans.

Booty, one of a lonely minority of Trojans who'd *not* been overjoyed by Leinart's decision to return for a fifth season, also foresees major contributions from "older guys that haven't gotten an opportunity," but who will now "get a chance to step up, and prove why they got a scholarship to USC in the first place."

He is doing more than describing his own circumstance. He is announcing, in a way, the theme of the upcoming season. *Matt, Reggie, LenDale? Thanks for the memories, guys—now don't let the gate to Howard Jones practice field hit you in the ass on the way out.* It's someone else's turn.

LIKE BOOTY'S THROWBACK crewcut, the tone of tonight's "Salute to Troy" is populist, democratic. It takes place two weeks before the season opener, on Cromwell Field, home to the 'SC track and field program. So they gather on a flawless summer's eve: the players and coaches, plus more than two thousand members of the Trojans extended family. A line forms outside the discus cage, where fans have their picture taken with Traveler VII, a 15-year-old Andalusian gelding who, like the Song Girls sweaters and the six Travelers before him, is pure white. At round picnic tables, the faithful dine on barbecued chicken while listening to a kerchiefed, dungareed country music band that is warming the crowd up for the Spirit of Troy marching band.

I have heard USC likened to a shrink-wrapped version of Orange County plunked down in the middle of South Central. While the university draws from all over the country—indeed, from around the globe—a large number of its students and alumni do hail from that 948-square-mile redoubt of affluence and Bush-Cheney bumper stickers to the south.

Certainly the OC is well represented at the Salute. From Tustin and Dana Point they have come; from Costa Mesa and Irvine; La Habra and Mission Viejo. If Trojan alums tend to be leaner than those from schools in the middle of the country, they are also more sun-damaged. Recent grads are outnumbered by lifers at this Salute: white-haired, gin-blossomed country-club swells whose wives secretly keep track of the beers they put away; men whose grappling-hook memories extend to the days of John McKay, who can tell you the pass route Rod Sherman ran when Craig Fertig hit him for the game-winning touchdown in the waning moments against Notre Dame in 1964. There are heavyweight donors and corporate sponsors. There are players, sitting at round tables with their families, not talking about their places on the depth chart, just happy to see their parents for the first time in weeks. (I can still see the mother of one offensive linemen—a kid who weighed not an ounce less than 290 pounds—absentmindedly running her fingers through his hair as if he were still her baby. Which, in her mind, he is.) There are members of the 1956 and 1981 Trojans squads, whose feats are celebrated tonight. And, as at all general admission Trojans football functions, there are those with no connection to USC other than an abiding love for a team that fills some void in them, makes them feel a part of something larger than themselves.

. . . .

THE BANDWAGON IS not quite so packed on the cusp of the new season. The team that missed out on its third straight national title by four points and a handful of seconds will be ranked No. 5 in *SI*'s college football preview. The upside to this absence of super-stars: it has resulted in a blurring of class lines on the squad. While no one has a bad thing to say about the departed Three Kings—Bush, Leinart, White—everyone is looking forward to hearing his name a little more often on the Coliseum loudspeakers. Booty, the humble transplanted Cajun, will oversee a more equitable distri-bution of touches, and glory.

While mulling over this populist theme, I cannot help but no-tice The Line—a massive, hundred-yard cardinal and gold queue snaking its way between tables all the way out to the buffet. Trav-eler has left the building, so this fuss is not for the mascot. No, at the terminus of this line is Jarrett, half his face covered by over-sized shades, a burly security guard keeping the rabble in order. Jarrett has come a long way since the early autumn of 2004, when he was a freshman so fiercely homesick for his native New Bruns-wick, New Jersey that he had to be repeatedly talked out of drop-ping out of school and jumping the first flight back to Newark. Two full seasons, 146 receptions, and 29 touchdown catches later, he is as comfortable in L.A. as he is against press coverage. As he flashes that killer smile while signing autographs, Jarrett reminds us that there remains some royal blood on this year's roster.

We hear from athletic director Mike Garrett, the school's first Heisman winner and the man who had the vision to hire Carroll (after first offering the job to Dennis Erickson and Mike Riley). We hear from members of those long-ago Trojan teams. We hear the band, and watch the Song Girls. Finally, with the crowd chanting "Let's go Pete!" Carroll bounds on the stage to kick off the main event. While honoring its past, the Salute is a forward-looking function—a kind of debutante ball, a coming out for "some big kids and some fast kids you've been reading about," says Carroll. Returning to the heights will not be easy, he warns. "There's a lot of people who think they have an opportunity to beat the Trojans this year."

This pronouncement failing to elicit sufficient outrage from the members of his AARP-intensive audience (many of whose members missed their naps), the coach then commands them, "Say 'No way!' "

"No way!" comes the vaguely feeble response.

Next up: the position coaches, who deliver briefings on their respective units—their players, that is—before calling each onto the stage. Linebackers coach Ken Norton, the ex–UCLA Bruins great, now sporting a cowboy hat that reminds us of his first NFL stop, declares himself "the luckiest coach on the staff. This group I have is ridiculous. It is the best group in the country. They've got it all."

Norton is followed by a man with a shaved head and—is there a polite way to say this?—a slightly *crazed* look in his eye (a distinct advantage in his line of work). First-year defensive coordinator Nick Holt also brings to his new gig a matchless Trojans pedigree: he is the grandson of Clarence (Buster) Crabbe, an All-American swimmer at USC in the early 1930s, who went on to an acting career that saw him play, among others, Tarzan, Buck Rogers, Billy the Kid, and Flash Gordon. Holt, who enjoyed a strong bond with his grandfather—Crabbe died in 1983—coached 'SC's linebackers from 2001 to '03, before taking the head coaching job at Idaho. He lasted two years in that thankless gig, resigning after the 2005 season to take an assistant coaching job with the St. Louis Rams. But something happened to Holt on his way to the NFL. Carroll got him on the phone and, by dangling the coordinatorship, talked him into a return to Troy.

For the first time in six seasons at 'SC, Carroll will hand the defensive coordinator's headset to someone else. Such is his confidence in Holt's grasp of his defensive philosophy. The departure of Holt after the 2003 season, followed by the departure a year later of assistant head coach Ed Orgeron—for the head job at Mississippi—resulted in an intensity deficit on the defensive side of the ball. Orgeron's departure in particular led to what my friend Dan Weber, the astute beat writer for the *Riverside Press-Enterprise*, describes as a lack of "adult supervision" on defense: an ass-chewing, fear-inducing ogre—a countervailing malevolent force to balance Carroll's upbeat happytalk.

I like Orgeron. He's an easy guy to like—provided you don't have to play for him. Mostly, he is a journalist's dream, a larger-than-life character with a short fuse, a checkered past, and a gumbo-thick accent. In one of his early full-squad meetings at Ole Miss, he reportedly removed his shirt and announced his willingness to take on anyone on the team. No one took him up on it. As news accounts had by then made clear, this is a man who knows how to take care of himself in a brawl. I remember talking to Coach O a couple days before the Orange Bowl that followed the 2004 season. He was kind enough to turn on the projector, pull out a laser pointer, and clue me in on how his guys might break down the Sooners offensive line. At one point, I felt comfortable enough to play devil's advocate, asking, "What if Patterson can't beat that guy?"

The question flipped a switch that ignited a kind of furnace behind Orgeron's eyes. "If he can't beat that block," said Orgeron of Mike Patterson, his superb nose tackle, "he better not come to the sideline." (*'E bednah cum't'sahdlahn* is how it actually came out.)

Later in the session, the coach had me stand and assume the position of right tackle. While demonstrating how Patterson would, in fact, defeat my block, Coach O seemed unaware of his own strength, like Lenny in *Of Mice and Men*. A couple times he almost knocked me over. It was awesome.

That was two days after Orgeron had gathered his charges around him following a subpar practice.

"Y'all a bunch of f____g pussies," Coach O informed them, according to a defensive end who was there. "If I was coaching this team, I'd make y'all go inside, shower"—*sha-oh-wuh*—"put your pads back on, come out here, and practice all over again."

Orgeron's successor, Jethro Franklin, was no shrinking violet, but did not last, leaving after a single season to take a job with the Tampa Bay Bucs (who fired him after one season). It remains a mystery whether the defensive line's flat-out no-show in the Rose Bowl against Texas had anything to do with his exit.

In addition to guiding the dee this upcoming season, Holt will coach the defensive line, which has never replaced the wrecking ball talents of Patterson and Shaun Cody, who terrorized Jason White in that Orange Bowl—'SC blew the Sooners out of the tub, 55–19—then left for the NFL.

Now Pete is back on stage, relating some rumors he's been hearing about how the defense is going to carry the offense while Booty gets things figured out. Carroll's response to those rumors: Screw that.

What he actually says to this well-heeled group: "We're not doing that. Our program has a system to it. As we fit new people in—as we have done over the years—we have expectations and standards" they will meet. Or they will sit. Yes, a pair of Heisman Trophies walked out the door after the 2005 season. "But there's more to this program than one player here, one player there," reminds the coach. "Don't get me wrong, those guys made some big plays. But here we come again!"

It is his best applause line of the night.

My favorite moment: The band, which has been sitting patiently in the bleachers behind Carroll, launches into "Tusk," the raucous number recorded by Fleetwood Mac in 1979. If it's in your library, give it a listen. Between the savage drumlines and the Burgundian chanting and Lindsey Buckingham fretting obliquely about a love triangle *in the band* (his ex, Stevie Nicks, and Mick Fleetwood were making the beast with two backs), you can hear the drums and horns of a kick-ass marching band. It is none other than the Spirit of Troy, which helped *Tusk*, the album, go platinum, and which has never stopped playing that song.

Two-thirds of the way through, "Tusk" devolves into a kind of organized chaos that is acted out here at the Salute: band members are out of their assigned seats, ranging all over the bleachers, blowing horns, banging drums, rocking out under a waning crescent moon. The Song Girls, usually so synchronized, are lost in their own, private fugues, like cage dancers at the Whisky a Go Go. Darkness has fallen: a primal, tribal moment has broken out in the heart of this Republican enclave.

EVERY COLLEGE PROGRAM has its unique tapestry of rites and songs; a catalog of talismans and traditions, heroes, and enemies all its own. Aside from better athletes, what does the NFL have? It has the braying of Hank Williams Jr. It has Super Bowl halftime shows featuring such past-their-prime performers as the insipid Paul McCartney (of whose performance David Letterman would say, "It was clean, it was wholesome, it was family-friendly. That's right—it sucked!"), the cadaverous Rolling Stones, or the Aunt Jemima–kerchiefed Prince. Long ago, when people got their news from magazines, it was posited that an appearance on the cover of *Time* signaled the peak of one's cultural relevance—that it was all downhill from there. When David Byrne showed up on the October 27, 1986 cover of *Time*, for instance, you knew he would never again write a song as haunting and edgy as "Once in a Lifetime." So does an appearance at the Super Bowl mark the performers as defanged, milquetoast, inoffensive.

The pageantry of college football is the opposite of those over-produced Super Bowl halftime shows. It is uncontrived, organic to the game, the program, the tradition. No one has a firmer grasp of this than Carroll, who after paying homage to the Spirit of Troy and the Song Girls, embarks on one of the Kerouackian riffs the Trojan faithful have come to expect from him. Not long after taking the 'SC job, he made it his business to vist Marv Goux, the former 'SC team captain and assistant coach, the quintessential Trojan, who by then had retired to Palm Desert. "I went out the desert, to visit with Marv," he begins, and the crowd is rapt: Goux has been dead for five years, but his memory is sacred to these people, many of whom knew him, all of whom know of him. "And I asked Marv, 'What about the heritage, what about the connection? Where is the life and the love and the spirit of this program?'

"And he couldn't stop talking about the music. And he couldn't stop talking about the band, and what [Spirit of Troy director] Art Bartner has done. This is a real relationship that we have. This is something that we count on and believe in. When you hear those songs—and they keep playing the same songs, you know?—it doesn't matter where you are, what you're doing, it takes you right back to those great feelings, to this program and the connection that we have."

Carroll's journey to the desert wasn't just a fact-finding mission. It was an opportunity for a mistrusted outsider to pay homage to, and bask in the mojo of, one of the seminal figures of a 113-year-old tradition. Carroll's visit carried a symbolic significance to alumni, hundreds of whom had phoned the athletic department to share their conviction that he was a wretched choice to replace Paul Hackett. The new coach grasped the importance of the Goux visitation, just as he understood that "Fight On!" and "The Spirit of Troy" and "Conquest" are more than mere songs to be blared, ad nauseam, to the immense irritation of opposing crowds and opposing bands. They are touchstones for 200,000 living alumni and many times that number of Trojans fans. They are part of the living fabric of what even the saltiest, bitterest UCLA Bruin would admit is a grand tradition.


I SKIP OUT just as the fireworks begin. I've got 350 miles to cover, and I want to be in bed by 2:00 a.m. I take the 110 to the 5, shooting the gap between Chavez Ravine and downtown proper, swinging north and west, through the San Fernando Valley—porn capital of the world!—up the Tehachapi Mountains and over Tejon

Pass, whose 4,183-foot vantage offers, on this clear night, a sweeping view of the fertile carpet that is the San Joaquin Valley: its rural byways, the winking lights of towns like Maricopa, Pumpkin Center, Weed Patch.

Also spread before me, as I crest the summit, is another season of America's best game. What will it bring?

It will take me to Austin, Texas, for the Brawl in the Royal. That, at least, is the nickname bestowed upon the Ohio State–Texas game by a scarlet-and-white-caped Ohioan named Buck-I-Guy, whom I meet moments before kickoff at Darrell K. Royal–Texas Memorial Stadium. (His drawl makes "brawl" rhyme with "Royal.")

While in Texas I will stand, pen posed over my notebook, beside Texas quarterback Colt McCoy, the apple-cheeked redshirt freshman quarterback who will be asked such probing questions as *Is it true you haven't had a soda since the sixth grade?*

McCoy's wholesomeness, on this day, stood in contrast to the nightcrawling of his teammate Tarell Brown, the team's top cover corner, who with a spasm of epically poor judgment six days before the Brawl, had gotten himself (1) Tasered, (2) arrested, (3) suspended from the game.

I will be in South Bend, driving around in a golf cart with Jeff Samardzija and Tom Zbikowski, the latter describing their respective gifts with his trademark brevity: "He catches good. I run into things."

I will fly into Dallas the day after Cowboy wide receiver Terrell Owens does or does not attempt to harm himself by overdosing on Vicodin; the day after Owens's publicist, Kim Etheredge, does or does not fish said pills out of his mouth. Fortunately, it will be someone else's job to cover the carnival at Valley Ranch. I will proceed to Fort Worth for a story on the Horned Frogs of TCU, where Associate Athletic Director Scott Kull will enlighten me on the school's distinctive mascot: "The horned frog—actually a spiny lizard—subsists on a diet of red ants." It has long been believed that this creature is capable, when angered or frightened, of directing a four-foot stream of blood from its eyes. Kull sets me straight: It's not blood, but rather, predigested red ants.

I will say thanks but no thanks, in the hours before TGFKAT-WLOCP (The Game Formerly Known as the World's Largest Outdoor Cocktail Party), when red-suspendered Georgia Bulldogs fan John Short offers me a cup of antifreeze-colored Gator Killer punch. We will chat beside a van to whose roof rack is tethered a 6-foot, inflatable "Hairy Dawg," kept firm, like the Jumpy at a child's birthday party, by a gas-powered generator.

I will fly to Detroit and drive to Ann Arbor for a feature on the Wolverines' dour head coach, Lloyd Carr, who cannot be bothered—the Ohio State game being 13 days away—to grant an interview. I will also request—and be blown off by—Bo Schembechler, who later in the week, on the eve of The Big Game, will suffer The Big One. The night of his death, I will attend a Hate Michigan Rally in Columbus, headlined by a punk band called . . . the Dead Schembechlers. (They have since changed their name.)

I will be hung over in South Bend the day UCLA snatches defeat from the jaws of victory; stunned in Pasadena the afternoon those same Bruins spoil the season of the 'SC Trojans; flu-stricken and jet-lagged while traveling to three BCS Bowl Games in eight days: Rose, Sugar, and the Tostitos Bowl Championship Series National Championship Game, whose title was conceived, clearly, by the Department of Redundancy Department.

I will share car rides of varying durations with Urban Meyer, the Florida head coach who never fails to tell me, when I ask about recruiting, "Can't talk about it. But it's going very well." (I guess it was. The Gators reeled in the best class any school has in the last decade.)

I will miss the best game of the year, but no matter. Two weeks after the season ends, I will find myself in Boise, and will ask the Broncos players and coaches: *How the hell did you guys pull that off?*

I would pose the converse question, far more tactfully, to Sooners linebacker Rufus Alexander, the Big 12 Defensive Player of the Year: *So, umm, Rufus—what happened?*

Rufus will explain it as well as he could. He'll recall the quiet bus ride back to the team hotel.

"I'm sitting on that bus," he will tell me, "and my [college] career is over. We'd lost to a team everybody said we were supposed to beat.

"But then I started thinking about it. This was a great game—a game people will be talking about 30 years from now. I wish it had gone the other way, but you know something? It was an honor just to play in that game."

It was an honor to chronicle it, Rufus.

But I'm getting ahead of myself.

# CHAPTER 3

# This Is the Day, and You Are the Team

**M**y first stop of the regular season is Georgia Tech's Bobby Dodd Stadium, a 93-year-old urban treasure hiding in plain sight in downtown Atlanta. Designed and built by the school's student engineers in 1913, this Fenwayesque old bowl exists in a different dimension, like Hogwarts or Middle Earth.

Organic to its surroundings, drenched in colorful history, it provides a stark contrast to the soulless and antiseptic Georgia Dome, which squats like a vast toadstool two miles away, and is the home of the Atlanta Falcons and their dazzling if occasionally distracted dual-threat quarterback, Ron Mexico.

That, at least, was the alias used by Michael Vick when the quarterback registered for treatment of a condition he is alleged to have passed on to at least one of his partners. On April 5, 2003, according to court documents posted on The Smoking Gun Web site, a woman filed suit in Gwinnett County Court against

**AP TOP 10**

1. *Ohio State*
2. *Notre Dame*
3. *Texas*
4. *Auburn*
5. *West Virginia*
6. *USC*
7. *Florida*
8. *LSU*
9. *California*
10. *Oklahoma*

"Michael D. Vick, a/k/a Ron Mexico." The plaintiff sought punitive damages "for Defendant's consciously indifferent and knowing failure to advise Plaintiff that Defendant was infected with genital herpes at the time he engaged in sexual contact with Plaintiff."

While denying that he and Mr. Mexico were one and the same, Vick settled with "Plaintiff" out of court a year later. His less-than-gallant behavior with this woman was overtaken in April 2007, when it was revealed that a property he owned in rural Virginia housed a professional dog-fighting operation. Pointing out that this domicile was occupied by his relatives, not by him, Vick denied any knowledge of the thirty or so pit bulls found on the premises, many with open wounds on their necks, ears, and front legs.

But let's not forget who was the victim here. "It's unfortunate I have to take the heat, " Vick told reporters. "Lesson learned for me." Ever the vigilant sentinel for its image, the NFL forbids shoppers on its online store from ordering Vick's No. 7 replica jersey with a personalized "Ron Mexico" on the back.


THE DOME WAS my home away from home eight years ago, my last season covering the NFL, when the Falcons made their last (only) Super Bowl run. It has been eight years, then, since Falcons players like Jamal Anderson and Ray Buchanan did "the Dirty Bird"; since coach Dan Reeves returned to the sideline three weeks after having his sternum cracked open for quadruple bypass heart surgery; since veteran safety Eugene Robinson got hauled in on Super Bowl eve for soliciting an undercover prostitute.

Atlanta, you'll recall, was the site of a double-murder early on the morning of January 31, 2000. Arrested and charged with the stabbing deaths of two Decatur men was Ray Lewis, the Baltimore Ravens linebacker and perennial Pro Bowler who later pled guilty to a misdemeanor charge of obstruction of justice, agreeing to testify against two men who'd been rolling with him that night. (Both of whom lawyered up and were acquitted for lack of evidence.) This grisly scene came 10 weeks after Rae Carruth, a sullen wide out for the Carolina Panthers, was arrested for arranging the contract killing of his pregnant girlfriend. (Prosecutors could not get the first-degree murder charge to stick; Carruth is now serving between 10 and 25 years at the Nash Correctional Institute outside Raleigh, North Carolina.)

I don't really miss covering the League.

I'm not saying there weren't great guys to work with. There was Dave Widell, the Falcons guard who tried to hurt my feelings by asking, "Now, if this was a really *big* game, would they have sent, like, Rick Reilly?" I respected that. I gave him props for an original insult, then asked him if he could help me find some actual *starters* to interview.

There was Drew Bledsoe, with whom I once played catch on the field before a Jets-Patriots game, while his head coach at the time, one Pete Carroll, played catch not far away. Before he became a head coach renowned for his grimace, Jon (Chucky) Gruden coordinated the Eagles offense. While breaking down film one night in 1995, he told me about his first few weeks at Veterans Stadium, that misbegotten, oversized concrete ashtray that was imploded, mercifully, nine years later.

Arriving at work in the small hours—I'm talking 4:00 a.m.—Gruden was spooked by the gigantic, feral cats that often crossed his path, turning their insolent gaze on him before padding away.

"What's the deal with those big-ass *cats*," he asked a custodian.

"The cats?" came the man's vaguely sinister reply. "The cats . . . eat the rats."

The problem was, they didn't eat all of them. Rats were known to scurry through the Eagles' weight room while the players pumped iron. Phillies third baseman Mike Schmidt used to complain about the smell of rat urine in the tunnels.

It was in the verminous bowels of this same stadium that the city assigned a Common Pleas Court judge to set up shop on game days. Such was the volume of drunken, loutish, criminal behavior that police were forced to set up a makeshift courtroom in the stadium during Eagles games—an NFL first. As ESPN's Sal Paolantonio reminds us, it was in the Vet that a fan named Torch Man would douse one of his sleeves with an accelerant, ignite himself, then wave his arm wildly, the better to arouse the passions of Eagles fans. These are the people who cheered when Cowboys receiver Michael Irvin lay motionless on the turf with a neck injury in 1999. "Raiders fans like to paint their faces and pretend to be crazy," Irvin told the *New York Times*. "Eagles fans really *are* crazy."

Like I said, I'm fond of a lot of the guys still in the League. But I speak of the entire NFL when I say, on the whole, I'd rather not be in Philadelphia.


AND SO I am in Atlanta for this season-opening contest between Notre Dame and Georgia Tech. We will find out, at long last, if this new-and-improved, less thinking–more tackling defense can actually stop anyone. "Everyone's telling me how bad our defense is," Weis had said with a tight smile several days before the game. "I guess we'll just have to wait till next Saturday night to find out. We'll see if we have any speed or not."

With eight starters back on offense, the question is not so much "Will the offense click?" as it is "How many records will it set this season?" Where Quinn had merely "grasped" Weis's system last year, according to the maestro, in 2006 he was ready to "take it to another level, mentally."

The biggest surprise of the preseason is Sam Young. At the practice I attended, the 6'7", 292-pound man-child from Coral Springs, Florida, more than held his own against his elders, and took a fair number of snaps with the "Ones." Asked what we ought to read into Young's getting time with the first team, Weis replied, "It means he's with the first team." He then paid Young what might have been the highest compliment he paid anyone that entire week: "He doesn't act like a freshman."

Under Weis, every incoming freshman was assigned an upper-classman "mentor." Young's was left tackle Ryan Harris, a four-year starter who came into camp nagged with a back injury. He is Young's tutor.

No amount of mentoring could prepare Young for what lies in store on September 2. No matter how precocious he's looked against the scout-team dee, his introduction to Division I game competition will be neither smooth nor glitch-free. Georgia Tech's defense is coordinated by Jon Tenuta, renowned throughout the land as a master of the zone blitz, a man who would bring blitzers from the secondary, from the press box, from behind the counter at the Varsity drive-in restaurant on nearby North Avenue. Tenuta's ability to confuse and frighten quarterbacks with on-field chaos recalls a compliment once paid to John Milton, who had no equal, according to Samuel Johnson, in "Enforcing the awful, darkening the gloomy, and aggravating the dreadful." Tenuta is, in short, a hell of an engineer.

I refer, of course, to Tech's internationally famous fight song, which was widely performed by big bands in the years after 1911, was sung by Richard Nixon and Nikita Khrushchev together at their 1959 Moscow summit, and includes the lyrics:

> *I'm a Ramblin' Wreck from Georgia Tech and a hell of*
> *an engineer,*
> *A helluva, helluva, helluva, helluva, hell of an engineer,*
> *Like all the jolly good fellows, I drink my whiskey clear.*

Befitting a school known for its engineers and innovators, Georgia Tech has given college football John Heisman, who coached the Yellow Jackets for 16 years and started the first prac-tice of each season with a rhetorical question. "What is this?" he would ask while holding a football before his squad. "It is a prolate sphere, an elongated sphere in which the outer leather casing is drawn tightly over a somewhat smaller rubber tubing." After a dramatic pause, he would add, "Better to have died as a small boy than to fumble this football."

In addition to his early advocacy for the forward pass, his pioneering use of shifts, motions, the power sweep, and the shotgun snap, Heisman set an all-but-unassailable standard for poor sportsmanship by allowing his 1916 team to score 30 touchdowns in a game against Cumberland. Leading 126–0 at the half, the coach told his team, "You're doing all right," according to Adam Van Brimmer's *Stadium Stories: Georgia Tech Yellow Jackets*. "But you just can't tell what those Cumberland players have up their sleeves."

The final score, 222–0, remains the most lopsided victory in the history of the college game. Heisman's career at Tech ended three years later, not because he was fired, we learn from Van Brimmer, but because his wife wanted a divorce. "Wherever Mrs. Heisman wishes to live," he told reporters, "I will live in another place." She wished to stay in Atlanta; he removed to Philadelphia, to coach at his alma mater, Penn.

It was against Georgia Tech, in the 1929 Rose Bowl, that Cal's Roy Riegels scooped up a fumble and, having lost his bearings, returned it 69 yards in the wrong direction. "I feel like I've earned this," said a smiling "Wrong Way" Riegels, 51 years later, upon his induction into the Georgia Tech Letterman's Club.

NOTHING CAPTURES THE spirit of this school so well as the sight of the Ramblin' Wreck proper—the 1930 Ford Cabriolet Sport Coupe that makes its quaint dash across Grant Field before every game.

There it is, resplendent in gold and white, oooogha-ing its way past the fraternities on Techwood Drive two hours before kickoff, drawing whoops and cheers from Yellow Jackets all around me. As at many schools in the South, the frat boy ensemble of choice here is khakis with a white shirt and tie—a cravat whose knot tends to loosen and drop as the undergraduate's blood-alcohol level ascends. That said, for all the intemperance of the fight song—

*Oh, I wish I had a barrel of rum and sugar three
thousand pounds,
A college bell to put it in and a clapper to stir it around*

—the levels of intoxication I'm seeing on fraternity row register below those I will witness, for instance, outside Jacksonville's Alltell Stadium before the Georgia-Florida game, or on the streets of Columbus, Ohio in the hours after the Buckeyes face down Michigan. Even as they nurse their moderate, sensible nascent engineer buzzes, the brothers of Delta Upsilon, Lambda Chi, and Sigma Chi coexist harmoniously with their across-the-street neighbors, the Christian campus fellowship and the Baptist Student Union, where hot dogs and hamburgers are on sale. (All proceeds "go to the missions.")

A favorite Notre Dame T-shirt features the Rockne-ism, THIS IS THE DAY AND YOU ARE THE TEAM. That optimism, it seems, has been co-opted by the Yellow Jackets. The Jackets upset Auburn in their 2005 opener, and believe they can make it two in a row. In wide out Calvin Johnson, they've got just the weapon to exploit Notre Dame's suspect secondary. And wouldn't it be lovely, goes the thinking, to smother Quinn's Heisman hopes in the cradle?

Early returns are encouraging. Intent, perhaps, on lulling Tech into the false impression that the Fighting Irish blew off training camp this year, Notre Dame commits three penalties on its first possession, and is quickly forced to punt on its second. The third time the Irish get the ball, Quinn finds tight end John Carlson on a crossing route for 12 yards. The crowd quiets down. Briefly.

Quinn's next pass is an overthrow of Samardzija, who wasn't open anyway, and who will struggle to get separation from Yellow Jackets defenders all night. Under fierce pressure on second-and-10, the quarterback throws the ball into the turf and is flagged for intentional grounding. On third-and-27, he puts another ball in the turf to end an ignominious possession.

I write in my notebook during Tech's next drive: *Who is the Heisman candidate, and who is the quarterback often ripped by his own fans?* Deftly mixing run and pass, Tech's Reggie Ball takes five plays to reach Notre Dame's 33-yard line. Ball, whose scattershot arm is a topic of much discussion among the Georgia Tech faithful, rifles a pass to the right sideline, where the cornerback is giving Johnson an obscene cushion. With a few jukes and a stiff-arm, Johnson is into the secondary. The play nets 29 yards.

Johnson is a very nice, very bright kid from nearby Sandy Creek, Georgia. His father is a conductor for Southern Pacific; his mother, a PhD of some sort, has a high-powered job in the Atlanta public school system. Their eldest son is nothing less than a postmodern prototype for his position, Randy Moss minus the misanthropy. Johnson goes 6'5", 235, and outruns defensive backs. He has great hands and better hops: His vertical jump was measured at 45 inches, although, his teammates tell me, it's probably closer to 47. The measuring device only goes up to 45.

Which is a roundabout way of saying that when Ball tosses Johnson an alley-oop from the four-yard line, Mike Richardson, the corner defending on the play, has no chance. Georgia Tech 7, Notre Dame 0.

Wispy third-receiver David Grimes gives his team a jolt with a kickoff return to midfield. With Quinn under clear instructions to stop scanning the far horizon and start taking the short stuff, he dinks and dunks down to the 23, but the drive stalls, and Carl Gioia hooks the 42-yard attempt wide left. On Tech's next possession I look down and see Walls, the freshman, singled up on Calvin Johnson. A little baptism by fire. But Ball does not attack the freshman on this series, and the Irish get off the field.

Not for long. Quinn orchestrates still another three-and-out. On Tech's next series, Ball and Johnson connect on a 45-yarder, with the receiver dragging Walls the last eight yards. Notre Dame stiffens, gives up a 30-yard field goal, trails 10–0 with under five minutes in the half. I'm babysitting this game for the magazine. That is, I'm writing in case of an upset. If Notre Dame wins, no story. I'm starting to think I'm going to be writing.

With duct tape and bailing wire, Quinn jerry-rigs an 80-yard drive to end the half. He converts a third-down pass to Carlson a millisecond before defensive tackle Joe Anoai drills him. The pickup is 15. He hits backup tight end Marcus Freeman for another 10. On another third-and-long he scrambles for 16, moving the chains. Darius Walker gets eight yards around right end. On first-and-goal at the seven and time running dangerously low, Walker gets stuffed. Weis calls his final time-out with 16 seconds in the half. Quinn lines up in the shotgun. I'm thinking he hits Carlson on a little dig route. Possibly Samardzija on a fade. Wrong. On a gutsy call, the 6'4" senior takes the snap and torpedoes up the middle on a quarterback draw. Touchdown.

The mood in the Notre Dame room at the break is, if not funereal, less than chipper. "People were acting like we were down 50 points," says Weis, who finds it necessary to remind his players, "Fellas, it's a three-point game. Relax. It's okay."

The Irish offense is marching early in the second half. But the drive loses its fizz when Quinn is stopped for a short gain on third-and-10. Ranging to his right, Jackets linebacker Phillip Wheeler knocks Quinn out of bounds with a fierce hit. Notre Dame will have to settle for a field goal attempt—not at all a sure thing. Gioia will miss two makeable kicks before the evening is over. It's a big stop for the Tech defense.

But it doesn't count. The side judge launches a flag, nailing Wheeler for a helmet-to-helmet hit which, replays show, he didn't commit. Even Weis will allow afterward, "On the replay, to me, it looked like a clean play."

Tech fans don't need instant replay to know they've been jobbed. They shower the field with refuse. Four plays later (including a pair of penalties on Notre Dame which reek of make-up calls), Darius Walker is in the end zone. With 6:33 left in the third quarter, the Fighting Irish lead 14–10, a dangerously thin margin on the road against a team with a player like Calvin Johnson, who will run a 4.35 forty at the NFL Combine the following February. Hardboiled scouts—men who pick nits for a living; who could find fault with Halle Berry's body—will tremble and gush over him. Johnson will be the second player selected in the NFL draft.

With the game on the line, however, he disappears from the radar of Ball and offensive coordinator Patrick Nix. Though he finishes with seven catches for 111 yards, Johnson pulls down just two passes in the second half, for a scant 16 yards.

THE BEST THAT can be said of Notre Dame's offensive performance for the rest of the game is that it manages, with a couple longish drives, to consume some clock. One drive ends with a missed field goal. The next is hamstrung by a rare leg-whipping call on Harris, the four-year starter at left tackle. When the night is done, Quinn will have been sacked twice and hurried at least ten times. His linemen are flagged six times for 95 yards in penalties. The first of those was the false start on Young—to be expected, considering his tender years. More surprising is the lack of composure shown by his on-field tutor, Harris, who was busted holding, in addition to that seldom-seen personal foul.

"How 'bout that leg whip!" I shout to John Latina on the field after the game. Weis does not allow his assistants to speak with reporters without permission, but I am hoping to catch Latina, the offensive line coach, in a moment of candor. I fail. A giant man whose default expression is one of guarded hostility, he looks at me as if I've asked to borrow $50. Seldom have I seen a coach on a victorious team look so unhappy. He is in for a long season, and he knows it.

With the win in his pocket, Weis cannot resist striking a slightly triumphalist note on behalf of his much-maligned defense.

"The big question mark coming into the year was whether we could play defense or not. I think they played some defense tonight."

This was the group that Ohio State had run up and down the field on the previous January. The total yardage allowed that day by the losers: 614, a stat that tailed the team like a poltergeist through the offseason; a number used as bludgeon by skeptics seeking to beat down the squad's high hopes in 2006. Fifteen minutes later, in a dank room with reporters, Weis speaks of how old it had gotten, hearing that unholy number: "If I heard [614] one more time, I was going to be sick," he says.

"That right there was a tough win," says Weis, making no effort to disguise his relief. "They're a good football team. They're gonna give a lot of people a lot of problems." Indeed, the Jackets will win nine games, go 7-1 in league play, and make it to the ACC title game.

"We knew it was gonna be a dogfight coming in here," adds Quinn. "So obviously we're pleased with the win, but we're in no way happy with our performance. Especially myself."

He engages in a brief session of self-flagellation for missing receivers on some of his long throws, and for lacking accuracy on some of the intermediate passes he was forced to unload on the run. "This game coulda been a lot more wide open," he added, "if I fulfilled my job better." He will not allow himself the luxury of seeing it the way most observers see it: a textbook example of how a Jon Tenuta defense can monkeywrench a prolific offense.

Before the start of another season, Quinn will sign a multimillion dollar contract, based on the strength of his lightning right arm. Among the more interesting aspects of this game is the fact that he did more significant damage with his legs, running for a touchdown, scrambling for a big first down, sneaking for a first on fourth-and-one. He threw for no touchdowns. But in a hostile atmosphere, the boys found a way. This victory is a harbinger of pitched battles to come. Unlike the surprise team of 2005, this squad, for whatever reason, will be forced to grind from behind for its most important victories, will dig deeper than it had to in Weis's first season. Of course there will be blowouts. And the 2006 Notre Dame team will know its share of disappointment. But its finest moments will rank with some of the sweetest in the annals of this program, because of how hard Quinn and his mates will have to fight for them.

Moments after the game ended, the visitors clustered at the west end of the stadium. Senior guard Bob Morton, whose father had died during fall camp, led the team in the alma mater, hoping to compensate with sheer volume for what he lacked in musical talent or pitch. When the singing stopped, he and Weis shared an embrace. When they parted, both wiped tears from their eyes.

After bear-hugging Morton, Weis is doing a stand-up for a local news station, raising his voice to be heard over the caterwauling of a group—hive?—of Tech supporters leaning over the railing behind him, decanting their bitterness to the summer night. And to Weis.

They are at once pigeon-chested and bare-chested. Just because they look ridiculous, coated with yellow body paint, their arms accessorized with black stripes, their yellow fright wigs trembling with indignation, does not mean they aren't seriously pissed. They scream accusations and insults at the visiting head coach, who cannot hear, or ignores them.

They remark on his physique, suggest he has undue influence on the officials, advise him to avail himself of nourishment. ("Have another sandwich, Charlie!")

Now the Atlanta police close in on them. "All right, game's over. Time to get out of the stadium."

Weis and the Fighting Irish are more than happy to oblige.

# CHAPTER 4

# The Brawl in the Royal, or The Blunt Truth

ooking out from between the cur-
tains of his dreadlocks, Michael
Griffin seems a little cranky. Not
being well acquainted with the Texas
free safety, I have no way of knowing
if he is always a bit prickly, or if he re-
sents showing up for an in interview on
Monday morning, or if he is already getting a good hate on for Ohio State. Texas
will kick it off against the Buckeyes in
five days.

**AP TOP 10**

*1. Ohio State*

*2. Texas*

*3. USC*

*4. Notre Dame*

*5. Auburn*

*6. West Virginia*

*7. Florida*

*8. LSU*

*9. Florida State*

*10. Michigan*

This one is shaping up to be the big-
gest game ever played in Austin. Ohio State is coming in ranked
No. 1; the defending national champions will be bumped up to
No. 2 the following day. For the first time in a decade, the top
two teams in the AP poll will meet in the regular season. "So
this," Mack Brown declared earlier this morning, "is a game of
magnitude."

It was a rare moment of understatement from Snoop Mack, as some of the beat writers had taken to calling him the previous season. In an effort to find more common ground with his players, the 55-year-old had downloaded a host of hip-hop onto his iPod. (When I asked him if it was true that he could rap out some lyrics by 50 Cent, Brown took immense pleasure in correcting me: "It's pronounced *Fitty* Cent. I can't discuss it with you if you can't pronounce it the right way.")

Ohio State at Texas, the Brawl in the Royal, to borrow Buck-I-Guy's coinage, is the most electric interconference matchup of the early season, and a neon advertisement for the superiority of college football. Too often, NFL teams stagger into the playoffs with .500 records, a pathetic testament to a lack of regular season urgency. But five days from now, one of these teams will find itself with a loss and greatly diminished chances to realize its most ambitious goal.

That urgency may be wearing on Michael Griffin. Do I detect a slight rolling of his eyes when he is asked about the program's recently departed star quarterback? "Without Vince Young," Griffin replies, pointedly, "we put up 50 points last Saturday" in a cakewalk against North Texas. Next question.

What about Ohio State's Troy Smith and Ted Ginn? Has Griffin met the star quarterback and flanker at off-season functions?

"I didn't go to any of those," said Griffin, channeling Miracle Max from *The Princess Bride*. "I'm not a good enough player." *Why don't you give me a nice paper cut, and pour lemon juice on it!* "Ask [nose tackle] Frank Okam. He got to go to the Playboy All-America thing. He probably met those guys. I just stuck around here, went to some dog shows." (He is serious. Griffin later tells me that he breeds pit bulls, and drives all over the Southwest attending American Kennel Club dog shows.)

What is eating Michael Griffin, I will later conclude, is the news the *Austin American-Statesman* has broken minutes before, but which Griffin has probably been aware of since early this morning: The Longhorns will be taking the field against Smith and Ginn without one of their best players.

You can break through to another level of excellence, as the Longhorns had done the previous season, stunning the Trojans in the national championship game. You can recruit your backside off, as Brown and his staff proceeded to do in the aftermath of the school's first national title in 35 years. You can bust your tail in off-season conditioning; you can forge powerful bonds with your teammates going through seven-on-seven drills in 100-plus-degree heat in the shadow of I-35, the elevated freeway that runs over the Longhorns' practice field.

You could do all those things and still find yourself at a disadvantage because, at the end of the day, or, more accurately, at the end of the night, at last call, there are guys on every college football team as deficient in common sense as they are blessed with speed and strength. To paraphrase Art Linkletter, kids do the darnedest things.

Not even eight hours earlier, just shy of 3:00 a.m. on Labor Day, police cruising I-35 had observed a white 2003 Mercury "swerving from lane to lane," according to the affidavit filed by Deputy A. Howard of the Travis County Sheriff's Office. "The driver was initially traveling in the center lane. On three occasions he swerved into the inside lane with half of the vehicle in each lane. On 2 occasions the driver swerved halfway into the outside lane. At one point the driver almost swerved into a car also traveling northbound."

After pulling the Merc over, Deputy Howard "observed three subjects in the vehicle." One was the driver, former Longhorns linebacker Aaron Harris. Riding shotgun was reserve safety Tyrell Gatewood. In the backseat was Tarell Brown. Both passengers were asleep, or, as less-charitable news outlets would later put it, "passed out."

It was only after Harris had passed a field sobriety test (but admitted that he'd been smoking weed—Doh!) that officers returned to the vehicle and noticed that Brown, asleep in the backseat, was holding a handgun in his lap. Howard: "I then instructed everyone to return to our vehicle as we called for more officers."

"We first woke up and detained the rear seat passenger identified as: Brown, Tarell 1-6-85."

What the affidavit doesn't mention is that, after getting Brown out of the car, the officers Tasered him in the chest, then Tasered Gatewood.

A search of the car turned up "a marijuana 'blunt' cigar under the front seat of the vehicle. I observed the 'blunt' and through my training and 7 years of experience believed it to be marijuana. The 'blunt' weighed approximately 1.1 grams."

Thank God for Deputy Howard's keen sleuthing instincts, I thought. A less experienced cop may have mistaken the "blunt" for a harmless panatella.

The gun, a 9mm pistol, belonged to Gatewood, who had a permit for it, and uses it for target practice. Brown was holding it so his friend would not forget he'd left it in the car.

That part of the plan worked to perfection. He won't be forgetting anytime soon. Brown was also charged with unlawfully carrying a handgun, a Class A misdemeanor (which matter went unresolved as this book went to press).

Mack Brown promptly suspended both players from the Ohio State game. Two days later, after Gatewood and Tarell Brown had passed university-administered drug tests, their attorney, Jamie Balagia, complained that the coach had been too quick to suspend them.

You think?

Six days before the team's biggest game of the season, you're out at three in the morning in a car driven by a guy who admitted to police he was high. There's dope in the car, and the cops find you with a loaded gun in your lap.

I think even Jesse Jackson would get behind Mack Brown on this one.

My gut feeling, as the game approaches, is that Tarell Brown will not cost his team this game so much as Troy Smith will take it from the Longhorns. It feels like his time.

I am in danger of missing the Jim Tressel Presser, which is not a steam iron, but rather the Buckeye head coach's weekly sit-down with the media—a function Tressel strives to complete, apparently, without providing a single sound bite.

I'd boarded a predawn flight from Austin to Knoxville, connected to Columbus, and found myself cruising north on Olentagy River Road around noon on Tuesday. But my customary entrance to the Woody Hayes Athletic Center is fenced off: the Buckeyes' football complex is under construction. The WHAC, which I had long viewed as one of the more spacious and opulent football complexes in college football, had been judged insufficiently palatial. Before its plainness, its ordinariness, turns off too many blue-chip recruits, it will undergo a modest, $19.5 million upgrade—modest in comparison to the $150 mill the university recently shelled out to overhaul (and close the open end of) The Horseshoe, a.k.a. Ohio Stadium.

When you are one of the superpowers in college football's arms race, it simply won't do to accept merely *very good* facilities. Hell, the football complex hasn't been upgraded in some 20 years— during which time, as one athletic department official explained, "other schools were building, too. Now it's time for us to add to ours and update it."

And that is just plain humiliating not just for the athletes, but for *the entire Buckeye Nation*, whose constituents include anyone who has ever corrected another person with the following admonition: "Actually, its proper name is *The* Ohio State University." (To which the only proper response is: Yeah, well, please feel free to kiss either of *The* fleshy protuberances otherwise known as my ass.)

The facility boasts a vast new weight room and players' lounge; injured Buckeyes can become whole again in the restorative waters of the 15,000 square foot aquatic therapy pool area, which includes the thermal plunge pool, the polar plunge pool (a.k.a. The Shrink Tank), and the Hydroworks 2000, an underwater treadmill that allows injured athletes to jog in the water, as if in a bad dream.

Players will also be able to avail themselves of the new racquetball and basketball courts, bowling alley, subterranean shooting range, and five-thousand-bottle wine cellar.

Yes, I made up the last three, to see if you were paying attention—but also to give architects some ideas for that moment, 10 or 15 years down the road, when the Oklahomas and Tennessees and Auburns of the world have pulled even in the arms race and it is time, once again, to escalate.

I HAVE PULLED to the side of the road and am placing an emergency call to the Buckeyes sports information office—If it's not in the WHAC, then where the hell *is* today's press conference, I will ask them—when an understated luxury sedan cruises past at precisely the speed limit.

The sedan is piloted by an upright burgher, a handsome man in wire rims whose jawline is well defined and whose hair, shot through with distinguished silver, appears to have been parted with a surveyor's laser, so true is the line. I close my phone and follow Coach Tressel to the press conference.

My friends on the Buckeyes beat bitch often about Tressel's pressers. In the stingy tradition of their larger-than-life forebears, Tressel and his Michigan counterpart, Lloyd Carr, close practices, limit player access, and generally part with as little information as possible. While he is downright Churchillian compared to Carr, Tressel's responses at these functions tend to range from the vague to the opaque.

On this day, he is better than average. He performs a brief Bill Parcells impersonation, giving a series of truncated, Tuna-like answers:

"Yep."

"Nope."

"Because I want to."

He is large-hearted, announcing, in the midst of an unprompted paean to Mack Brown and the Longhorns, that "I've got them ranked number one on our ballot because I think they deserve that."

Brown had earlier informed reporters that he voted Ohio State No. 1 on his ballot, on account of the Buckeyes' surging finish in 2005, and their wealth of returning offensive starters. With this gallant, reciprocal gesture, Tressel is merely returning the favor.

This pleasing tale suffers the disadvantage of not being true. Later that afternoon, *USA Today* will bust Tressel, announcing that the coach actually voted his own team No. 1. (Votes cast by coaches are usually secret; the paper announced it is correcting Tressel's account in the interest of maintaining the "integrity" of its poll.)

Honest mistake, comes the explanation from the Ohio State camp. The task of phoning in Tressel's ballot had been delegated to Stan Jefferson, the team's director of player development, a highly respected former high school principal with a master's degree in education. While Tressel and the staff had decided to rank the Longhorns No. 1, when it came time to fill out his boss's ballot that morning, he had called an audible, elevating the Buckeyes to the top spot "because we were number one in the preseason poll that came out."

I'm guessing that Jefferson is quickly forgiven his "error." This, after all, is a man with a great many responsibilities: "orchestrating the day-to-day operations" of the program; keeping tabs on the academic progress of the players; overseeing "community relations and outreach," according to the Buckeyes' football media guide. Plus, when the need arises, he must fall on his sword for the head coach.

Whether or not Poll-gate is an honest mistake or an example of a PR-savvy man trying to be a little too slick, the fact remains that many longtime Tressel watchers are disinclined to give him the benefit of the doubt.

Give him this, though: On those occasions when his players commit infractions and Tressel is made aware of it in a timely fashion, the punishment is swift and harsh. Sort of.

When Troy Smith confessed to having accepted $500 from a booster in December 2004, Tressel suspended him for two games. That may have seemed like a mild rebuke, compared, for instance, to how Oklahoma's Bob Stoops dealt with a similar issue. (When Rhett Bomar took money for a no-show job, Stoops threw his ass off the team.)

There was a method to Tressel's mildness. Where Stoops was like Charlton Heston in *The Ten Commandments*, angrily dispensing Old Testament justice, Tressel was more of a New Testament kind of coach. In the Ohio State football family, players' "bad decisions" were used as teaching opportunities. You had to screw up *big time* not to rate a second chance.

That worked for Smith, whose journey from Cleveland to Columbus was serrated with peaks and valleys: intervals of high achievement and model behavior interspersed with hardship and false steps. When Troy was 9, his mother's personal problems rendered her unable to take care of him or his older sister, 13-year-old Brittany. Troy's small-fry football coach Irvin White and his wife Diane welcomed him into their home. For four years, while Tracy battled her demons, the Whites were Smith's foster family.

Reunited with his mother in high school, Smith faced anger issues. "I was so bitter about her being away," he told Ken Gordon of the *Columbus Dispatch*. "I was still a baby, and I still wanted my mother and she wasn't there. But through our growth as family members, we got through it."

His temper got the best of him during a basketball game in December 2000. Smith was then a junior at St. Edward High, a predominantly white private school the Whites had encouraged him to attend. A guard on the basketball team, Smith threw an elbow that knocked out a player from Toledo St. John's. Smith would later say the St. John's player used a racial epithet—an accusation the player has adamantly denied ever since.

With the looming likelihood of expulsion from St. Edward, Smith transferred back to the 'hood. While not exactly a lateral move, it was, as biblical scholars describe Adam and Eve's original sin, a fortunate fall. For it put him in the corridors of Glenville High, under the watchful eye of an American hero named Ted Ginn Sr.


TED GINN *Jr.*, a future Top 10 NFL draft pick, was simply one one of most electrifying players to ever don an Ohio State uniform. Yet the success of the son is eclipsed by the success of the father. Ted Sr. is not a college graduate. He is head football coach (and moonlights as a security guard) at this all-black school on Cleveland's east side, just south of St. Clair Avenue, not far from an old LTV steel mill. Yet there he was, No. 14 on the *Plain Dealer*'s list of the 25 most powerful people in northeast Ohio sports, published early in 2007. Ginn is a football coach in the sense that Frank Lloyd Wright was a contractor. The nine straight league titles clinched by his football teams, the two state championships in track—these feats pale in significance beside the young men whose lives he has transformed, and in some cases, saved.

What he does at Glenville transcends mentoring. In a community with too many single-parent homes, at a school whose percentage of economically disadvantaged students is 100, he has been a surrogate father for more young men than he can count. Standing on the sideline under Friday night lights is one of the easiest things he does.

I met him in August 2005. I was in Cleveland to work on a feature on his son. "Xs and Os are the last things we're concerned with," he told me. Ginn is all about bird-dogging guys to get to school; making sure they've eaten breakfast, eaten lunch; staying on them to take the right classes, do their homework, keep their grades up, train in the off-season. "We make it a total business," he says. "Nothing is recreational about being a student-athlete."

The pipeline he has established from Glenville to Ohio State— there are seven Tarblooders on this season's Buckeyes roster alone—turns out to be nothing more than a good start. Convinced that deserving players were being overlooked by D-I schools, Ginn was proactive. In the summer of 1998, he took out a second mortgage on his house and drove a handful of of his players around the Midwest, taking them to various college football camps. That road show has evolved into the Ted Ginn Sr. Foundation "Road to Opportunity Division I Combine Tour." In the summer of 2006, he took 47 players, from numerous area high schools, on a 13-day trip to 13 Midwest college camps, including Notre Dame, Purdue, Ohio State, Wisconsin, and Illinois. Twenty-five of those kids ended up getting scholarships—an astounding 21 from Glenville alone.

Once one of his guys gets a scholarship, whether or not the kid ever plays a down of football becomes a secondary concern. "You've got your education paid for," he says. "Now the worst thing that can happen is, you get a degree."

A lot of guys share Troy Smith's feelings for him. As Smith told *SI*'s Stewart Mandel before the 2006 season, "He is one of the angels in my life."

IT DIDN'T SEEM that way at first. Smith was unaccustomed to the plain talk he got from Ginn Sr., who quickly tired of the quarterback's belligerence and bad attitude. Before Smith's senior season at Glenville, the coach told him he was "poisoning the program." Humbled, Smith adjusted his attitude and led the team to a strong season.

Rivals.com had him pegged as the 12th-best "dual-threat" quarterback coming out that year, but did not see fit to rank him among its top hundred players. In a strong Buckeye recruiting class that included Maurice Clarett, Mike D'Andrea, and Justin Zwick, Smith was an afterthought. He got the last scholarship, with the understanding that—because of the presence of the more highly regarded Zwick—he was joining the program not as a quarterback but as an "athlete."

Smith was a utility man for his first two seasons in Columbus—a part-time wide out, running back, and kick returner. He was switched to quarterback full-time in the spring of 2004, and lashed out after the annual Scarlet and Gray game, embittered by the fact that Tressel had forbidden him from scrambling—had censored his freedom of expression, his artistry! Displeased with his lack of playing time early in the following season, he vented to reporters, informing them that in his view, everything was not "peaches and cream . . . I'm not going to say [the coaches] are playing with my life, but it's sort of like they've got puppet strings on it."

When opportunity knocked midway through that 2004 season—Zwick separated his left shoulder in the sixth game, at Iowa—Smith tore the door off the hinges, leading the 3-3 Buckeyes to victories in four of their next five games. The last of those wins—a beyond-sweet 37–21 upset of Big Ten champion Michigan—became the foundation for a legend he would burnish over the next two Novembers. Smith would leave Columbus with many trophies and titles: Fiesta Bowl MVP, All-American, Heisman winner. Ohio State fans will recall him most fondly for his prowess on the final Saturday of the season. The guy was a Wolverine killer.

Nineteen days after that huge win over Michigan, Ohio State got a call from a whistle-blower at a company called Poly-Care Services. Employees there had described a disturbing scene: A Buckeye player not employed by the company (later identified as Smith) was seen leaving the offices with an envelope. Shortly thereafter, according to an account published in the *Cleveland Plain Dealer*, an Ohio State booster was heard boasting, "Now I own him."

As punishment, Smith was suspended from the last game of that season (the Buckeyes scarcely noticed his absence in a 33–7 romp past Oklahoma State) and the first game of 2005. Smith would later speak of the desolation he felt, sitting in the Ginns' basement, surrounded by trophies, medals, plaques, and team photos—many including him, smiling out at himself—watching his teammates roll over Oklahoma State.

EIGHT MONTHS AFTER that game, three days before the start of the 2005 season, I sat on that same sofa, amidst those same mementos. Above a set of weights hung a poster celebrating Ted Jr. as "Defensive Player of the Year," just a few feet from a *Plain Dealer* headline identifyng Ginn Sr. as Football Coach of the Year. Another clipping, accompanied by a photo of Ted Jr. airborne over a high hurdle, boasted the headline, "Best Since Jesse Owens?"

I was there to report a cover story on Ted Jr., who was three days from kicking off his second season as a Buckeye. Ginn had starred at quarterback and defensive back for his father, intercepting eight passes as a senior—and returning five of those for touchdowns. In the frenzied courtship for his services, Ohio State narrowly beat out USC, mainly because, as Ted Sr. told me, his wife, Ted's mother, could not bear the thought of him so far away.

Ginn went to Columbus hoping to duplicate the success of Chris Gamble, a two-way player who'd become one of the nation's top lockdown corners. "As time went by," Tressel had told me, "you could see that Chris Gamble was going to make his livelihood as a defender. He had extraordinary abilities on that side of the ball. With Teddy, it happened just the opposite."

Where it was obvious Ginn could be "a very good defender," the coach told me, it also became obvious that "he could be out of this world with the ball in his hands."

As a true freshman, Ginn returned an astounding four punts for touchdowns. (The NCAA *career* record is eight.) With the

Buckeyes down to one quarterback in the Alamo Bowl—the erst-while starter sitting in the Ginn family basement in disgrace—Ted Jr. lined up under center for seven plays, scoring on a five-yard draw. He caught six passes for 78 yards, rushed for 51 and—according to the cover story I wrote—"gave 2005 opponents a glimpse of what lies in store for them." The sophomore Ginn would line up at flanker, as a running back, or in the so-called shot-Ginn formation, as a kind of single-wing quarterback.

It was the jinx at its most potent. Several days before the Buck-eyes hosted Texas for their second game of the 2005 season, Ted Jr. appeared on *SI*'s cover in midstride, running effortlessly through the tackle of a Miami of Ohio Redhawk. Ginn and the Buckeyes, the subhead proclaimed, were "gunning for a showdown with Texas."

Ginn would catch two passes in that game, a 25–22 loss in the Horseshoe, for a total of nine yards.

Smith did not start against the Longhorns that evening. He was rusty, having taken fewer snaps than Zwick in fall camp. And truth be told, he was still being punished for taking those five Benjamins from the booster.

With Ohio State trailing 10–0 late in the first quarter, Tressel inserted Smith, who promptly rallied the Buckeyes to a 19–16 lead. When the Longhorns reclaimed the advantage in the game's final minutes—remember Vince Young's perfect pass to the backward-falling Limas Sweed at the side of the end zone?—it was Zwick who got the chance to save the game, Zwick who fumbled on the very next snap. Texas recovered, and the Buckeyes faded, for all practical purposes, from the national title race. For the remainder of his college career, Smith started every game. He comes into this season as the Heisman frontrunner.


AT THE CONCLUSION of the Tressel Presser—Tresser?—I take a knee four feet from Smith, remarking, in my notebook, on his transformation. Coming into college—coming into his third season, for that matter—Smith's default mode was hothead. (Recall his indignation at being jerked around like a "puppet.")

There will be no more colorful rants. The serene and smiling senior sitting before us has bought into the system, embraced the rhetorical boilerplate of his head coach. "Once you start thinking about what's created around you," Smith warned, in response to a question about the Heisman, "you can take your eye off what's really at stake."

Ohio State opened its 2006 season with a 35–12 tune-up win over Northern Illinois. A Buckeye defense featuring nine new starters gave slight cause for concern, surrendering 171 yards rushing and 285 yards of total offense to Huskies scatback Garrett Wolfe. For his part, Smith was in supreme command, leading the offense to touchdowns on each of their first four possessions. He completed his first five passes, three of which were touchdowns.

With the ascension of Vince Young to the Tennessee Titans, Smith has been hailed as the country's top returning *dual-threat* quarterback. I get the sense that something about that modifier sticks in his craw. Whenever the subject of Young arises—it happens a lot this week—a cloud passes over Smith's features.

Whenever asked to compare himself to Vince Young, Smith flinches, almost imperceptibly, then answers by not answering. "He's a great guy, but I play for a totally different team," he says on one occasion. "He's 6-6, I'm 6-1," he replies on another (inadvertently spotting them both an inch). My theory is that he dodges the question because there's no upside in answering it truthfully: *I'm better at reading defenses, better at getting through my progression. I have a more fluid motion, and throw a better, more accurate deep ball—a more accurate ball, period.*

"I am," Smith says, "my own man."

He'll be attacking a weakened secondary. Although both Tarell Brown and Tyrell Gatewood passed university-administered drug tests—and police dropped the marijuana charges against them—coach Mack Brown has stood by his decision to keep them out of Saturday's game.

. . . .

One injury to keep an eye on going into the Armageddon in Austin: Ohio State senior Dan Wanders is suffering from pain in both hip flexors. "As soon as I get home," he reports after Thursday's practice, "I'm going to take some Tylenol." Is he worried about Saturday night? "Nahh. Once you're on the field, adrenaline takes over."

Wanders, of course, is a fourth-year sousaphonist from Hudson, Ohio, who will be living out the dream of every childhood tuba player in the Buckeye State. (A sousaphone, Dan and some of his buddies explain to me, is simply the marching band version of a tuba.) In one of college football's most beloved pregame rites, he will dot the *i* in the Band's famed script Ohio. Sixteen measures from the end of "Le Regiment de Sambre et Meuse," drum major Steward Kitchen will strut toward the top of the *i*, with Wanders high-kicking several paces behind. As the cheering reaches a crescendo, Kitchen will point dramatically to that sacred spot atop the lower-case *i*.

Having completed the ritual, Wanders will doff his hat and bow deeply to the east and west sides of the stadium, drinking up the adulation. . . .

Such are the daydreams that have sustained him during marching band two-a-days. The student-musicians have been going nine to noon, then two to five since August 30. (If NCAA rules forbidding teams from practicing or meeting more than 20 hours a week applied to marching bands, the Buckeyes would've received the death penalty long ago.) He's sore from that backward-leaning kick-strut.

"It's kind of a jump-kick," he tells me. "While I'm kicking my feet out, I'm leaning back and swinging my upper body in opposition to the leg I'm kicking."

He's doing that while leaning back so far that the bell of his 35-pound instrument is pointing toward the sky. It is a motion that isolates and aggravates the hip flexors. When Wanders was a rookie, he recounts, some of the older sousaphonists advised against practicing the jump-kick until the week you were actually scheduled to dot the *i*.

How much stock did he put in that superstition? "I've been practicing for this all summer."

It is small—minute, even: We are talking about a dot, for Christ's sake. And it is immense. It will number among the highlights of a sousaphonist's life, right up there with (in no particular order) graduation, marriage, losing one's cherry. Dotting the *i* in the band's script Ohio is profoundly serious and completely whimsical: a tuba-lugging undergraduate directed to a spot by an extravagantly plumed drum major whose headgear approximates the length and shape of Marge Simpson's hairdo. Both students employ gaits that are on loan from Monty Python's Ministry of Silly Walks. Impugn this ritual, however, suggest a revision, and feel the wrath of a million Ohioans. This is the distilled essence of college football, and has no analogue in the NFL, or any pro sport. No wonder Wanders isn't complaining about pain in his hip flexors.

WHEN IT COMES to rowdy, drunken, sofa-torching behavior, I would put Buckeyes fans—and I distinguish here between Ohio State fans and Ohio State *students*—in the 95th to 99th percentile. They did nothing to harm their reputation for loutish behavior before, during, or after last year's Longhorns-Buckeyes game in Columbus. "I had unprovoked cursing of my mother on High Street," another Longhorns fan told the *Columbus Dispatch*. "It made me feel really, really sorry for Michigan fans. If we got treated that poorly, I can only imagine how Michigan fans get treated. They're nuts."

One outraged Texas student told the paper, "I have never been anywhere like that," before adding the unkindest cut: "Even Arkansas fans weren't that rude."

What retaliatory fireworks await in Austin? Even though Ohio

State had been allotted only 4,000 tickets in Royal–Texas-Memorial's 85,000-seat stadium, some 40,000 Buckeyes fan are said to be converging on the Lone Star State.

The atmosphere in Austin turns out to be far less toxic. Texas fans seem determined to show the Buckeyes how things are done at a class program. Yes, the Longhorns' fans partake of a few adult beverages on game day. The difference was, they invite the visiting Buckeyes to drink with them.

Perhaps they've decided to take a small measure of pity on the visitors. As one sign in the stadium read, Austin - babes & sunshine = Columbus.

No one bothers John Chubb, a.k.a. Buck-I-Guy, whose ensemble includes white shoes, white shorts, and a scarlet and white cape. A half hour before kickoff, he stands at the railing behind the Texas bench, striking heroic poses and issuing such overblown proclamations as: "This is the Game of the Century! This is Ali-Frazier! You've heard of the Thrilla in Manila—this here's the Brawl in the Royal!"

Questions about Ohio State's run defense loom especially large on the Longhorns' second drive. On successive rushes, Texas tailbacks Jamaal Charles and Selvin Young gash the Buckeyes for 12, 13, 9, and 12 yards. A pair of completions by McCoy, the apple-cheeked second-year quarterback, and a pass-interference on the Buckeyes, give Texas a first-and-goal at the Ohio State seven. The defending national champions, it seems, have picked right up where they left off.

This game—and, by extension, the 2006 college football season—turns on what unfolds in the moments that follow. On second-and-goal from the seven, McCoy throws to flanker Billy Pittman, who is struggling for extra yards when middle linebacker James Laurinaitis, late to the ruck, pops the ball out. Nimbly scooping it up at the two is Buckeye cornerback Donald Washington, who is run down, 48 yards up the field, by none other than McCoy, who later makes a good point: "You never want to be on the tackle chart as a quarterback."

Smith makes the Longhorns pay, moving the Buckeyes 50 yards with three completions to Anthony Gonzalez, whom Texas corners were giving a 30-foot cushion. On his 14-yard touchdown catch, Gonzo shakes cornerback Brandon Foster with a double-move—one fake, followed by another. He doesn't really need the second juke to lose Foster, who's having a tough day at the office, filling in for the suspended Tarell Brown.

McCoy shows moxie late in the half, leading the Horns on a 78-yard touchdown drive kept alive, at one point, by a bogus roughing-the-quarterback call. Pittman's redemptive, two-yard touchdown catch ties the score with just under two minutes to play.

Any buzz the Longhorns hope to take into the locker room is killed by Smith, who proceeds to direct a textbook two-minute drill, connecting on five straight passes. Just before the last of those throws, on first-and-10 from the Texas 29, he looks left and sees Aaron Ross lined up in press coverage on Ginn. (Ross, by the way, is dating former Longhorns track star Sanya Richards, who at the time is the world's top-ranked 400-meter runner, and who may have had more success covering Ginn on this play.) The Buckeye flanker jukes right, then left, then right again before bursting past Ross on the inside. Safety Marcus Griffin arrives too late to prevent Ginn's over-the-shoulder basket catch, in the end zone, of the most beautiful pass of the night.

Texas is finished, for all practical purposes, then and there. The Longhorns are shut out in the second half by a defense that appears to be coalescing before our eyes. Yielding 326 yards, 172 of those on the ground, Ohio State's defenders bend but never break. In holding Texas to a single touchdown—the final score is 24–7—they make a statement: If the Buckeyes don't contend for the Big Ten and national titles, it won't be because the defense sucks out loud. With 13 tackles, two forced fumbles, and an interception, Laurinaitis is defensive MVP.

There is even less debate about the Buckeyes' most valuable player on offense. Smith is masterful, forcing nothing, managing the game like the cagey vet he is. He completes 17 of his 26 passes for 269 yards. He throws for his fourth and fifth touchdown passes of the season, against zero interceptions. When he finishes spouting bromides at his postgame press conference—"Aaron Ross is a great cornerback . . . he had some great plays today"; "I just put the ball in the air and Teddy made a great play"; "Week in, week out, we just try to execute the game plan"—I follow him from the visitors' dressing room to the team bus.

After rushing for 950 yards on 218 attempts over the previous two seasons, Smith has now carried eight times for minus 14 yards in the first two games of 2006. By turning his nose up at the run all the sudden, is Smith making a point? Is this his response to the tiresome comparisons to Vince Young?

He lets me get the question out. He even starts to answer it—"I try not to think about things like that, but"—then catches himself. "You know," he says, side-eyeing me, "we're not supposed to be giving interviews."

Congratulations, I feel like telling him. You have now completely, officially bought in to the Jim Tressel belief system. Did someone say puppet?

Meanwhile, a time zone away, the skyline of Columbus has taken on an extra glow. Celebratory fireworks and floodlights? Umm, not exactly. Police will report that 35 to 40 fires are set in student neighborhoods. Couches and mattresses are the sacrificial items of choice, although at least one car goes up in flames. Seventeen people are arrested.

Buckeyes fans in Austin are better behaved. Trudging toward my rental car after midnight, I hear a chorus of slurred voices raised in song—a ragged but joyous profession of faith celebrating a huge win even as it points to the next monster game on the schedule:

*We don't give a damn about the whole state of Michigan,*
*We're from O-HI-O.*

# CHAPTER 5

# "We few, we happy few . . ."

September 1, Fayetteville, Ark. — Two weeks and a day after being called onto the stage at the Salute to Troy, the Trojans are in team buses, attracting salutes of a different sort as they make their way up Razorback Road on the campus of the University of Arkansas. A year earlier, 'SC had simply annihilated the Hawgs, rolling up 736 yards of total offense in a 70–17 slaughter. Scoring on four of their first *eight plays* in that game, Leinart, Bush, White, & Co.

**AP TOP 10 WEEKS**

*1. Ohio State*

*2. Texas*

*3. USC*

*4. Notre Dame*

*5. Auburn*

*6. West Virginia*

*7. Florida Fl*

*8. LSU*

*9. Florida State*

*10. Michigan*

didn't just hand Arkansas its worst loss since 1918. To hear Razorbacks defensive coordinator Reggie Herring tell it, they had emasculated the program, taken its "manhood."

Herring is the crack assistant whose cutting-edge idea it was to force players whom he judged to be "loafing" to wear pink jerseys at practice. Asked by the *L.A. Times* to recall that 2005 rout, he showed potential as a country-music lyricist: "It was like having your dog run over, your wife left you and your house burned down . . . it was about as bad as something can happen to you in life and still be breathing."

Redemption is finally at hand. "One way or another, we're going to get our manhood back," Herring vowed to the *Arkansas Democrat-Gazette* on the eve of the 2006 opener, before adding a brief disclaimer: "Or we're not."

If the Trojans are at all concerned about walking into a buzzsaw in the Ozarks, they give no indication of it the day before the game. Filing through a tunnel into Donald Reynolds Razorback Stadium, whose towering, steeply banked stands call to mind vast, breaking waves, the Trojans are laughing, razzing, smiling, joking—almost as if they find the expression "Whoo-pig-sooie!" more comical than threatening.

Some members of the Trojan family—the biggest members— already have game faces on. Near the beginning of the walk-through, offensive and defensive linemen line up against each other for a game of touch football, a weekly contest otherwise known as "Fat on Fat," which left tackle Sam Baker insists be spelled "Phat on Phat." To conserve their energy, the big uglies play the equivalent of a half-court game—53 yards across the width of the field. To further conserve their energy, running is strictly forbidden. If someone would loan them enough golf carts, these guys would play the game sitting on their duffs. With two dozen 300-pound post-adolescents speed-walking and shouting nearby— "You didn't tag me!" "Bullshit! That's a sack!"—I make the acquaintance of one Chester Caddas, a friendly ex–football coach from northern California who is responsible, indirectly, for the renaissance of football at Southern California.

Now 71 AND retired to Murray, Kentucky, Caddas was the head coach at the University of Pacific in Stockton, California, from 1972 to 1978. The Tigers would terminate their football progam in 1995, following a long, slow descent into futility. Pre–death spiral, however, Pacific often overachieved, knocking off more than its share of name opponents and turning out an inordinate number of celebrated coaches. Amos Alonzo Stagg held his final head-coaching job at Pacific from 1933 to '46; he would die in Stockton at the age of 102. Buddy Ryan made a stop at Pacific, as did future NFL head coaches Mike Martz and Jon Gruden.

In 1971, on the advice of Tigers secondary coach Walt Harris, Caddas offered a scholarship to a juco player from Marin County, that ruggedly spectacular tract of land just over the Golden Gate Bridge from San Francisco. Then as now, Pete Carroll was a restless, carefree spirit whose hair was longer than his attention span. Even then, Caddas recalls, Carroll dealt with his pregame butterflies by playing catch on the field.

"On and off the field, he sparkled," Caddas recalls. "He covered lots of ground, was very instinctive, and intercepted a bunch of passes, I think nine," as a junior. And he would bring the wood. "You think he's happy-go-lucky?" says Harris in David Wharton and Gary Klein's 2005 book, *Conquest*. "Well, he would knock you out. He would hurt you and love it."

Once he ran out of college eligibility, Carroll took a shot at pro ball, trying out with the Honolulu Hawaiians of the World Football League. He was cut, and took a job peddling roofing materials in the East Bay. Later that year, Caddas was picking up a transcript at the College of Marin when he dropped some change into a phone booth to make "a courtesy call to Pete's parents." Jim and Rita Carroll lived in Greenbrae, 10 miles or so north of the Golden Gate Bridge. Rita insisted that he join the family for lunch— "We're just having sandwiches on the patio," he recalls her saying. An hour later, between bites of a bologna sandwich, Caddas asked how Pete was doing. Jim replied, "I think he'd really like to coach."

As it happened, Caddas had a spot on his staff open. "This is full-time," the head coach warned. "Not a grad-assistant job." It only paid like one: $2,800.

"That was on a Friday," recalls the old coach. "On Monday or Tuesday, Pete Carroll walked into my office."

Carroll coached three seasons at Pacific while moonlighting as a grad student: he received his secondary teaching credential and his master's in physical education in 1976. For Carroll, it was a bracing, exhilarating time—"a time of exploration in sport," write the authors of *Conquest*. "People were looking at the jock world in new ways, delving beyond the merely physical, examining connections between mind and body."

"At the time," recalls Glen Albaugh, a professor and sports psychologist who mentored Carroll, "I was really interested in the Human Potential Movement and how it might reflect itself in sport." He describes his former grad student as "very inquisitive, bright, willing to take risks and willing to go into territory coaches don't normally go into. And so, away we went."

Albaugh remembers being impressed by Carroll's ability to knowledgeably discuss *Cutting Through Spiritual Materialism* by the Buddhist meditation master Chogyam Trungpa Rinpoche. It wasn't the fact that his student had read the book that stayed with Albaugh, who'd assigned Carroll works ranging from George Leonard, whom *Newsweek* would describe as "the granddaddy of the consciousness movement," to that polestar of humanistic psychology, Abraham Maslow. It was *how* Carroll plowed through the Trungpa tome: with the book flat on his dashboard, while driving south on 1-5 from Stockton to Southern California to visit Glena, his future wife.

After three years at Pacific, Carroll heard from a former colleague. Ex–Tigers coach Bob Cope was an assistant to Lou Holtz at Arkansas in 1977 when his bespectacled boss gave him permission to hire a part-time assistant.

Carroll's initial response: "Man, I don't want to go to *Ark*ansas."

After pointing out to Carroll that he would be sextupling his salary while landing a job at one of the hottest programs in the country, Caddas informed him, "If you don't take this, you're not as smart as I think you are."

Thus did this son of Marin find himself at the only university in America whose mascot is named for a feral pig. In Fayetteville, Carroll found another mentor, a thin-faced defensive guru named Monte Kiffin, from whose fertile mind would spring a widely imitated scheme called the Tampa Two (and from whose loins would spring Lane Kiffin, future USC Trojans offensive coordinator and Oakland Raiders head coach).

For the first time in nearly three decades, Carroll is back in Hawgs country, which, due in large part to the Wal-Mart-induced economic boom, is all but unrecognizable to him. "I sure don't remember it like this," he tells Dan Weber of the *Riverside Press-Enterprise*. The stadium itself had undergone a dramatic makeover, adding 25,000 seats since Carroll last coached here, plus a vast new Smartvision LED scoreboard known to the locals as "the Pig-Screen."

ADDRESSING THE TEAM at midfield at the end of the walk-through, strength coach and cancer survivor Chris Carlisle harks back to the best pep talk in history. He tells the Trojans about the Battle of Agincourt, fought on October 25 (St. Crispin's Day) in 1415 between the armies of English King Henry V and Charles VI of France.

"Before the battle," Carlisle informs the team, "he gave a speech, and Shakespeare wrote about it in his play *Henry V.* And it went something like this:

> *We few, we happy few, we band of brothers.*
> *For he today that sheds his blood with me*
> *Shall be my brother. Be he never so vile,*
> *This day shall gentle his condition.*
> *And gentlemen in England now a-bed,*
> *Shall think themselves accurs'd they were not here,*
> *And hold their manhoods cheap whiles any speaks*
> *That fought with us upon Saint Crispin's day."*

After supplementing the Bard's verses with a few historical tid-bits—such as the fact that the French were fond of cutting off the fingers of the British longbow-men—Carlisle brings it home: "To-morrow, with 76,000 against us, we come together as a family, this group right here, this band of brothers."

Some brothers are newer than others. The following evening, on the basis of his consistency in camp, C. J. Gable becomes the first freshman in Trojan history to start at tailback for Tailback U. The 18-year-old from Sylmar, California, is one of three true freshmen to score touchdowns in the Trojans' opener. While that statistic presages a logjam at that glamour position, it also speaks to the talent of 'SC's recruits, and Carroll's willingness to put them on the field when they are babies.

Unlike the previous matchup between these teams, the out-come is not decided in the first quarter. On its first three posses-sions of the season, USC kicks a field goal, surrenders the ball on downs, and punts.

The story of the first half is the Trojans' defense, a unit that had done a highly creditable impersonation, in its previous game, of eleven cardinal-and-gold pylons on Vince Young's private play-ground. In the off-season, to take advantage of 'SC's embarrass-ment of riches at linebacker, Carroll green-lighted a switch from a base 4-3—four down linemen and three linebackers—to a 3-4. During his tenure as the 49ers' defensive coordinator, he'd used Charles Haley as a so-called elephant—a stand-up rush end who sometimes dropped into coverage. (A reprobate even by NFL standards, Haley was best known for picking fights with team-mates, one of whose cars he used as a urinal. And yet, he never had trouble finding work. Dude may have been bipolar, but he was a bipolar Pro Bowler who finished his career with 100 sacks.)

Carroll's latest elephant is Brian Cushing, a 6'4", 245-pound true sophomore whose Captain America physique and Fabio-like mane have made him a favorite over at Boi From Troy, a Web site devoted to politics, 'SC athletics, and gay issues, though not nec-essarily in that order. While Cushing may have been a bit uncomfortable seeing his picture posted next to ads for Firefly "personal lubricant" and ManCandy.com—he is, after all, 19, and barely a year removed from Bergen (New Jersey) Catholic High—such is the price of his precocity.

With Cushing looking exceptionally comfortable in his new role—"He's a monster," Carroll told reporters, "he needs to be out there"—the newfangled 3-4 had outperformed the Trojans first-team offense in preseason. How would it fare when it mattered?

Admirably, it turns out. The Razorbacks fumble three times in their first three possessions, losing two. With Booty and the offense taking a bit longer to find their sea legs, the Trojans' half-time lead is a modest 16–7. On the Hawgs' first series of the second half, nose tackle Sedrick Ellis, who already has a sack in the game, bats a Robert Johnson pass into the air. Junior cornerback Terrell Thomas makes the pick.

Before throwing his first touchdown pass as a starter, Booty throws a minor tantrum. Or so it seems. Coming out of a time-out, on first down at the Hawgs' 14-yard line, the redshirt junior approaches the line of scrimmage and starts waving his arms and chewing out his teammates. What is up with that?

"Oh, that?" he will tell the *L.A. Times* after the game. "No, I was only pretending to be yelling."

By faking a hissy fit, Booty hopes to deflect Arkansas's attention from the fact that the Trojans are lined up in the same formation they'd shown *before* the time-out. Steve Smith is wide left, with flanker Patrick Turner in the slot to that side. After going in motion to the right, Smith reverses course at the snap of the ball, heading for the left flat, drawing a cornerback with him. Turner, a true sophomore and native Tennessean, sprints for the left corner of the end zone. Undeterred by the fact that Turner isn't open—is, in fact, double-covered—Booty rifles the ball low and away from the defenders, where only Turner can dig it out.

He does, and the Trojans lead 23–7 with 9:24 left in the third quarter. It is the first highlight of a half in which he will throw three scoring passes and announce himself a worthy successor to

Leinart and Carson Palmer before him. Booty is incandescent in the third quarter, completing nine of his 10 passes, two for touchdowns. The first of those passes is a frozen rope to the far side of the field—a throw, his teammates don't mind telling reporters, that Matt Leinart did not have in him.

Arkansas will score once more. While that touchdown has zero effect on the outcome of the game—'SC cruises, 50–14—it has disproportionate influence on the outcome of a bizarre season in Razorback Nation. That scoring drive is led by Mitch Mustain, the true freshman and local boy who was named the 2005 *Parade* magazine prep player of the year after throwing for 47 touchdowns as a senior at Springdale High, just up the road. Despite throwing a pick on the following drive against 'SC, Mustain will be named the starter for Arkansas's next contest, a gimme win against sacrificial lamb Utah State. While Mustain will win eight straight games, head coach Houston Nutt will bench him late in the season. The ill will created by that decision is but an appetizer for the full-scale tumult to come, a surreal interval during which a booster close to the Nutt family will send a toxic e-mail to the 18-year-old Mustain, encouraging him to transfer. Later, Razorback fans will use the Freedom of Information Act to obtain Nutt's phone records. Those records revealed that the married 49-year-old had exchanged 1,063 text messages with a local female sportscaster between November 30 and January 11. Both parties forcefully insisted that all those messages were perfectly innocent—even the one sent by Nutt just 19 minutes before kickoff of the Capital One Bowl.

The following April, Mustain will announce that he is transferring.

To USC.

After losing their opener by 36, the Razorbacks take solace where they can find it. A list of postgame notes typed up by the Arkansas sports information office celebrates the "vast improvement" of Reggie Herring's defense. Whereas the 2005 unit had yielded those 736 yards of total offense, this year's crew "held" USC to 472 total yards.

Two games, 120 points, 1,208 yards. That's a lot of unreclaimed manhood. It would be only fair, I believe, for Herring to spend the following week in a pink jersey.

The Trojans are greeted with hosannas. The 50 points they'd hung on the Hawgs is one more than the 49 points per game averaged by the celebrated 2005 offense. Booty completed 24 of his 35 passes for 261 yards, three TDs, and no interceptions. Clearly, the Trojans' quarterbacking machine hasn't missed a beat. Somehow Booty has bypassed the learning curve required of most first-year starters. As one columnist put it, "Booty isn't as tall as Leinart, but he throws a much stronger ball, and he already has the poise that it took Leinart several months to develop."

A committee of backs rushed for 192 yards against a very good front seven. Moody averaged 8.3 yards per carry; Chauncey Washington, 6.9. Gable, who went against the Arkansas defense when it was freshest, averaged 4.2 yards per carry. The defense had been a revelation.

There are slivers of disturbing news to temper the euphoria. Josh Pinkard, a terrific, instinctive, ballhawking free safety and the most experienced member of the Trojans' secondary, blew out his right knee late in the game. He is lost for the season, and will be replaced by Taylor Mays, a 6'4", 225-pound true freshman who appears to be out of position in the secondary—why is that linebacker 20 yards off the line?—until the ball is snapped.

At a late August practice, I'd noticed a towering presence in the Trojans' secondary. "Who the hell is 29?" I asked Weber.

"Taylor Mays," he replied. "Pete loves him. He's playing so well they can't keep him off the field." The son of ex–NFL defensive lineman Stafford Mays, Taylor had twice swept the 100 and 200 meters in the Washington State 3A track meet. A fan of Charles Woodson, Mays was leaning toward Michigan until he took a visit to USC. It was then, according to an account in the *L.A. Times*, that Trojans athletic director Mike Garrett had advised him not to bother becoming a Trojan if he feared competition. "If you're scared you're going to get lost in the shuffle, don't come here," warned the sly AD, knowing precisely the effect his warning would have. As Mays told the *Times*, "In my mind I said, 'All right. I'm coming here.'"

It is a good thing that the 18-year-old relishes a challenge. His first college start will come in front of 92,000 fans at the Coliseum against resurgent Nebraska.

SEPTEMBER 16, Los Angeles —Having begun their 2006 season with a pair of wins, the Men of Corn are standing taller than they have in years. True, they have yet to pick on anyone their own size—those wins had come at the expense of Louisiana Tech and Nicholls State—but a victory over the Trojans will signal to America that Nebraska's exile from the college football elite is at an end.

Actually, the Huskers don't need a victory to make that statement. They have the Mouth from the South, Andre Jones, a loquacious cornerback who'd arrived in Lincoln from Fort Walton, Florida, by way of Kentucky and Fresno City Community College.

Jones isn't sweating the fact that 'SC has won 46 of its previous 48 games. "When we beat this team," he vows, "we can show the world that we are a great team and we restored the order."

Gosh, Andre, what about Trojans receivers Steve Smith and Dwayne Jarrett?

"My friends have all been calling me, blowing up my phone, talking big noise and everything—saying how they're going to beat us, saying all these threats they have on their team," Jones said. "We've got the same amount of threats over here."

At least one person agreed that 'SC receivers were, for the time being, overrated. Lane Kiffin, the Trojans offensive coordinator and wide receivers' coach, had been one of the least happy people on the charter back from Fayetteville. Kiffin didn't care that his guys caught 15 passes for 143 yards; he gave them a collective F. His displeasure was focused on one in particular.

Jarrett had come through a rough off-season. There had been that suspension levied by the NCAA for his failure to pay his full share of the rent at the apartment he shared with Leinart. (The suspension was lifted three weeks before the opener.) On the morning of August 15, he and offensive tackle Thomas Herring were mistakenly detained by Los Angeles police as the pair made their way to practice. Police reported that the two players had accepted a ride in a car that may have been used in a crime, which is why they were swarmed and handcuffed upon stepping out of the vehicle. (It probably didn't help Jarrett and Herring that they are both African American.)

And he was nagged throughout August by his left quadriceps, which he strained early in camp. "It never totally healed up," Jarrett would later tell me. "So I went into the Arkansas game about 80 percent. I was hurting, and it was really hard for me to get open like I normally do, but I didn't tell anybody."

Which was fine, because Kiffin wasn't in the mood for excuses, acidly observing that "We didn't bring him here all the way from New Jersey to catch five passes for 35 yards."

The coach saved his most biting indictment for Steve Sipple of the *Lincoln Star-Journal*. "He might be living in the past," said Kiffin of Jarrett, who'd pulled down 91 catches for 1,274 yards as a sophomore in 2005, "and that doesn't do us any good right now."

Message received. On USC's second play from scrimmage, Booty hits him on a 19-yard gain, in front of the voluble Andre Jones, who becomes decidedly less talkative as the evening unfolds. Jarrett catches three more balls on the Trojans' final possession of the first quarter. On the third of those, he is lined up wide right. Jones is 10 yards off him, apparently thinking fade. Eagerly purchasing Jarrett's fake to the flag, he has an excellent view of the play as the All-American plants hard with his right foot, cuts across his face, and casually gathers in a 12-yard touchdown pass.

Trojans corner Cary Harris recovers a Nebraska fumble early in the second half. Four snaps later, Booty finds Jarrett for his second touchdown of the night. The junior finishes with 11 receptions for 136 yards and those two scores, giving him 31 touchdown catches, two games into his junior season.

"You could see him really coming this week in practice," Carroll gushes in the postgame. He is proud of his defense, proud of Taylor Mays, who "survived"—Carroll's word—his first collegiate start. Aided by the on-field counsel of fellow safety Kevin Ellison, Mays put in a solid night's work, making six tackles and giving up no big plays.

MAYS'S DEBUT WAS made smoother by the mystifying tactics of Cornhusker head coach Bill Callahan, who devised an offensive game plan so recondite that its brilliance was evident only to him. Having spent the better part of three years installing the most effective passing attack in the history of Cornhusker football, facing an opponent missing not one but two starting defensive backs—Harris was filling in for Kevin Thomas—Callahan set the Wayback Machine to the late '70s. Evoking the days of such departed I-backs as Jarvis Redwine and I. M. Hipp, the Cornhuskers got very conservative in the Coliseum, rushing the ball 36 times while attempting just 16 passes.

It's one thing to keep it on the ground when Dean Steinkuhler is punching vast holes in the defensive line. Against USC, Nebraska managed three first downs rushing. All day. Three. Cornhusker backs averaged 1.9 yards per carry.

"We continued to run the football," Callahan will later say, growing testy when inferior football minds question his methods, "and we did what we planned to do to win the game."

They ran the ball after they went ahead, 3–0. They ran—four times in a row, to run out the clock—while trailing by 11 at the end of the first half. They ran after they'd fallen behind, 21–3. They ran on first down—every time, until the final minute of the third quarter. The first time Taylor *threw* on first down, he completed a 25-yard pass.

"We felt we could come in and run the football," the head Husker will later repeat, staying faithfully on message.

"We were pounding the ball and doing a good job." (One-point-nine yards per carry.) "That was just the game plan, and if you stick with it, you have a chance to win."

Perhaps. But it seemed, at times, as if Callahan was more intent on keeping the score respectable, avoiding an Arkansas-type blowout, than giving his guys a legitimate chance to win.

Jones, the self-assured Cornhusker corner, had vowed to "restore the order." In his own small way, he had: Jarrett once again looked All-World. While Jarrett is out of Kiffin's doghouse, the latest Trojans coach to be displeased is offensive line coach Pat Ruel, who holds his hogs responsible for the fact that the Trojans couldn't get much going on the ground, either. That had much to do with Nebraska's formidable front seven. It had something to do with the fact that 'SC continued to rotate tailbacks into the game as if each series were a casting call. And it had something to do with 'SC's fifth play from scrimmage, which produced the most disturbing injury of the college football season.

BACK UP THREE weeks. During an intrasquad scrimmage on a chilly night at the Coliseum, I saw No. 37 take a swing pass out of the backfield and turn on the jets. Ryan Powdrell was finally ridden down, but only, according to my notes, after "dragging 6 guys @ 10 yards." So pleased was Carroll with this effort that he performed a brief jig, then smacked the fullback's rump as he jogged past.

Carroll was feeling equal measures pleasure and relief. Early in camp, he'd lost the services of starting fullback Brandon Hancock, who tore ligaments in his left knee for the second time in two years. Hancock, a.k.a. the Hulk, was a workout beast who didn't have muscle groups so much as he had federations. Coalitions of muscle. But it was the Hulk's destiny to be as fragile as he was ripped. His senior year was over before it began. The loss of this Phi Beta Kappa was as harsh a blow to the offense—when he was healthy, Hancock was as fine a blocker as he was a receiver—as it was to the team's cumulative GPA.

It was almost heresy to say it, so beloved was Hancock by members of Trojan Nation, but it didn't look like they were losing much with Powdrell—or, as he was known on message boards, POWdrell—in the backfield. A 6-foot, 255-pound ex-linebacker who'd switched to offense to get on the field, Powdrell had a fullback's body with a tailback's burst. He was the talk of the spring game, rushing for 81 yards on 10 carries. Going into fall camp, Carroll had said, "We need to get him the ball, both handing it to him and throwing it to him, because there's something special about the way he runs."

Three weeks later, on USC's first possession against Nebraska, Kiffin calls his number on third-and-two. Finding not even a crease of daylight up the gut, Powdrell bounces the play outside. As middle linebacker Corey McKeon pulls him down from behind, Powdrell's ankle is trapped beneath the linebacker at a bad angle. What Powdrell hears, as his connective tissue rends and his fibula snaps and his ankle joint explodes, is "a sound just like when you crack your knuckles."

Lying on the field, he screams at the sight of his foot pointed 90 degrees inward, like an unmoored prosthesis. He grows calmer after 'SC team physician James Tibone rotates his foot, then pops the dislocated ankle back into joint. Even as he suffered this injury, Powdrell had hung on to the ball. He had not fumbled. Now, as he leaves the field on a cart, he flashes the school's two-fingered victory salute to the fans.

He receives a pain-killing injection and two Vicodins in the locker room. He is x-rayed, splinted, and handed a pair of crutches. After hobbling in and out of the shower, he lies on the floor of the locker room with his leg elevated, watching the game on TV. That is the only time he cries. "It wasn't the pain," he will recall.

"It was the frustration and disappointment. After all the years, all the hard work, I'd finally gotten where I wanted to be. And it was over so fast."

The next morning his ankle is reconstructed. Two weeks later he is in the weight room. The NCAA will turn down his request for a medical redshirt. All he can do is prepare for the Trojans' NFL Day, and hope to impress some NFL scout enough to spend a late-round draft choice on him, or sign him as a free agent.

To the people sickened by his injury, Powdrell had reassuring words: "It didn't hurt as bad as it looked."

The converse is true of the loss of No. 37: it hurts the Trojans more than anyone first realizes. The significance of his absence will become apparent in the fullness of time.

# CHAPTER 6

# Losin's Losin'

September 16, South Bend, Ind. — He had pureed Purdue, massacred Michigan State, bullied Boston College. In three years, however, Brady Quinn had never had a big game against Michigan. He threw 10 passes in the Big House as a wide-eyed freshman, coming on in relief of his battered roommate, Carlyle Holiday. He completed four of those throws—one to a grateful Jon Shaw, the Wolverine free safety. As a sophomore Quinn tossed two touchdown passes but three picks in a 28–20 win. A year later he passed for just 140 yards in Weis's second game, a stunning, 17–10 upset of the No. 3 Wolverines in Ann Arbor. The simple fact was, the guys in maize and blue hit Quinn hard and made him earn every yard, every pissant completion. It was almost as if the Michigan coaches took secret pleasure in making his life miserable.

That would be the karmic wheel coming full circle. Before Ohio State began its belated courtship of him; long, long before

**AP TOP 10 WEEKS**

1. *Ohio State*
2. *Notre Dane*
3. *Auburn*
4. *USC*
5. *West Virginia*
6. *LSU*
7. *Florida*
8. *Texas*
9. *Florida State*
10. *Georgia*

Notre Dame chose to acknowledge his existence, Wolverines head coach Lloyd Carr and his staff had studied Quinn's high school tape, and they were smitten.

They were smitten because in the spring of 2001, Coffman High in Dublin, Ohio, hired a new football coach. The new guy was Mark Crabtree, who announced to the Shamrocks at his first team meeting, "We *will* throw the ball here." At that moment, he recalls, "every set of eyes swung to a guy to my left. I remember thinking, That must be the quarterback. I didn't know what I had yet. But the players knew."

As a junior in Crabtree's first year, Quinn threw for 2,200 yards and 21 touchdowns, against just four interceptions. In leading the 'Rocks to the state semifinals, Quinn thrust himself onto the radar of Division I coaches across the nation.

No major power was on him earlier than Michigan. By the end of what Robin Quinn calls "his World Tour" the following summer—she chauffeured her son to football camps at Louisville, Ohio State, Michigan, Kentucky, Tennessee, and South Carolina, among others—he'd fielded dozens of scholarship offers.

It was a source of some disappointment to the Quinns that none of these overtures came from South Bend. Brady's go-to receiver at Coffman was Chinedum Ndukwe, whose older brother had attended Notre Dame. Several times Quinn had accompanied the Ndukwes to the school for football games, piling into the backseat with his buddy for the four-hour drive to South Bend.

The campus worked its magic on him, but the affection was unrequited. While scores of schools had offered him scholarships, Quinn got little more than generic mailings from the Irish. On the heels of Bob Davie's dismissal on December 2, 2000, following the five-day tenure of George O'Leary (he was forced out after admitting that he'd padded his resume), Ty Willingham had become the school's third head coach in less than a month. Recruiting was a mess; Quinn had fallen through the cracks.

The situation was rectified in July 2002, when Ndukwe and

his parents made an unofficial visit to South Bend (Nedu, as he is known, would go on to become a two-year starter at free safety for the Irish). At the end of the visit, Willingham asked them if they had any questions. They did not. But Ndukwe's father Stephen did have a suggestion: "You need to get Brady Quinn up here." After reviewing video of Quinn, Willingham agreed. An invitation was extended.

"I was *so* close to going to Michigan," Quinn told me. "I'd been up there a bunch, I'd built a nice relationship with the staff. And, at the time, I had *no* relationship with the coaching staff here. They hadn't said much to me that entire spring, and I wasn't that interested in them."

As he was squired around the campus he'd already come to love, Quinn had a change of heart, as did his hosts. Acknowledging they'd "made a huge mistake" by not recruiting him hard earlier, the Irish staff now sought to make amends. By the time he got back to Dublin, Quinn had made up his mind.

When Robin asked him to justify jilting the Wolverines, Brady ticked off his reasons. "Quality of education . . . Networking opportunities . . . The opportunity to get on the field quickly . . . Genuinely like Willingham."

It was the final reason that made the strongest impression on Robin.

"I think I could grow there, spiritually," said the 17-year-old.

"Then go make your calls," his mother said.

FOURTEEN MONTHS LATER, I was dispatched to Ann Arbor for Michigan's third game of the 2003 season. After outscoring their first two opponents, Central Michigan and Houston, 95–10, the Wolverines were expecting their first tough test of the season. Notre Dame had won the previous year, 25–23. Its margin of victory: a safety the Irish were awarded when a Wolverine offensive lineman was called for holding in his own end zone. That cruel and unusual punishment was of a piece with the bizarre twists that have made this series so maddening for Michigan down through the years: blocked field goals, phantom touchdowns, a fierce wind which—Wolverine fans swear this is true—died the moment Notre Dame kicker Harry Oliver lined up to boot the winning, 51-yarder in 1980. The Irish had made a habit of derailing Wolverine national title hopes in September.

Not in 2003. While Michigan's own quarterback, Douglas C. Neidermeyer look-alike John Navarre, looked sharp as a pledge pin completing 14 of his 21 passes for 199 yards, a touchdown, and no picks, the Wolverines' mobile, attacking defense held poor Caryle Holiday to a single passing yard through the first half. One yard. Michigan running back Chris Perry rushed for 133 yards, caught passes for another 44, and scored four touchdowns as the Wolverines romped, 38–0. In that week's story, I advised Michigan fans to remain calm. It wasn't like this hadn't happened before. The maize and blue had shut out Notre Dame, I noted, as recently as 1902.

Outside the Big House after that game, Brady's father, Ty, walked past an inebriated Michigan undergrad who remembered that Quinn had spurned the Woverines. "This kid was standing on a soapbox," Ty recalls, "screaming, 'Brady Quinn went to the wrong school!' " It looked, for long stretches of that season and the next, that the shitfaced kid had a point.

After two more losses, Willingham pulled the plug on Holiday, handing the team to the 18-year-old Quinn, who played well in spots, but still dropped four of his first five starts. He finished with three wins in the final four games, and carried that improvement into the following season. It was not enough to save Willingham's job. Like most of his teammates, Quinn took issue with the way the university treated Willingham, for whom he retains much respect. Still, there were times during his sophomore season, recalls Quinn's uncle, Dave Slate, that "Brady would say, 'I really don't feel like I'm being coached.' "

Slate, who played college football at Brown and coached his

nephew from fourth to ninth grade, would reply, "You're 19 years old. What do you know about it?"

"In hindsight," Slate reflects, "I think Brady had a point."

The inadequate instruction would end the moment Notre Dame officials brought Willingham's successor on board, which proved more difficult than expected. Athletic director Kevin White and Father John Jenkins, the university president, had flown to Salt Lake City to meet with Utah coach Urban Meyer, the stern-visaged offensive mastermind who was the "it" candidate of the moment. Meyer would be an ideal fit: He'd spent five seasons in South Bend as one of Davie's assistants, and had insisted on including an "out" clause in his Utah contract, should he ever be offered the Irish head-coaching job. The guy was named for a pope, for Pete's sake. But in a stunning decision that served, for some, as a barometer of how far Notre Dame had fallen in the world, Meyer left the Irish at the altar, pledging his allegiance to Florida instead.

CHARLIE WEIS BEGINS his recent book with an account of the Sunday afternoon in 1975 when he placed a call to the office of university president Theodore Hesburgh. Weis was a smart-aleck undergraduate from New Jersey who wasn't happy with the way the football team had played the previous day. "For some reason, I believed that being a student of the university entitled me to issue a complaint," he writes. Thinking he would get Hesburgh's machine, young Charles was alarmed to find himself on the line with the man himself, who summoned him to his office that instant.

The good father informed Weis that he should "go back and be a good student who was loyal to the school and its teams, and not consider my opinion one that mattered."

Thirty years later, Weis was the offensive coordinator for the New England Patriots, working on getting to his third Super Bowl in four years, when his office phone rang. It was senior associate athletics director John Heisler, asking if Weis would be at all interested in speaking to Kevin White, the school's athletic director, about replacing Willingham.

One of the reasons Weis was attractive was his work with Tom Brady, who'd come out of Michigan as a sixth-round draft pick. Tall, cerebral, and with just enough mobility to make somebody miss, Brady was a guy whose work ethic earned him the respect of his teammates. Brady Quinn had all that in common with Tom Brady, and a stronger arm. If Weis could do even a fraction for Quinn what he'd done for Tom Brady, the echoes would be awakened sooner rather than later.

"I beat 'em down so bad here, in the beginning," Weis told me. "Physically and psychological. It was gonna hit rock bottom before it got better. There was going to be a turning point sooner or later, and [Quinn] was one of the reasons it started to turn."

Even as he did right by his former coach, Quinn was bright enough to see that the new guy was his ticket out of the rut he'd been in. "The thing is," Weis says, "he was hardened already. He'd been playing for two years. He's a physical specimen. He's smart. He was tough, had all the tools. And he was hungry."

"The best thing that happened to this kid was that we put in the same offense I'd been running in New England, and he had the last four years of Tommy Brady to watch." Weis arrived with countless digitalized cut-ups of Brady executing every play in the Patriots'—now Notre Dame's—playbook. "Very few people in college football will ever have that tool—being able to watch a potential Hall of Fame quarterback run the same plays. It's one thing to tell him. It's another thing to show him." *This is what it's supposed to look like.*

The payoff came on September 3, 2005. Exhibiting a crispness and discipline unseen at Notre Dame since the Holtz era, the Irish eviscerated Pitt, 42–21. In the second quarter against the Panthers, Quinn completed 10 of his 11 passes for 109 yards and a touchdown, spreading the ball among seven different receivers.

A week later came that 17–10 win in Ann Arbor, where two

years earlier the drunk Michigan student had proclaimed the error of Quinn's ways.

"Didn't see him this year," Ty Quinn noted afterward.

Trailing by three touchdowns with 20 minutes to play against Michigan State on September 17, Quinn calmly led the offense on three touchdown drives to tie the game. In all, he threw for 487 yards and five touchdowns against the Spartans, but Notre Dame still lost the game, 44–41, when Jason Teague broke containment and went 19 yards for the game-winning score in overtime.

THE FINEST MOMENT of Quinn's junior season came in a defeat. As night fell on the heartland on October 15, he guided the Irish on a methodical, inexorable 87-yard drive to give the Irish a 31–28 lead over No. 1 Southern California. The Trojans took over with two minutes to play, and Quinn was forced to watch as Matt Leinart one-upped him. With under a minute to play and 'SC's 27-game winning streak on life support, Leinart faced a fourth-and-nine from his own 26. In a display of cool reminiscent of Joe Montana—who could be seen nervously pacing the Notre Dame sideline—Leinart looked over the defense and . . . *changed the play.* I still can't get over the chutzpah of that. A moment later, he feathered a perfect pass into the outstretched hands of Jarrett, whose 61-yard catch-and-run gave 'SC the ball on the Notre Dame 13.

On first-and-goal at the two, Leinart was drilled just shy of the goal line by middle linebacker Corey Mays, whose monstrous hit popped the pigskin from the quarterback's arms like a cork from a bottle of Moët. The ND faithful counted down the remaining seconds—"Three! Two! One!"—then poured onto the field. Their euphoria was fleeting. The ball had sailed backward, out of bounds. After a tense confab, the referee instructed that seven seconds be put back on the clock, setting the stage for the Bush Push.

Final score: 34–31. After congratulating the Trojans in their dressing room, Weis took a pass when offered the chance to declare a moral victory. "Losin's losin'," he said.

Notre Dame beat the teams it was supposed to beat in 2005. That was an improvement over DavieHam, as cynical Domers refer to the conflated reigns Davie (1997–2001) and Willingham (2002–2004). The team went 56-40 during this tumultuous epoch, for a winning percentage of .583, which comes in about .400 shy of the number most Domers regard as their birthright.

The next step would be to take a lead on one of these highly ranked opponents and *finish*. For that to happen, the defense would need to get some big stops, for a change. The off-season was spent upgrading the speed on the defensive side of the ball, streamlining the scheme so the Domers could "play faster."

So far, so good. The dee had provided the highlights of that narrow escape at Georgia Tech, holding the Yellow Jackets scoreless in the second half. Things only got better in the home opener against 19th-ranked Penn State. The Irish were up 41–3 in the fourth quarter before the Nittany Lions punched in a pair of window-dressing touchdowns. Travis Thomas, the running back transplanted to linebacker, looked more comfortable than he had against Tech. Ndukwe intercepted Penn State quarterback Anthony Morelli, who never found his rhythm against the Irish. And strong safety Tom Zbikowski had lived up to his big-play reputation, forcing one fumble and returning another for a touchdown.

Quinn had cruised, completing 12 of 16 passes for 150 yards and a pair of touchdowns in the second quarter alone. But unsettling questions lingered. Early in both games, against Penn State and Georgia Tech, the senior had been scattershot. He seemed slightly out of sync with his receivers—in particular Jeff Samardzija, the consensus All-American whose 15 touchdowns the previous season had set both the season and *career* records at Notre Dame. There was grumbling in Domer Nation that Samardzija's summer job—we're coming to that—was the reason he wasn't achieving the separation from defensive backs he'd gotten the previous season.

It didn't help that the quarterback was often throwing under duress. For a unit with three returning starters, the offensive line lacked cohesion and, well, *competence*. On the other side of the ball, Notre Dame's veteran defensive line had rung up exactly one sack in two games. And the team looked vulnerable at linebacker. At six feet and 220 pounds, Maurice Crum was undersized to be playing the middle. Travis Thomas, the converted running back, was having trouble getting off blocks. Strong side linebacker Mitchell Thomas, who had no tackles against Georgia Tech, tended to disappear for long stretches.

THE FRIDAY PEP rally on the eve of the Michigan game is a hoot, as always. Weis introduces a surprise guest, a burly alumnus who jogs from the tunnel to the podium to raucous applause. "I was born and raised in Detroit," Jerome Bettis reminds the crowd, "and I *hate* Michigan. *This* is my home."

Victor Abiamiri, the imposing-looking defensive end, is downright surly, looking and sounding as if he wished to suit up this instant. "They even got the punter talkin' smack," he complains to the crowd. "The punter? You kiddin' me? What's he talking about? How hard he's gonna *kick* the ball?

"They talk about how they're gonna outscheme *our* coach!" He pauses, allowing the outrage to build. "Well, the last time I checked, you can't spell Lloyd without two *l*'s."

Weis himself is the picture of jowly restraint, informing the congregants that the team's focus all week had been inwardly directed. "We have not said one word about Michigan. We have not talked about their coach. We have not talked about their players."

Pregnant pause.

"We'll do our talkin' tomorrow."

I'm not here to write a game story. I'm reporting a feature on Zbikowski and Samardzija, into which I will artfully weave game action. Charlie had given them permission to spend some time with me the day before the game. It had gone well. I met with the guys in the team's meeting room at the Guglielmino Athletics Complex, then puttered around campus with them on a golf cart.

While we waited for Zibby to finish with an ESPN crew, Samardzija riffed on their similarities: "We've both got hard-nosed families with similar backgrounds. It feels like we coulda switched families and been the same people growing up."

And he pointed out their differences: "I'm a little laid back, Tommy's a little . . . not so laid back."

Zibby walked in carrying a garment bag. In a half hour, both the guys would be speaking at the kickoff luncheon at Joyce Center. Of the change of clothes he brought along, Zbikowski boasted, "I've never been so organized in my life." In 20 minutes he would sprint to his car in a panic: the garment bag contains his suit jacket, but not the pants.

I explained the proposed angle of the story: tough kids from the Chicago area helping the Irish wake up the echoes. Plus, they both had interesting summer jobs. After finishing his junior season as Notre Dame's all-time career leader in receiving yards and touchdowns, Samardzija was taken in the fifth round of the Major League Baseball draft by the Chicago Cubs. (A fireballing right-hander on the Notre Dame baseball team—he's been clocked in the mid-90s—Samardzija would have been gone sooner, had clubs not been under the impression that he was intent on pursuing an NFL career.) Samardzija pitched for a pair of the club's Single-A affiliates: the Boise Hawks, followed by a few outings with the Peoria Chiefs.

Zibby, a Golden Gloves boxer so accomplished that university officials have barred him from participating in the school's intramural Bengal Bouts out of fear he might maim someone, had fought his first professional bout at Madison Square Garden the previous June.

The other, obvious hook, I told them, is that you're close friends and roommates. I'd heard they shared an off-campus apartment.

"Umm, I don't live there," says Zbikowski, fixing me with his dull, flat, assassin's gaze. (Seriously. When he is not on the field, Zbikowski's eye of the tiger morphs into an impassive, shark-like expression, which is confusing, because Samardzija's nickname is Shark, although, as Zibby noted while introducing his friend at that evening's pep rally, "the guys on the team don't call him that.") It seems that Zbikowski has on-campus housing and would like, very much, to prevent university officials from getting the impression that he lives off-campus.

"That's right," lectures Samardzija, "he doesn't *live* there. It only seems that way because he eats all my food and sits on my couch."

"And, if he were to nod off over a textbook late in the evening," I added, helpfully, "he would be welcome to crash in the guest room, whose closet and drawers contain, by coincidence, his clothing."

"Yes," said Zibby.

"Exactly," said Samardzija.

I prompted Zbikowski, who is the kind of subject who requires prompting: "Tell me more about the bout." The previous June, he'd dismantled one Robert Bell, a palooka from Akron who'd had the poor judgment to enter the ring sporting an Ohio State jersey. Zibby took 49 seconds to knock him out. "I was way too pumped up for the fight," he recalled. "I never get that much adrenaline. You gotta be as calm as possible. If it had been a longer fight I would've been done after two rounds."

It was Weis who'd speculated, while standing at the microphone in front of 35,000 people at the Penn State pep rally, "I probably could've beaten that guy." But when I referred to Bell as a "tomato can," Zbikowski defended him. "I give him respect. He still took the fight. I have a certain respect for guys that get in the ring."

. . . .

After lunch we hooked up with *SI* photographer Bill Frakes, a Nebraska alum who is soon wearing everyone out with stories of Tom Osborne and the Cornhusker glory days. First, he took some shots of the guys over at the stadium. When things got slow—it didn't take long—Samardzija launched into his Austin Powers impersonation. "Be a tiger, baby! You're great! Now be a lemur! You're a ring-tailed lemur!"

Later, they were posing in the quad, Touchdown Jesus looming in the background, a ring of onlookers closing in. The shot was missing something. You're too static, Frakes told his subjects. I need more energy. That's all Zbikowski needed to hear. Like the ex-wrestler he is, he "shot" Samardzija's legs, driving his head into the quads and executing a flawless double-leg take-down. As they grappled in the grass, sports information assistant Mike Bertsch approaches Defcon 4: "You guys. You GUYS!" If one of them were to break a wrist or dislocate a finger while roughhousing on a photo shoot, Charlie would not be pleased.

Obviously, I assured him, we would just blame the photographer.


Johnny Lujack is at midfield with the captains to flip the coin. Notre Dame wins the toss, elects to receive. And that's about as good as it gets for the Fighting Irish on September 16. Three plays into the game, tight end John Carlson runs a little square-out toward the left sideline. Quinn's throw, slightly behind him, is eminently catchable. Instead, the ball caroms off Carlson's hands into those of linebacker Prescott Burgess, whose 26-yard touchdown return puts the Irish in an early hole. (Burgess, by the way, is a graduate of Warren G. Harding High, whose head football coach, Thom McDaniels, is father of one Josh McDaniels, the wunderkind coach who replaced Weis as the Patriots' offensive coordinator.)

Ndukwe picks off Michigan quarterback Chad Henne's first pass, setting up the tying touchdown. But Notre Dame can't hang on to momentum today, can't hang on to anything. On a first-and-10 at his own 31, Henne sends No. 86 in motion toward the right sideline. This is true sophomore Mario Manningham, a 6-foot, 187-pound bundle of fast-twitch muscle fibers. Coming into this contest, he was best known for reeling in the game-winning touchdown pass from Henne as time expired against Penn State 11 months earlier. That loss, that catch, spoiled the Nittany Lions' perfect season.

A wiry wide out with 4.39 speed in the 40, Manningham accelerates toward the sideline, as if intent on beating the defender around the end. Suddenly he "sticks" the cornerback, Ambrose Wooden, planting hard with his right foot and going vertical. The fake literally turns Wooden around, spinning him like a dreidel. Wooden is fifteen feet behind Manningham when Henne's pass catches up with him.

Wily, undersized defensive tackle Derek Landri fights through to block the extra point, but David Grimes fumbles the kickoff. Six snaps later, Mike Hart catapults into the end zone—Zbikowski tries to stuff him, but whiffs—putting the Wolverines up 20–7 with more than a minute left in the first quarter.

Michigan is back in the red zone on its next possession when Manningham splits out wide to the right, where he is covered by Terrail Lambert, whom he loses with a head-and-shoulder fake at the line of scrimmage. Lambert can only wave despairingly at the ball, like one of the damned in Michaelangelo's *Last Judgment*, as it falls into Manningham's arms for Michigan's fourth touchdown of the half.

The news isn't all bad for the Irish. Quinn finds Grimes for an 11-yard completion. Four minutes into the second quarter, Notre Dame has a first down—its first of the game.

. . . .

Is THAT THE theme from *Jaws* I hear? With just under three minutes to play in the half, Manningham splits wide to the left, where Lambert awaits. Mesmerizing the corner with a farrago of stutter-steps, Manningham jukes right before busting his move down the left sideline, toasting Lambert to the outside. Zibby is a step late with deep help, and Manningham has his third touchdown of the half.

But the receiver's momentum sends him sailing into a grove of horns. Preparing for its halftime performance, the Michigan band has mustered behind the end zone. Taking the brunt of the collision with Manningham is Heather Vogt, a senior clarinetist from Mason City, Michigan. "He pretty much knocked the wind out of me," she will tell me later in the game. "Maybe I'll feel it in the morning, but right now, I've got a lot of adrenaline going." The resilient Vogt recovers quickly, missing not a single rendition of "The Victors." The conclusion is inescapable: Vogt and her bandmates have more success slowing Manningham down than Notre Dame's secondary.

The final score, 47–21, is but one of a host of ugly statistics awaiting the Irish. While surrendering more points at home than any Notre Dame club since 1960, the Irish netted all of four yards rushing, while committing 11 penalties for 84 yards. Gold-helmeted receivers dropped seven passes, which helps explain why the offense had eight three-and-outs; why the offense converted two of its 14 third downs. Quinn's four turnovers—three picks and a fumble—resulted in 24 Wolverine points as the Irish plunge, quite deservedly, from No. 2 in the AP poll to No. 12.

Asked to gauge the level of his concern with his porous secondary, Weis gets a laugh at his postgame press conference by replying, "I got concerns with everything right now. You name it, I got concerns with it."

Appropriately so. In announcing themselves as a Top 5–calibre squad, the Wolverines exposed the Irish, whose worst fears have been realized. They are not national championship material. Despite Weis's preseason suggestion that Quinn would be able to "mentally take it to another level" this season, the offense has somehow regressed from a year ago. Despite an off-season spent "simplifying" and "streamlining" schemes so that embattled defensive backs could "react" rather than "think," the secondary was toasted just as crisply as it had been against Ohio State in the Fiesta Bowl.

GREAT THINGS HAD been forecast all week during Wolverines practices by the eerily confident Hart, who rushed for 124 yards on 31 carries.

Standing outside the visitors' dressing room in the House That Rockne Built, where the Wolverines had not won since 1994, where Carr had never won, the junior running back recalls the strong positive vibes he'd been picking up in practice all week. "I'd ask the other guys, 'Do you all feel it? Do you feel what I'm feeling?'

"We knew we were gonna come down here and win this game. We *knew*." How did they know? "Last year they were hunting us. This year we were hunting them."

Hart's hunting analogy gets at the root of Notre Dame's biggest problem. A year earlier, the Irish could sneak up on people. Well, goodbye to all that. Michigan was the underdog coming into this game—the Wolverines' reward for underachieving so epically in 2005. With Hart and every member of the offensive line missing significant time due to injuries, Henne struggled to recapture the magic of his freshman season, when the Wolverines had shared the Big Ten title. While his statistics were similar, the result—a 7-5 season—was not.

The only Wolverine who took more abuse than Henne from impatient Wolverines fans was Carr, long a piñata for Internet posters named sickofcarr and firelloydyesterday on such Web sites as FireLloydCarr.us and SackLloydCarr.com. Yes, the man had won 105 games in his dozen years as head coach—including the 1997 national championship—against just 34 losses. But Carr bashers dwelt on his shortcomings: he is predictable, conservative, plays not to lose, and has but a single victory in his last five games against Ohio State.

The critics kept up their chorus even as Michigan opened the season with wins over Vanderbilt and Central Michigan. The team's aerial attack in those victories barely qualified as popgun: Henne threw for 135 yards against the Commodores, followed by a career-low 113 against the Chippewas.

It turned out that first-year offensive coordinator Mike DeBord (on his second tour of duty in that job) had been playing his cards close to the vest. The absence of a vertical passing attack was by design. Why show the Irish anything if they didn't need to?

It had taken Henne exactly one pass—that interception by Ndukwe—to get his detractors fired up, warming up their vocal cords, logging onto the message boards to flame his ass but good. He responded to that bad play by leading touchdown drives on four of his next five possessions.

Far more surprising than the travails of Notre Dame's defense is the egg laid by Quinn. Asked after the game what the Wolverines had done to confuse him, he replies, "Nothing. We flat out didn't execute."

Quinn can shoulder all the blame he wants, but truth is, Michigan has a seriously ornery defense. It has been transformed under the glowering leadership of first-year coordinator Ron English, a highly regarded 38-year-old who joined Carr's staff in 2003. English took a job with the Chicago Bears after the '05 season—a gig he held for less than a week. That's how long it took Carr, on bended knee, to woo him back, by offering the coordinatorship.

English replaced Jim Herrmann, whose preference it was to install opponent-specific packages each week, sometimes overwhelming his players. English simplified the scheme. In exchange, the intense, excitable Coach E requires his guys to practice and play at a higher tempo. Taking note of what lousy finishers they were last season—four times the Wolverines lost by allowing opponents to come from behind in the fourth quarter—he and the staff put a renewed emphasis on nutrition and off-season conditioning. The result: streamlined athletes working from a streamlined playbook allowing fewer yards and points.

THE STUNNING, 26-POINT home-field loss is a reminder that Weis's hard work and football intellect cannot close the biggest gap between the Fighting Irish and the *real* contenders for the national title. Notre Dame has plenty of very good athletes, but lacks the difference makers, the four- and five-star studs that teams like Michigan, Ohio State, Florida, and USC attract en masse. Today, the contrast was particularly acute at one position. While the travails of Notre Dame's linebackers have been duly noted, Michigan boasts one of the finest linebacking corps in the country.

It was LaMarr Woodley, a 6'2", 268-pound senior who lines up at both defensive and rush linebacker, who delivered the coup de grace. With under for minutes left to play, he returned Quinn's fumble 54 yards for a touchdown. Shawn Crable, an outside 'backer with 4.5 speed, sacked Quinn once and pasted him on several other occasions. Converted safety Prescott Burgess intercepted Quinn twice.

Really, the only Wolverine who had a better game than Burgess is his former high school teammate, Manningham, who was a sophomore at Warren Harding when Burgess was a senior. "That was the year he scored four touchdowns against Massillon-Washington," recalls their head coach, Thom McDaniels, when I speak to him that evening. "One on a punt return, one on a kickoff return, and two touchdown receptions. We won 31–28. You can't tackle that guy in a phone booth. He's the best receiver I've seen in 33 years of coaching."

He may also be the most reticent. It is clear, when I approach him 45 minutes after the game, that he wants to throw me a little head-and-shoulder fake and walk on by. I tell him I just want to hear, in his own words, about the routes he'd run on those three touchdowns. "I can't remember," he says with a sigh, before informing me that he is undergoing a mild medical emergency. "I just drank a bottle of lemonade too fast and now I've got a really bad stomach ache. I need to get on the bus."

I congratulate him on the win, wish him a speedy recovery, and head over to the Notre Dame room.

By this time it's pretty empty. I do get a chance to pat Zbikowski on the shoulder. I thank him for his time the previous day, and tell him the feature on him and Samardzija will be on hold for a while.

He laughs, as if to say, *No shit.* We shake hands. He and his boys have just gotten their heads handed to them. Their national title ambitions are out the window, and that's the least of their problems. The way the Irish played today, it's an open question whether they'll win more games than they lose this season. But Zbikowski's chin is up. Even in defeat he cuts a proud, impressive figure.

He took the fight. To paraphrase a boxer I know, I have a certain respect for guys that get in the ring.

# CHAPTER 7

# Redeemed

September 23, East Lansing, Mich. —Before the players' sweat has dried after the Michigan disaster, Weis addresses them as a team. The first thing he does, he will later recall, is forbid guys from hanging their heads. "Look at me," he commands. He does not scream, does not rant. Is there some general berating, some sarcasm? Almost certainly. This is Weis, after all. But no individual is called out. Weis doesn't believe in "creating scapegoats," he explains in a press conference the Sunday after the loss. You don't pick "five guys out of a 105" and make "sacrificial lambs" of them. "That's not how a professional handles that."

Asked if his confidence is shaken, Weis gets off one of his better ripostes of the season, His confidence "might be stirred," he allows, paraphrasing Sean Connery, "but it's not shaken."

"One of the things that gives you a little credibility with your team," he goes on to explain, "is when the first person you blame

**AP TOP 10**

1. *Ohio State*
2. *Auburn*
3. *USC*
4. *West Virginia*
5. *Florida*
6. *Michigan*
7. *Texas*
8. *Louisville*
9. *Georgia*
10. *LSU*

is yourself." It isn't clear from this statement whether Weis actually blamed himself, or whether he was taking the fall to preserve his team's fragile psyche.

Either way, it works for the beat writers, one of whom is more than pleased to follow up by asking (I'm paraphrasing), "Okay, you're taking the blame. Talk about why you deserved it. How did you screw up? Be as specific as possible."

Weis, a stand-up guy, dives in: "You say you want to take care of the ball. We have five turnovers. You say you want to run the ball. You run the ball for less than a yard [per carry]. You say you want to stop big plays on defense. [They scored on] three touchdown passes."

He takes the fall for the team's 11 penalties. "A lot of those penalties come from a lack of discipline. Who else can you fault for the lack of discipline but yourself?"

Consuming as much blame as possible does not prevent Weis from taking a few guys aside and letting them know that if they don't step it up, "we'll just have to move you out, move somebody else in.' "

Oh yeah. It's going to be a fun week of practice on Cartier Field. This is a team with big problems, but also a team that cannot afford a minute of self-pity. Next up on the schedule is Michigan State, 3-0 and coming off a 38–23 spanking of Pittsburgh.


MICHIGAN STATE HAS always had great athletes. Over the last decade alone, the program has turned out wide receivers Charles Rogers and Plaxico Burress, defensive end Demetrius Underwood, linebackers Percy Snow and Julian Peterson, running backs DeAndra Cobb and TJ Duckett. It's just that, like all the other teams flying coach in the Big Ten, they haven't had *as many* great athletes as Michigan and Ohio State. Catch the Spartans late in the season and you should be okay. Catch them after they've had a few key injuries; after head coach John L. Smith has presided over some of his trademark come-from-ahead losses; after they've phoned it in at the end of another bowl-less season, they'll roll over like good dogs for you. When things go bad for the Spartans, they know the way home. But Notre Dame doesn't catch them late. Because the Big Ten insists that its members get their nonconference games out of the way early, the Irish get the Spartans early.

Upon further review, Weis has concluded that his defense played better against Michigan than the final score would indicate. Yes, the Wolverines put up points. But, as Weis points out, Michigan defenders had scored two touchdowns, and the Notre Dame offense had given the visitors the ball in the red zone on two other occasions. Yes, Hart rushed for 124 yards, but did most of his damage on five carries. *Other than that, Mrs. Lincoln, how did you enjoy the play?*

While this line of reasoning may spare the defense's feelings, it calls attention to the fact that the offense sucked worse than anyone realized. The biggest problems are the biggest guys.

Rare is the offensive line coach who has not shared some version of this metaphor with his leviathans: *A good offensive line is like five fingers working together, to make a fist.* The Fighting Irish hogs were making a fist. The problem was, it looked like it belonged to Stephen Hawking. Quinn was sacked three times and pressured—flushed, clobbered, or otherwise harassed—on a dozen other occasions against Michigan. Notre Dame had averaged .2 yards per rush in the game.

Not quite as eager as Weis to shoulder blame, running back Darius Walker is more than happy to discuss what needs to happen if the ground game is to be resurrected: "We've gotta stay focused, know blocking schemes, make sure we know who we're blocking. We've gotta understand who we're blocking."

Did he mention the importance of linemen knowing their assignments, then executing their blocks?

After Tuesday's practice, offensive line coach Latina is escorted to the press area, where he is more than happy to answer questions about the woes of his unit.

"We gotta be more physical. We gotta run the ball better, protect the quarterback better," says the coach, exuding determination. "But that's an ongoing process. . . . You gotta just get better and better every week and hope that the next week is a week that you put things together and start to gel, and play better as a unit. That's where we are. . . . All the problems are fixable, but you gotta fix 'em, and sometimes fixin' 'em overnight . . ."

He doesn't finish that thought, but makes it clear that a quick fix isn't really in the cards for these five fingers.

It had not helped, he notes, that Notre Dame fell behind early against the Wolverines, forcing the offense to abandon the run and thus making it one-dimensional and predictable. That must not happen in East Lansing. Playing at night, in possibly the most hostile environment in the Big Ten, it will be critical not to fall behind early. So it is discouraging and alarming, four nights later, when the Irish find themselves trailing 17–0 before the first quarter is over.

THE OFFENSE IS getting too many three-and-outs, Weis had said after the previous game. At Michigan State, the Irish go three-and-out on their first possession.

The defense needs to cut down on big plays, Weis had emphasized after the Michigan debacle. Against Notre Dame it takes the Spartans three snaps to cover 73 yards—a 29-yard rumble by rhino-like running back Jehuu Caulcrick; a 10-yard scramble by dual-threat quarterback Drew Stanton; and a 34-yard scoring pass from Stanton to wide out Kerry Reed—to take a 7–0 lead on their first possession.

Following four giveaways the previous week, Weis had harped on the need to eliminate turnovers. There is Zbikowski, midway through the first quarter, muffing a punt, recovering it, *then* fumbling—the rare muff-fumble, a.k.a. mumble—to set up the Spartans' second touchdown. There is Quinn, coming off a three-pick performance, somehow failing to see defensive end Ervin (Magic) Baldwin dropping into coverage. In one of the worst decisions of his career, Quinn lobs a pass toward Walker which Baldwin gratefully intercepts and returns 20 yards for a touchdown.

Notre Dame is down 24–7 with nine minutes and four seconds remaining in the half. Domers are starting to feel nostalgic for the Michigan game, beginning to wonder if they should begin making arrangements to attend the Sun Bowl, or the PapaJohns.com Bowl, or the Alamo Bowl. On ABC, Kirk Herbstreit is shocked by what he is seeing from Quinn:

"This is a mental thing right now for Brady Quinn.

"It's not just that the plays aren't working. Brady Quinn is not executing the short throws."

If you've been watching, you agree with him.

How do they win this game?

WHEN IT IS over, true believers will describe the outcome of this contest as miraculous. The real miracle was that Ty Quinn only gets in one physical altercation in East Lansing that evening. During the six- or seven-block walk from the parking lot to Spartans Stadium, the father of the Notre Dame quarterback and his buddies—also sporting the colors of the Fighting Irish—absorb a jumbo ration of abuse from certain Spartans fans.

"Maybe it's just me," he would later speculate, "but when fans from other teams come to the Notre Dame campus, you welcome them. You're glad to see them. You're proud of the place—you want to show it off." Was that not his experience in East Lansing? "I've been up there twice now. And both times have been terrible. We fought our way in, and we fought our way out."

He is barely exaggerating. "Two blocks from the stadium, pedestrian traffic was halted at an intersection while police directed traffic," Ty recalls. "Right in front of us, there was a sweet old man" in Notre Dame colors.

Quinn describes the kid as "18 to 20, six feet, thinks he's bigtime. The old man didn't step off the curb fast enough for him, so he put his hand on the guy's back and pushed him." The oldster went off the curb and fell to the ground. As Ty Quinn recounts it, he gave the punk a shove that sent him flying into his buddies. When the fellow lunged at him, "I had to take him down," he recalls with a what-are-you-going-to-do? shrug. "You pushed him down," he lectured the bully, "so why don't you help him up?"

"I couldn't believe how callous they were," he says of the Spartans fans around him. "Even the women." Surely he is referring to the tiny minority of drunken, disorderly Michigan State fans when he describes them as "spiteful, vicious little people, [who have been] drinking like fish all day. The only way to shut them up is to beat them on the field."

That part isn't going so well. The Irish aren't doing everything wrong. It just seems that way. When Stanton goes around left end on a first down early in the second quarter, Ndukwe lights him up like a Roman candle at the sideline, drawing a flag for a late hit. The fireworks are only starting.

Realizing his quarterback is running the ball, stud receiver Matt Trannon throws a nice cut block on the play. Seeing Ndukwe's hit, the 6'6" Trannon hauls ass over to the Irish bench area, where he seeks out, chest-bumps, and generally lords it over the 6'2" safety. Trannon is soon joined on the visitors sideline by most of the Spartans' offense. After 20 or so seconds of jawing, critical mass is reached. A roar goes up in the stadium as players from both teams began shoving.

The zebras are on it quickly; a Miami-type melee is avoided. After a confab, referee Bill LeMonnier sorts it all out: "Two fouls on the play, both dead ball. Dead ball, late hit on sideline on the quarterback. Following action on the sideline, dead ball, personal foul"—he has to raise his voice to be heard over the howls of outrage—"NUMBER SIX."

That's Trannon, who was a tad zealous in Stanton's defense. Now the penalties will offset. Smith is batshit on the far sideline, pitching a Bob Knight–calibre fit. The officials having robbed him, in his mind, of 15 yards, Smith spikes his cap, madly gesticulating like Lear on the heath, only slightly more in control than the bald Britney going after the paparazzi with her umbrella.

Notre Dame cuts the lead to 10 thanks to the gutsiest call of the game. Facing a fourth-and-one at his own 37-yard line, Weis pushes all his chips to the middle of the table. Travis Thomas, the ex–running back converted to linebacker, now enters the game as a short-yardage back. Quinn takes the snap, puts the ball in Thomas's belly . . . then deftly withdraws it, nonchalantly concealing the rock on his right hip before delivering a strike to Carlson, his tight end, 27 yards downfield. There is Samardzija four plays later, high-stepping into the end zone on a 17-yard touchdown catch, then thanking McKnight for the block.

Before the Irish can take heart Stanton slaps them back down, leading a 59-yard touchdown drive capped by his scoring pass to Reed. Now trailing 31–14—*how do they win this game?*—Notre Dame answers with a series that goes like this: two penalties, two incomplete passes, punt.

Even as this slapstick is unfolding, boos are raining down, oddly, on poor old John L. What gives? Well, with less than two minutes left in the half, Michigan State has the Irish on the ground, standing with the heel of its hobnailed boot on Notre Dame's neck. The fans want Smith to finish them off, *now.* They want another score before the half. But there is Smith, standing beside a wrecking ball of a back Notre Dame has not been able to even slow, sitting on all three of his timeouts, letting the Irish burn clock. As Spartan alum and Detroit talk show host Mike Valenti would rage on the air two days later, "Note to John L. Smith: YOUR TIME-OUTS ARE NOT LIKE CELL-PHONE MINUTES! THEY DON'T CARRY OVER!"

Down 17 at halftime, Weis stands before his players and asks a simple question: "Well, fellas, which is it gonna be?" The Fighting Irish are at a fork in the road. One path leads to mediocrity, four or five losses, a second-tier bowl. If this team is to even approach the goals for which it has been working since the previous January, it will have scant margin for error in the second half. "Don't worry about the plays," Weis told them. "I'll call the plays. That's not going to be the issue. The issue is going to be how important it is to you."

Up in the bleachers, Ty Quinn likes the way his son keeps counterpunching. "I had a feeling we were going to win this thing," he remembers. "But then, right at the third quarter, the rain started coming down in sheets. In buckets. And I thought, How are we going to do this if Brady can't throw the ball?"

Don't worry about the rain, Weis would have counseled him. *I'll handle the rain.* Stanton & Co. go three-and-out to start the half, and Quinn goes to work. He moves the chains on a third-and-nine, finding Samardzija for 14. Two plays later, with Spartans defensive coordinator Chris Smeland bringing a blitzer off the left edge, Carlson slides behind the linebackers, latches on to a dart from Quinn, and glides 62 yards for the touchdown that brings the Irish within 10.

Getting smart midway through the monsoon that is the third quarter, Spartans offensive coordinator Dave Baldwin starts calling Caulcrick's number. A 260-pound juggernaut of a back, the junior batters the Irish defense for 18 yards on one carry, 30 yards and a touchdown on the next. Zbikowski bounces off him as if the Spartan is equipped with a cowcatcher. You would think that a sure-footed blunt instrument like Caulcrick would be the perfect weapon for these conditions. But what do you know about football? The Spartans will run 23 more plays over the course of the game. Caulcrick will touch the ball on three of them. With 14 minutes left to play, he barges nine yards for a first down, giving him 111 yards on *eight touches*. And he is done. Forgotten. Stanton and Javon Ringer will take all the carries the rest of the way.

Later in the fourth: Quinn fumbles twice on the same possession. The Irish go three-and-out. While the quarterback explains himself to Weis on the sideline, Weis refuses to look at Quinn. That is his punishment.

Mike Richardson, maybe the most improved player on the Irish roster, erases Quinn's mistake by blowing up Stanton five yards behind the line of scrimmage with a highlight-reel open-field tackle.

On his first full series of the fourth quarter, the rain abating, Quinn can't miss. He finds Carlson again, this time for 32 yards. He hits Samardzija for 12, and Samardjiza again on a right-to-left slant. With the defense flowing left, the wily Serbian-American stomps on the brakes, then motors against the grain for the right corner of the end zone. Even with this 43-yard touchdown, the Irish still trail by 10.

Now Ndukwe atones for his cheap shot earlier in the game, ripping the ball from Stanton's grasp, then pouncing on the fumble—a sensational play. McKnight is well covered on Notre Dame's ensuing touchdown—hell, he is double-covered—but Quinn feathers the ball into the only place it can go: a two-square-foot area over his receiver's left shoulder. McKnight makes the catch, his butterfingers from the Michigan game a distant memory. Walker is stopped short on a two-point conversion. Irish still trail, 37–33.

I'D VISITED EAST Lansing a year earlier to write a Stanton feature. Great guy, tough guy. "A linebacker trapped in a quarterback's body" is how Smith described him. Before my eyes, the junior completed 20 of 26 passes in a 61–14 demolition of an atrocious Illinois team. Unable to help myself, I reported that Stanton had "thrust himself into Heisman contention." Further down in the story I made noise about how Michigan State would contend for the Big Ten title.

The Spartans lost six of their next seven games. They enjoyed many leads, but couldn't seal the deal to save their lives. Embedded in their green-and-white DNA, it seems, are instructions to panic when time is short and the game is on the line.

Now, with three minutes left to play on this miserable night, Stanton takes a shotgun snap at his own 12-yard line and finds himself in immediate distress. With blitzing linebacker Maurice Crum getting very big in his windshield, Stanton uncorks a misbegotten throw off his back foot. The ball barely clears the outstretched paw of Landri, a tackle who'd dropped into coverage, before falling into the arms of cornerback Terrail Lambert, his skin presumably tender where it was repeatedly singed by Mario Manningham. Now Lambert loops to his right and weaves his way 27 yards into the end zone, where he is tackled by euphoric teammates.

Up in the bleachers, Ty Quinn is feeling a little less hypothermic. The Old Testament deluge of the third quarter has given way to drizzle. The word is out among the Spartan fans seated around Quinn. They know whose father he is. Some offer their ponchos.

The Spartans get one last shot, but Lambert—delighted to donate his goat's horns to Stanton—nails down the victory with his second interception. Quinn takes a knee to run out the clock. While seventy-some thousand Kelly green–clad homers file glumly out of the stadium, their hangovers beginning to kick in, the Fighting Irish gather in a corner of the end zone, raise their helmets, and sing the alma mater with their fans.

CONSPICUOUS BY HIS absence is the Leprechaun. Kevin Braun, the 5'8", 140-pound red-bearded, green-vested, knickered, shillelagh-wielding mascot, is nowhere to be found.

"When we were down 17 in the monsoon," he tells me later, "I'd promised the [cheerleading] captain that when we took the lead, I was going to take my vest off and dive through the end zone, like a Slip'n Slide."

To celebrate Lambert's last pick, Braun dove into the crowd, and was passed up "a bunch of rows. But the game was about to end, so I said, 'Get me down!' My coat was off, my hat was off. I was all disheveled. When I jumped over the fence, these two state troopers grabbed me.

"I told them, 'Umm, guys, I'm the mascot,' but one of them just said, 'This is no time for messing around, son.'"

Braun was marched into the bowels of the stadium, hands behind his back. "This guy was rushing the field," reported one of the troopers to his lieutenant.

"Actually, I'm the mascot," Braun explained.

"Do you have any ID?" she inquired.

"I don't," he said, with an air of apology. "My knickers don't have any pockets."

It's a tough crowd in East Lansing. Earlier in the game, the Michigan State mascot Sparty had parked himself behind the Notre Dame cheerleaders, mugging and pointing to the scoreboard. "We were down by 17, and he wouldn't leave," says Braun, who finally resorted to "an old elementary school tactic." To wit: "One of the cheerleaders got down on all fours behind him while I distracted him with my shillelagh. Then we just pushed him right over. He fell on his butt."

There was a rumor circulating on the message boards that the Leprechaun had been arrested for beating up Sparty. "My cheerleading coach was saying, 'We don't want that to get out,'" says Braun, who didn't necessarily agree. "Actually," he said, "I'm pretty pleased with that story."

Less pleased with the outcome—indeed, made physically ill by the outcome—is Valenti, who'd sat in the upper deck, shouting himself hoarse in the monsoon, pleading with elderly fans in his section to get off their desiccated backsides and cheer.

Valenti takes the loss hard. He brings it to work on Monday, having arrived at the WXLT studio via the Detroit Metro Airport, where he'd dropped off his father, who'd flown in from upstate New York to see the Spartans once again snatch defeat from the jaws of victory.

What results is the single finest rant I've ever heard on sports talk radio, a 12-minute philippic in which he took a flame-thrower to the entire roster. A sampler of his outrage:

On Stanton: "Now, I love Drew Stanton. But [now addressing Stanton] I can't defend you when you play that way . . . you *have* to make better decisions.

And you know what? It's time for Drew to step up in a big game. It's time for Drew to play [in a big game] the way he plays against Kent State and Indiana."

On Stanton's teammates: "Every single stereotype about Michigan State football came true on Saturday night. They *choked*. They *absolutely gagged*. While Notre Dame played with fire, emotion, poise, and tact, Michigan State sat there, and *choked on applesauce*. They *choked!*

I'm disgusted with the guys who strap on those uniforms. Make plays! [His voice here reaches, if possible, a higher, more deranged register.] YOU'RE AT HOME. AT NIGHT. THIRD LARGEST CROWD IN THE HISTORY OF THAT STADIUM! WITH A 37–21 LEAD! MAAAKE PLAYS!!! DON'T SIT THERE AND PUCKER. MAKE PLAYS! [Now thumping the desk in front of him.] Don't sit there and turn to your quarterback with a puppy dog look and say, 'Help us, we don't know what we're doing out here!' MAKE PLAYS!"

On Smith: "Michigan State is pounding Notre Dame, and they took their foot off the accelerator. They mismanaged the clock—AGAIN. They didn't use their timeouts right—AGAIN. And they allowed an opponent to get into halftime and make adjustments, AGAIN. It's the same, tired-ass story."

Valenti is downright gentle with John L., compared to his treatment of Spartans defensive coordinator Chris Smeland, of whom he says: "I would rather have H. R. Pufnstuf . . . in the booth."

And so on. By the end of his scorched-earth oration, his voice is all but gone. It is a cri de coeur that transcends its genre, reaching the level of performance art. Valenti goes home early and doesn't come to work the next day. He's lost his voice.

I give him a week to calm down. When I reach him on the phone, he is rational, reasonable, off the ledge—nothing like the guy in The Rant. He tells me about how, growing up in upstate New York, he'd somehow cultivated a passion for the Spartans. "There was something about them," he relates. "They fought hard. I was drawn to them. I like pulling for the underdog."

He raked leaves to earn the money to buy a Spartans windbreaker, and so he could afford Michigan State football games on pay-per-view. By the time he was 13, he knew he wanted to go into sports talk radio. When he was 16, he and his father visited East Lansing. "Once we set foot on campus," he recalls, "we looked at each other and I said, 'This is where I want to be.' "

He was there from 1998 to 2002. "I saw the Mateen Cleaves national championship," he recalls wistfully, "saw the Nick Saban 10-2 season."

State football got tied up, somehow, in Valenti's bond with his father, who never went to college. "I carry the torch for him" is how he puts it to me. Thus, he feels the program's failures on a personal level. "I feel, in some twisted way, that if State could just get it right, my dad would be able to enjoy it the way I do."

When the Spartans spit the bit against Notre Dame, Valenti saw the disappointment in his father's face, and felt responsible. Then he sat down in front of a live mike. And someone had to pay.

This being Michigan State, it's going to get worse before it gets better. The Spartans will win a single game the rest of the way. They will find a way to lose to Illinois, which had not beaten a Big Ten opponent in years. Indiana will beat the snot out of them. Having started 3-1, they will finish 4-8. Smith will be fired with 17 days left in the season. There will be no bowl for the Spartans. Again.

Like I said, if you're going to play these guys, you want to get them late in the season.

# CHAPTER 8

# Meet Me in Frog Alley

September 27, Fort Worth —It's time to find out how the other half lives, to leave the four-star environs of college football's landed gentry. My purpose holds to chronicle the plight of D-I football schools who are not members of the six power conferences—to give voice to the benighted athletes who do not have dedicated indoor practice facilities, who must share their weight rooms with men's cross-country, with the women's tennis team, with intramural athletes.

**AP TOP 10**

*1. Ohio State*

*2. Auburn*

*3. USC*

*4. West Virginia*

*5. Florida*

*6. Michigan*

*7. Texas*

*8. Louisville*

*9. LSU*

*10. Georgia*

What of these teams looking in from the outside of college football's aristocracy, programs overseen by athletic directors who reflexively ask, when ESPN informs them they will be kicking it off on a Tuesday, "What time?"

This year the overlords have deigned to throw a sop to the campesinos in Conference USA, the WAC, the MAC, the Mountain West. This year there is this added hope for teams from have-not leagues who've had to content themselves since 1998—the year the BCS was thrust on college football—with table scraps left by the superpowers, your SEC, your Pac-10, your Mr. Bigs (Big Ten, Big Twelve, Big East). We are in Year One of something the grasping, tin-eared Solons of the Bowl Championship Series have dubbed the "double-hosting" format. Starting this season, the four BCS bowl games (Orange, Fiesta, Sugar, Rose) will be augmented by a national title game, the clunkily named Bowl Championship Series National Championship Game (BCSNCG). The other four used to take turns hosting the title game, but that, apparently, has been deemed insufficiently convoluted. So, once every four years, if you're one of those four elite bowls, you host two BCS games: your traditional bowl game and the BCSNCG.

The net effect of the "double-hosting model" is that it adds one more lucrative bowl to the BCS stable. Room at the table has been promised to qualified teams from non-BCS conferences. It's not like the commissioners of the power conferences did this willingly. *And one day we asked ourselves, How would Jesus divvy up all these windfall millions the networks are throwing at us?* They simply didn't want to get their asses sued, which the smaller conferences were threatening to do.

Who among these Davids has a legitimate shot at doing some BCS-busting, at making it to a BCS bowl? A month into the season, the path seems clear for the Horned Frogs of Texas Christian University.

So BEFORE DAWN on September 27, I board an obscenely early flight to DFW, flash my driver's license at the Hertz attendant, decide against the fuel-purchase option, then point my midsize Alero toward a distant, unfamiliar skyline. I've flown into the Metroplex maybe 40 times on assignment for *SI*. That's a lot of Cowboys and Longhorns and Lance Armstrong, with some Dallas Stars and Texas A&M Aggies and Baylor Bears thrown in. But in 22½ years at the magazine, I've never been assigned a story on TCU.

So I motor west, toward Fort Worth, where the construction cranes on campus are but one measure of the good things happening at this thriving private university. "There's 130 million dollars in construction going on right now," athletic director Danny Morrison will be happy to inform me, later this afternoon. Projects include four new student dorms and an indoor practice facility for the football team, which will be completed this spring. "Our business school was just ranked number one in the state by *The Wall Street Journal*. This university, as an institution, is really hot." (He is not talking about the sauna-like Texas heat that puts the Horned Frogs' opponents at a distinct disadvantage, or about the pulchritude quotient on campus: *Men's Health* recently declared that Fort Worth has the second-most attractive women, per capita, in the nation, behind only Honolulu, a distinction Horned Frog coaches seldom fail to mention to recruits.)

It's impossible to say how much of TCU's renaissance has been driven by the success of the football team, but the influence is probably greater than you think. The average SAT here may be more than 1100, the student-faculty ratio an impressively low 15:1, but this is still Texas. Head coach Gary Patterson, the guitar-playing defensive savant who had a bit of an outburst following his team's last victory—more on this later—has won 10 or more games in three of his last four seasons. The undefeated Frogs, who kick it off against BYU in tomorrow's Thursday night game, might be the best team from a non-BCS conference in the land. I look forward to meeting Patterson, and possibly hearing him do a bit of guitar picking.

Sharing a market with Stars, Mavs, Rangers, Astros, and Longhorns makes it an uphill pull for TCU to grab media attention—attention that has been diverted by the latest scandal to beset the Dallas Cowboys.

AT 7:51 ON the night before my arrival, according to the Dallas Police Department report, officers "were dispatched on a call by

Dallas Fire and Rescue regarding comp"—Dallas Cowboys wide receiver Terrell Owens is identified throughout the report as "comp," short for complainant—"attempting suicide by prescription pain medication." Owen's publicist, the overmatched Kim Etheredge, informed the officers that Owens had told her he was "depressed." Etheredge told police she "noticed that comp's prescription pain medication was empty and observed comp putting two pills in his mouth. [Etheredge] attempted to put her fingers in comp's mouth to retrieve the pills."

This was a bottle of generic Vicodin filled September 18, after Owens had broken his hand in a game against the Washington Redskins. The report goes on to say that Etheredge told police Owens had only taken five of the pills "up to this date," and that he'd downed the remaining 35 that night. "On further interview of comp, comp was asked if he was attempting to harm himself, at which time the comp stated 'yes.' Comp was treated by Baylor Medical staff for a drug overdose."

That was Tuesday night. Now, it was Wednesday, and Owens and Etheredge were gazing haggardly at the media circus they had wrought. It was all a big misunderstanding, they explained at a press conference at the Cowboys headquarters in Valley Ranch. Owens had merely had "an allergic reaction" when he combined "a couple pain pills" with some health supplements that he takes. Etheredge denied telling responding officers that her client was depressed; denied having tried to fish pills out of his mouth. And those extra pills? Owens had taken them out of the bottle and put them in a drawer.

What about reports that he told the cops he intended to harm himself? "I really wasn't as coherent as they probably thought I was," he replied.

It was all riveting theater, and very sad. This guy belonged on a suicide watch. Instead, the big question was, *Would he suit up against the Tennessee Titans the following Sunday?* (He did, and caught five balls for 88 yards in a Cowboys rout notable for two things: 1) It was the first NFL start of Vince Young, who showed flashes of brilliance in defeat, and 2) After a third-quarter touchdown run by Dallas's Julius Jones, Titans defensive tackle Albert Haynesworth stomped and raked his cleats across the face of Cowboys center Andre Gurode, whose helmet had come off on the play. Gurode needed 30 stitches to close the lacerations. Haynesworth was ejected and suspended five games by the NFL. My question: Why wasn't he arrested and charged with assault?)

I'M TEMPTED TO drop in at Valley Ranch, just to see the feeding frenzy as it happens, to sit in on one more Bill Parcells press conference. It would be worth it, just to see the dyspeptic expression on the Tuna's face, and possibly inquire after his health. (In an upcoming story by Michael Lewis in a *New York Times* supplement called "Play," we will learn that the coach is divorced, "living alone in what amounts to a hotel room," and that he's not sleeping well. He keeps waking up choking on his own bile. Have I mentioned that the college game is more fun?)

I've got a more wholesome story to cover. I've got a date with Gary and the Stepchildren.

With each passing season under TCU head coach Gary Patterson, now in his seventh year in Fort Worth, the bitterness subsides a little more. TCU alumni and fans are getting over the hurt of not being invited to join the Big Twelve a decade ago, after the Southwest Conference, having become synomous with "under the table payments," imploded under the weight of its own corruption. Cast into the college football diaspora, the Horned Frogs have won titles in three different conferences—Conference USA, the WAC, and the Mountain West—in the past six years.

Right now they are trying not to think about, but cannot help thinking about, a BCS bowl. They're 3-0 and ranked No. 15 in the coaches' poll. They are sitting (squatting?) on a 13-game winning streak, the longest in Division I. A win over BYU would tie a school record set by the Horned Frogs of 1937 and '38. While John Heisman never won the Davey O'Brien Award, Davey

O'Brien carted off the 1938 Heisman for quarterbacking that year's TCU squad to the national championship.

Their most recent victory was a big one—a shocking 12–3 victory over the offensively prolific Red Raiders of Texas Tech, whom the swarming, blitzing Frogs held without a touchdown for only the second time in 79 games under Tech head coach Mike Leach, who could not contain his disgust after the game.

"That was the sorriest offensive effort I've ever seen," he declared. "Today, I coached the worst offense in America, which makes me the worst offensive coach in America."

Patterson blew a gasket. Would it kill the guys he beats to give some credit to the players who just beat them? "People have been underselling our kids for years," he fumed, with TV cameras rolling. "All they ever want to do is talk about the Big Twelve. We're not the Big Twelve, just a Texas team playing with Texas players"—and beating every Big Twelve team that shows up on their schedule.

Then, the money quote: "I get tired of being treated like the stepchild in this state and in this town. My kids do, too."

Patterson seems slightly sheepish, when I meet him, recalling that brief outburst. "My point was," he says, "we've got great kids here doing the right thing. You've gotta give these guys a little bit of respect."

We are on the field at Amon Carter Stadium, where the team has just finished its walk-through for tomorrow's game. Patterson is sporting black pants and a black shirt in 88-degree heat and high humidity. "This?" he says, when I mention the discomfort index. "To people around here, this feels like December."

I ask him about his fiendish 4-2-5 defensive scheme. It's like asking Robert Oppenheimer for the particulars of the Manhattan Project. Three safeties, two corners . . . blitzes, dogs, fire zones, deep thirds—my notes trail off. On offense, "we've got a little bit of everything," he says, helpfully. "Some option power game, some read option, like they do at Florida. We're gonna find out what you didn't work on."

It was after a loss to the Horned Frogs in 2005 that Air Force head coach Fisher DeBerry gave a Denver TV station a glimpse of the keen intellect and powers of perception required to make it at the D-I level. "It just seems to be that way, that Afro-American kids can run very, very well," observed the coach, having noted that TCU had more black players than he did. "That doesn't mean that Caucasian kids and other descents can't run, but it's very obvious to me they run extremely well."

I guess, by Afro-Americans, he means citizens of this country with kinky, teased-out hair, like the actor who plays Napoleon Dynamite. While I haven't seen any truly formidable Afros in my short time with the Frogs, I am noticing they're not a huge team. Patterson doesn't recruit size, he recruits speed. TCU has five guys along its defensive line who played running back in high school. Everybody can run, everybody's obscenely fit. Through last season and the first three games of 2006, TCU has given up a total of 31 fourth-quarter points. The Horned Frogs had 40 takeaways in 2005, a season that began with their upset of Oklahoma and ended with a win over Iowa State in something called the EVl.net Houston Bowl.

AMON CARTER STADIUM is surrounded by a loop of pavement called "Frog Alley," a fun place to kill time before the game. Companies pay for the right to "brand" themselves in the Alley, setting up booths and tents. There is a petting zoo, with goats, a donkey, pot-bellied pigs, and a horned frog—a critter that, I am informed by helpful associate AD Scott Kull, is actually a spiny hazard capable of expectorating a four-foot stream of predigested red ants from its eyes when alarmed.

There is an inflatable bouncy, outside which a child is receiving treatment for a cut on her chin. There is a face-painting area. IHOP has sponsored a tent; the pancake palace is raising awareness for an upcoming fundraiser for the Ronald McDonald House. "Latin Fraternity Inc." has set up a table. This is in keeping with an overarching theme. For every home game, it has been explained to me, the university reaches out to a different segment of the Fort Worth community. Today, TCU is embracing the city's Hispanic population. The pregame festivities have been dubbed Fiesta de los Frogs.

A fair number of Amon Carter's 44,000 seats remain unoccupied a half hour before game time. The cruel and unusual 5:00 p.m. kickoff, mandated by ESPN, is not helping. As a subtle nudge to get fans to the stadium on time, the athletic department took out a tongue-in-cheek ad in yesterday's *Fort Worth Star-Telegram* asking readers, "Have you caught Frog Fever? You might need to get out of work early." Attached was a "coach's note" from Patterson allowing the bearer to get out of work early "this Thursday, September 28."

All college programs have developed their own unique traditions. No football culture is quite so distinct as at BYU, the Mormon university whose 32,000 students make it the largest private church-sponsored university in the country. While BYU might not be the whitest team in the country, you can bet Coach De-Berry has never attributed a loss to the Cougars on the profusion of "Afro-Americans" on their roster. As in the student body at large, most of the athletes are members of the Church of Jesus Christ of Latter-day Saints. Sixty-one players on this year's team have served two-year full-time missions for the church. That means BYU has the oldest college team in the country, which cuts both ways. Yes, the guys are more mature. Late bloomers have grown into their bodies. On the other hand, a lot of them haven't played football in three years. "When we're good," BYU spokesman Jeff Reynolds points out, "opposing coaches always bring up the age factor. When we've struggled, no one says anything about it."

BYU fans have a reputation for their willingness to travel to away games—all the more impressive considering that, unlike the rest of us, they can't mainline caffeine on long road trips. They're out in force tonight: I'm guessing there are 10,000 Cougars fans in the north bleachers. It makes for an obvious, and ever so slightly uncomfortable divide: Mormons on one side of the stadium, everybody else on the other. The lines are blurred by the Reverend Angela Kaufman, who delivers the pregame invocation. Normally I am leery of such exercises. But Kaufman's words, intoned as evening shadows creep into the east end zone, stay with me a while: "God, we come here a passionate people from two teams but of one heart. Tonight, Lord, grant us community, even in our fiercest competitions. . . . Remind us of our shared unity as your children—a unity that crosses all geographies, differences, and divides."

And the band strikes up "Deep in the Heart of Texas," and a fog machine is cranked up, so the Frogs might take the field through a daunting curtain of white mist. And none of it matters, because BYU is quarterbacked by a cool-headed senior named John Beck, and this is his night.

Hobbling around like a peg-legged pirate—Beck has a pair of badly sprained ankles—he threw for 436 yards in his previous game, at Boston College. Tonight, playing with what appears to be two pounds of athletic tape on either ankle, he is masterful, clinically dissecting Patterson's scheme. On a fourth-and-one early in the second quarter, BYU head coach Bronco Mendenhall gives Beck the green light to call his own play.

What are you thinking? Sneak? Fullback dive?

Beck calls a play-action pass, then finds wide out Matt Allen for a 16-yard completion. Patterson, who cannot be said to have a gentle bedside manner, can't chew out the cornerback who's surrendered the first down, and must content himself with unloading on the poor defensive back who happens to be standing next to him. The Cougars are in the end zone two plays later. Beck only gets sharper in the second half, throwing for three touchdown passes in 31–17 victory that snaps the longest winning streak in Division I.

Afterward I stand on the field with Beck, whose parents attended BYU before him. Many was the December the Becks road-tripped from their home in Mesa, Arizona to San Diego to see the

Coogs play in the Holiday Bowl. John has a picture of himself as a 10-year-old, posing with Ty Detmer. Winning the starting job at BYU fulfilled his dreams.

But there was nothing dreamy about his debut against Georgia Tech. "My first three snaps as a collegian went like this," he recounts: "Sack, fumble, interception." He suffered a concussion against USC in his next game; he threw two picks in his first start, an 18–14 loss to Stanford. Since then, he's developed into one of the best quarterbacks in BYU history.


I'M HAPPY FOR Beck, but sad for the Frogs, and for myself, frankly. My four-pager has just fallen out of the magazine. Unable to win on the day of the Fiesta de los Frogs, the Frogs have blown their shot at the Fiesta Bowl. To cheer ourselves up, Kull and Rudy Klancnik and I find ourselves at a table on the patio at Joe T. Garcia's in downtown Fort Worth. We graze on appetizers and decant our woes. There may even have be a Margarita or two on the table.

Kull can't get over how sharp Beck was. "Guy looked like Tom Brady out there," he says, shaking his head. "Same number and everything."

Klancnik, who works for a company called ISP as its "General Manager for the TCU Property," has put in a long day. One of his jobs is to oversee corporate sponsorship for the Frogs. Just because he commands quite a bit of authority doesn't mean Klancnik enjoys using it. But when he began receiving reports of a rogue pancake in Frog Alley, it was time to dispense some law.

As he told it, IHOP had hired an eight-foot pancake mascot—not a problem, in and of itself, although mascots have been known for their willful ignorance of corporate strictures governing branding rights in the Alley. And this particular pancake had boundary issues. IHOP had paid for a tent. For an extra premium, companies can purchase the privilege, as Klancnik put it, "to reach out and touch people *all over* Frog Alley." IHOP had not purchased such "roaming" rights.

Not getting the memo was this outlaw pancake, who ranged far afield—hundreds of yards!—from its assigned tent, forcing Klancnik into sheriff mode.

"Hey, Pancake," he'd scolded, "you've got to get back to your tent. You've got stay in your area." The pancake had apparently retreated with insolent silence, although, since one of the cardinal rules of being a mascot is that you never speak while in character, the pancake may in fact have been exhibiting professionalism, rather than insolence.

"Damn," I tell Klancnik, my tongue loosened by a margie-with-salt. "You guys are *strict*." I thought about it some more. "Down here in the mid-majors, nobody gives you anything."

"That's right," he agrees. "Gotta earn it."

# CHAPTER 9

# Toomer's Corner

October 14, Auburn, Ala. —"He's got a presence," Florida athletic director Jeremy Foley says of Urban Meyer, his head football coach. "You walk into a room and you can tell he has a little something about him."

He's talking about the Meyer charisma, which tonight I am witnessing for the first time in person. A former Division I strong safety who spent a summer in baseball's minor leagues, Meyer is tall, dark, athletic, and handsome. But so are a lot of guys. To me, his most arresting feature is the Medusan stare. Meyer fixes his subjects with a gaze so direct, so penetrating, that it is capable of introducing doubt in the mind of an umpire. (*Maybe I am missing a bunch of holding calls!*); of melting the heart of a recruit's mother; of stirring obedience and urgency in his players. After my first audience with Meyer, I come away thinking: Here is a guy with the Right Stuff.

But on this night in Jordan-Hare Stadium, he doesn't have

**AP TOP 10, WEEK 7**

1. *Ohio State*
2. *Florida*
3. *USC*
4. *Michigan*
5. *West Virginia*
6. *Texas*
7. *Louisville*
8. *Tennessee*
9. *Notre Dame*
10. *California*

enough of it. Even as he emerges from the visitors' locker room to address a clutch of fidgeting reporters—it is well after 10:00 p.m., and some of these scribes will now have about 20 minutes to file their stories—hundreds of delirious undergraduates, several of whom are sober, are filling the night air with bathroom tissue a mile away. Wordsworth wrote that each of us comes into this world "trailing clouds of glory." Tigers football victories come into this world trailing clouds of Charmin and Angel Soft, Cottonelle and Scott. The rolling of Toomer's Corner is underway.

The intersection of College Street and Magnolia Avenue is the Rockwellian cynosure of "the loveliest village on the plains," as Auburn (with uncharacteristic immodesty) refers to itself. It is named for Toomer's Drug Store, which, like the twin oaks lording over it, is more than a century old. After parking in one of the nearby diagonal spaces—shades of Mayberry—you can get some fresh-squeezed lemonade at the Drug Store. Or you can proceed down the street to Cambridge Coffee, where they make a respect-able cappuccino, bake some nice muffins, and carry the *New York Times.*

It is into and over these ancient trees that roll upon roll of bath-room tissue is hurled until white filaments hang from every limb like some exotic, local species of Spanish moss. Hours later, after they shut down the press box at Jordan-Hare Stadium, after the Saturday night crowd has dissipated from downtown, but before workmen pressure-wash the tissue out of the trees, I will stroll into this two-ply microclimate and find it beautiful and a trifle surreal, like strolling through a just-shaken snow globe. It's not a good idea to get in the business of ranking college football cus-toms, but none is more kick-ass than this.

Unless, of course, you are the rollee. All the toilet paper is probably reminding the Gators that their hopes of playing in the BCS title game have just gone swirling down a figurative commode.

Or so it seems. They've just lost, 27–17, to an Auburn squad that held quarterback Chris Leak to 108 passing yards and forced him into a pair of brutal, morale-crippling turnovers that cost his team both the game and, it appeared, a chance to play in the national championship.

Now Meyer stands before a roomful of reporters who wonder if he will throw his quarterback under the bus. Leak's interception with three minutes left in the game had been especially catastrophic: wide out Andre Caldwell had his man beaten, but Leak's badly underthrown ball was easily picked off by Eric Brock. Quite justifiably, for Leak had been God-awful, a reporter asks the coach to share his thoughts on the senior's poor play.

This particular scribe, it bears noting, is clad in that sartorial staple of sportswriters: a gratis windbreaker from a charity golf tournament. This one commemorates the "Steve Spurrier Scramble for Kids"—a reminder that, regardless of his popularity around Gainesville, Meyer labors in the shadow of a legend.

It was Spurrier, now the coach at South Carolina, who led the Gators to their last national title, a decade ago. In addition to his many positive attributes, the Ol' Ball Coach was not above hanging his players out to dry after a tough loss. Meyer isn't going there.

"If you're looking for someone to point fingers," he tells Windbreaker, "you're talking to the wrong guy."

I LIKED MEYER even before I met him. Readers will recall that even before he coached Utah to a smashing victory in a BCS bowl after the 2004 season, it was clear he would have his pick of prestigious jobs. After allowing the Notre Dame athletic director and university president to fly to Utah for an audience with him, Meyer jilted them to take up with that floozy, Florida.

The high regard in which I hold Notre Dame is nearly as high as the regard in which Notre Dame holds itself. As previously mentioned, Domers can be susceptible to a low-grade institutional

smugness, which malady made it easier to take mean-spirited pleasure in Meyer's heartless rejection of the Irish. Meyer's stiff-
arming reminded me of the Lending Tree commercial where the
couple sits on their sofa, summoning from the kitchen banking
executives whom they mock, cut short, and otherwise bring low
before dismissing them with callous disregard. *Hey, you've got a nice
tradition there—Touchdown Jesus, what a concept!—but I think I can
accomplish my goals more quickly at Florida. Can you guys find your own
way out?*

When asked by reporters, Meyer graciously points out that by
the time the Irish got into the game, his courtship with Florida
was so advanced that consummation, as it were, had become inevitable.

Next came the hard part: lifting a once-proud program from
the slough of despond into which it had sunk under the enigmatic
Ron Zook, a man afflicted with a worse case of the Mack Brown
Syndrome than Mack Brown himself. If the guy could coach half
as well as he recruited, Meyer would be working in South Bend
and Zook would still be in Gainesville, where people would barely
remember Steve Spurrier.

Meyer brought to Gainesville a reputation for brutal candor
and offensive wizardry. His "spread offense" averaged 45.3 points
per game in 2004 at Utah, and created coast-to-coast buzz. All
"spread" means, really, is that you force the defense to line up all
over the field. By spreading the defense, Meyer creates lanes and
space for his fastest players to exploit. "If you recruit athletes"—by
which he meant hand-picked, quicksilver difference-makers found
in abundance on his roster—"it would be a mistake to put them in
a small, compressed area." While making this point, Meyer creates a little box with his hands.

Playing in a small, compressed area, of course, was the doctrine
of one of Meyer's heroes. Growing up in Ashtabula, Ohio, Meyer
had idolized Woody Hayes, the Buckeye head coach who epito-
mized conservative, strength-against-strength football; who expressed his mistrust of the forward pass with the observation,

"There are three things that can happen when you pass, and two of them ain't good."

As tailback and defensive back at St. John High, Meyer wore No. 45, an homage to Archie Griffin. He played in the secondary at Cincinnati, where he graduated in 1986 with a degree in psychology. Weeks later, he drove north to Columbus. He would be a graduate assistant for the football team while pursuing his master's in sports administration.

Upon Meyer's arrival at the Buckeyes football complex, a fellow graduate assistant gave him the skinny. Two g.a. positions were open: one with the tight ends, the other with the secondary. If he took the job with the defensive backs, Meyer was told, his responsibilities would consist of making coffee and drawing up scout-team plays. "On offense," his new colleague told Meyer, "you actually get to coach."

He took the tight ends job. To make a sparkling impression on then–head coach Earle Bruce, Meyer spent the summer devouring the Buckeyes playbook. "I memorized that son-of-a-gun from A to Z," he recalls with a grim smile.

At the first day of practice, Bruce barked at him "give me a four-technique." The eager young coach put a blocking dummy directly over the tackle—just as it said under "four-technique" in the Buckeyes playbook he'd painstakingly committed to memory. In Bruce's mind, however, the bag should have been shaded to one side of the tackle or the other. "He just started cursing and screaming at me," recalls Meyer. "He berated me and beat me to death."

Thus began a meteoric rise through the coaching ranks, from Ohio State to Illinois State to Colorado State, where Meyer's mentor Earle Bruce was fired in 1992. Bruce was replaced by Sonny Lubick, who had no intention of retaining Meyer until he sat down across from the young man who exuded intelligence, confidence, and ambition. "You might not know me now," Lubick recalls him saying, "but you'll never be sorry if you keep me on."

Meyer spent six seasons with Lubick, whose most lasting influence on him is best boiled down to two words: lighten up. Meyer was a graduate of the Hayes-Bruce school of fire and brimstone coaching: "I never knew it could be done another way," he now says. Lubick showed him, as the older coach put it, "you catch more flies with honey than vinegar."

Meyer became adept at dispensing both, as the need arose. After five years at Notre Dame under Lou Holtz, then Bob Davie, Meyer landed his first head-coaching job in 2001, at Bowling Green. There, he orchestrated the first of what would be three dramatic turnarounds.

With each stop he broadened his horizons, deepened his understanding of how to reach young men—how to motivate them, as he put it to me, "to do some very uncomfortable things, whether it's lifting weights, battling through pain, becoming unselfish. Love, fear, and hate are the three strongest forms of motivation, and we try to use all three."

Unsure how to reach his most important player at Florida, he tried hospitality. Quarterback Chris Leak had been recruited by, and subsequently befriended, the fired Zook. Their relationship, he would later say, "went way beyond football." Zook's dismissal meant the junior would be learning his third offensive system in three years. While he was capable of running for first downs, Leak saw himself as more of a traditional, pro-style, drop-back quarterback. He was nervous about the arrival of Meyer and his spread offense.

Little wonder, then, that Leak tended to keep his own counsel in the early weeks and months of the Meyer regime, despite the new head coach's attempts to draw him out. To allay his quarterback's anxieties, Meyer invited Leak to his house shortly after he was hired. They would have some refreshments and watch some game tape. They would bond.

That, at least, was the idea. As it turned out, coach and player stared straight ahead at Meyer's big-screen TV while enduring excruciatingly long silences.

"When I say he didn't say a word," Meyer recalls of those sessions, "I mean he didn't say a word."

Part of that could be chalked up to the natural reticence of Leak, whose default mode is a meditative silence easily mistaken by those who don't know him for catatonia. And part of it was "a lack of trust," according to Meyer. "He didn't know who we were. All he knew was that he was playing for his third offensive coordinator in three years, and that everybody was saying he wouldn't fit the system."

STATISTICALLY, THE GATORS offense backslid in Meyer's first year. Leak threw nine fewer TD passes (20) than he had as a true sophomore. His 219 passing yards per game in 2005 was 47 yards less than his average from the previous year. Part of the problem was Leak's steep learning curve. Under Zook, incredibly, Leak could get through an entire game without making a single call at the line of scrimmage.

"We wanted to take as much off his shoulders as we could," recalls Larry Fedora, who served on Zook's staff as running game coordinator, then offensive coordinator. From his press-box vantage, Fedora would read the defense, then relay an audible to a coach on the field. That coach would signal in the play. Changing the protection was the job of the center. Even the snap count was silent: to signal his readiness, all Leak did was lift his leg.

None of that was going to cut it under Meyer. It was fine to coddle an underclassman quarterback, to hold his hand and give him shortcuts. But now, Meyer decreed, it was time for Leak to become The Man. He would change the protections and handle the audibles, or he would finish his college career on the bench.

After leading the team to victories in its first four games, Leak—and the Gators—fell on hard times. Right around the time three top receivers went down with injuries, the offense began listing badly. In a stunning 31–3 loss at Alabama, Leak completed just 43 percent of his passes, and threw a pair of interceptions. The Gators lost twice more in their next five games, at LSU (Leak completed 11 of his 30 passes and was sacked four times) and, more galling, at underdog South Carolina, a team coached by Spurrier, in whose shadow all Florida coaches labor until one of them could return a national title to Gainesville.

By closing out the season with a roar—a 34–7 thrashing of underachieving Florida State, followed by a 31–24 win over Iowa in the Outback Bowl—the Gators took momentum into the off-season. By crushing in-state rivals Miami and the Seminoles in the Sunshine State recruiting wars—19 of the Gators' 27 commitments came from Florida—Meyer and his staff put together what at least one recruiting analyst rated as the nation's top class. Two players stood atop that class: Rivals.com's top-ranked player in the nation, Percy Harvin, a hard-nosed wide out with game-breaking speed, and Tim Tebow, a freakishly big, strong, fast southpaw quarterback who was as outgoing as Leak was reserved.

Those blue chippers safely in the fold, Meyer took the opportunity to coast for a few months.

Actually, no. The man was breathing fire before spring ball, making headlines by excoriating his tailbacks, whose collective performance in 2005 he likened to garbage.

From a distance, Florida appeared to have an okay ground game. The Gators had averaged a credible 146.8 yards per outing. But that was a hundred yards per game less than Meyer's offenses rang up at Utah in 2004. Plus, it was the inability to consistently establish a ground game that allowed top defenses to tee off on Leak. (Recall, if you will, his 11-for-30, four-sack outing in Baton Rouge.) Meyer's solution was to call out his running backs. The choicest vitriol: "I get very upset thinking about that position. That's not what is expected. If that continues, we'll play without a tailback. I'm not going to sit and watch that trash I watched last year.

"Fred Taylor and Emmitt Smith played tailback here before. I keep checking that. That did happen, right? I want to see that. We have to recruit that, we have to develop that. There's got to be a standard set. Right now, we don't have a standard. That has to happen or we will not play with a tailback.

"That's maybe the most disappointing position on our team.

Florida has a nice tradition of great running backs here. We are not fulfilling our obligation of upholding that great tradition. We're very poor at the tailback position. I've been around football for 21 years and we've always had a back you could count on. [Last season] we didn't have one."

Recall that one of Meyer's motivational methods was "hate," as in, "You challenge 'em to the point where they wanna prove you wrong and they hate you."

By going so far out of his way to publicly humiliate his tail-backs, Meyer seemed especially determined to excite that emotion in them. "The truth hurts," Florida running backs coach Stan Drayton told me during two-a-days. "The passion and leadership was not there. Guys were not playing to their potential."

The guy they were really talking about was DeShawn Wynn, the senior from Cincinnati whose flashes of excellence had always been interspersed with injuries, questionable effort and attitude, weight problems, suspensions, and fumbles (note to editor: am checking to see if he also suffered the heartbreak of psoriasis). Despite undergoing, by all accounts, a serious attitude adjustment in fall camp, Wynn split carries with sophomore Kestahn Moore through Florida's first two games, tea parties against Southern Miss and Central Florida.

Wynn appeared to have a breakthrough on the night of September 16. With the Gators trailing Tennessee at Rocky Top five minutes into the fourth quarter, Wynn slashed for 26 yards, the longest play in what would become Florida's game-winning touchdown drive. On a third-and-four with under two minutes to play, the senior quieted a hundred thousand voices at Neyland Stadium by pounding for six tough yards, allowing the Gators to run out the clock.

Florida had trailed by 10 with two minutes left in the third quarter. This was a watershed win, for Meyer and for Wynn. "It's time he became a tailback," declared the coach of his doghouse-prone senior, "and he did."

Wynn got to enjoy his alpha dog status for six quarters, at which point he wrenched his right knee in the second half of a vengeance-fueled victory over Alabama. That sprain kept him out of the following game, a mondo tilt at home against No. 9 LSU, but opened the door for Moore. The sophomore shook loose for 15 yards on his first carry, but fumbled on his third. That giveaway led to an LSU touchdown, and seemed to remind Meyer of his preseason screed against the tailbacks. For long stretches of this Homecoming game, he made good on his threat to field a tailback-free offense.

Because he could. In Harvin, Dallas Baker (the Touchdown Maker), and Andre (Bubba) Caldwell, he had a sleek collection of blindingly fast wide outs to whom Leak could hand the ball on end-around plays. And he had the un-Leak, the X-factor, Tim Tebow. Whereas the mild-mannered Leak stood just over 5'11", Tebow was large (6'3", 229) and in charge, a linebacker with a low jersey number and a disposition to pump up his teammates and the crowd.

Leak never pretended to relish the physical aspect of the game; he slid to avoid contact so many times in one game that one cruel blogger referred to his "10 stolen bases." Tebow, conversely, seemed to seek it out, as evinced on his first play against LSU. After taking a shotgun snap and turning his head to the right, as if searching for a receiver, he pulled the ball down and bulled forward. Apparently mistaking would-be tackler Jessie Daniels for a hitchhiker, Tebow carried the LSU safety for most of a 15-yard gain. Four plays later, Florida faced a fourth-and-goal at LSU's one-yard line. Disdaining the field goal attempt, Meyer put the ball back in the hands of Tebow, who led with his head, stoving in LSU's interior line for the game-tying touchdown.

There was plenty of machismo to go around in the Gators' 23–10 victory. An active, ornery Florida defense held the Bayou Bengals to 90 yards rushing and picked off JaMarcus Russell, the future first pick in the NFL draft, three times. But the player on the tips of Gators fans' tongues in the hours and days after the game was Tebow, who followed that goal-line plunge with two more touchdowns. One of which you probably remember.

Tebow may go on to throw a hundred touchdown passes for Florida, but none of them will be quite so memorable, so lovely and ungainly all at once, as his first. Lowering his head and charging the goal line just before halftime, he suddenly went airborne, pogoing more than two feet off the ground, looking for tight end Tate Casey.

It was a jump pass, a retro throw last seen with regularity in the days of Bronko Nagurski and Red Grange. "We practiced it all week," said offensive coordinator Dan Mullen, "but in practice the tight end got off the line a little quicker."

The play was a jump pass, but Tebow seemed to think it was a jump *shot*: that if he didn't get of the rid of the ball before he returned to earth, he might be called for traveling. While Casey struggled to get off the line of scrimmage—he got hung up with an outside 'backer—Tebow pumped once, *then* flicked a free throw caught by Casey in the back of the end zone.

LSU's defenders bit again early in the third quarter. Tebow approached the line as if to run a belly option, with which he'd gashed a team or two already. That action sucked up the secondary, allowing Tebow to fire a rope to reserve receiver Louis Murphy, whose 35-yard touchdown put the Gators up 23-7.

"You have to respect his running ability," admitted exasperated LSU defensive tackle Glenn Dorsey afterward. "Then he passes like that?" How was this fair?

Gator Nation had come into the LSU game on October 7 nursing a keen infatuation with its quarterback of the future. They knew that he was born in the Philippines, that he was homeschooled, that he returns every summer on a Christian mission. Now, having watched him create three touchdowns in his 15 plays against LSU, their affection threatens to spill out of control; into the realm of man-crushes and restraining orders. "Tim Tebow's Tears Cure Cancer," claim the producers of one YouTube homage.

"Too Bad Tim Tebow Has Never Cried." The video goes on to posit that "There Is No Theory of Evolution. Just a List of Species Tim Tebow Allows to Live."

While Leak had thrown 79 touchdown passes at Florida, one columnist opined, none had the pizzazz of Tebow's jump pass. Both quarterbacks appeared on the *College Football GameDay* set after the win. Talk of Florida's two-headed quarterback buzzed throughout the Republic, as did speculation about a possible coup d'etat at the position. The only place where there was no such talk, it seems, was inside the Florida football offices. "Chris is our quarterback," offensive coordinator Mullen assured reporters, describing Tebow as "just a fun kid."

Meyer wasn't worried about Leak's ego. The coach's focus, as the Gators got ready for Auburn, was on the other side of the ball. Even though it ended well for Florida, with a Brandon Siler fumble recovery, the staff was troubled by LSU's 17-play geological epoch of a drive. If they wanted to stay undefeated, the Gators would need to force more three-and-outs.

Even by the physical standards of the Southeastern Conference, Auburn's 7–3 victory over LSU on October 7 had been a spectacularly violent slugfest. On the strength of that win, Auburn had jumped to No. 2 in the nation, only to sleep through its wake-up call the following Saturday. Still yawning midway through the first quarter on account of a CBS-mandated 11:00 a.m. kickoff, the Tigers somnambulated through a 27–10 home loss to unranked Arkansas—the same Razorbacks who'd been annihilated by USC 50–14 in their opener.

So mystifying was that loss that Auburn head coach Tommy Tuberville felt compelled to reassure the Tiger faithful, "We're not that bad of a football team."

They weren't. They just weren't morning people.

That won't be a problem against the Gators tonight. Kickoff is scheduled for 7:45 p.m. Auburn will be playing to save its season; Florida will be playing in a famously hostile, noise-trapping venue in which it has traditionally struggled.

The nocturnal kickoff works for Auburn fans, many of whom use the daylight hours to fortify themselves with fermented beverages. And it works for me. I've been in Atlanta, hustling to finish my *SI* story on Calvin Johnson, the All-Cosmos wide receiver for Georgia Tech. I leave my hotel around 4:30 p.m.—plenty of time to make the 109-mile drive to Auburn. Unless, that is, I hit obscene traffic on that circle of hell known as I-285. Which I will. Unless I misunderstood the kickoff time. Which I did: it was 7:45 *Eastern* time. Auburn is in the Central time zone.

AFTER WEDGING MY car into space on someone's lawn along College Street, I've got a mile's walk to Jordan-Hare. I cut across a beautifully manicured lawn, which appears, as I study a campus map, to have been the grounds of the university president. Striding past residence halls—Hollifield, Burton, Dobbs—I discern marching band music; hear the PA announcer, see the silhouette of Jordan-Hare rise dramatically above the plains. There are still some stragglers on campus—PhD candidates hunched under book-stuffed packs, shuffling to the library, to the science building, oblivious to the looming human drama. Seeing them I cannot help but think: If I'd studied just a little harder—20 minutes a night!—maybe I would have an advanced degree. Maybe I'd be cruising to an opera in a 700-series BMW instead of sweating through my shirt on a Saturday night, speed-walking across a campus where drunken good ol' boys look at you funny because you're not wearing Auburn colors, which means you must be "one of them Gay-tors."

The pop-up tents are everywhere, but most of the tailgaters have long since made their unsteady way to the stadium. Left behind, along with a general tang of grilled meat and booze, are skeleton crews: those without tickets. Left behind to guard the supplies, they slump in their folding chairs like Dali timepieces. They need the game to start. They need a second wind.

I share an elevator to the press box with two state troopers, one of whose uniform has been slimed with an oleaginous white substance, possibly mayonnaise. He confides to the elevator operator that, while escorting ESPN's Lee Corso from the *GameDay* set to the stadium, his detail had come under fire from liquored-up Tigers fans pelting "the Coach" with garbage. My guess is they had not appreciated Corso's picking Florida over the home team, although it is entirely possible they knew nothing of the prediction, and showered him with refuse on general principle.

THE TOUCHDOWN MAKER outleaps Tigers cornerback Jonathan Wilhite for Florida's first touchdown, a 15-yard lob from Leak early in the second quarter. Then, strangeness.

Tony Joiner snuffs a promising Auburn drive with his monster hit on tight end Tommy Trott. Joiner, the Florida strong safety, jars the ball loose. Velociraptor defensive end Derrick Harvey recovers on the Florida three-yard line. Those two are still getting congratulatory claps on the shoulder when Jim Tartt, a road grader of a guard from Sopchoppy, Florida, is flagged for holding on the next play. The infraction occurs in the end zone, leaving the referee no choice but to press his palms together over his head, signifying a safety. Florida still leads, by the vaguely ridiculous score of 10–5.

The score is 10–8 when The Freshmen take the stage. Harvin devours 64 yards on successive rushes around left end. On first down at Auburn's 16, No. 15 in white jogs onto the field, and a surge of electricity runs through Jordan-Hare. They've heard about this kid. Let the Tebow Show begin.

"We were in a double-eagle front," Auburn defensive coordinator Will Muschamp will later explain. "We wanted to be able to flush the ball outside, make him run east and west."

Tebow does precisely that, faking a run left, then charging

toward right tackle, turning the corner, and scoring easily on a 16-yard run.

BY HALFTIME, FLORIDA has run 18 plays for 194 yards. Tuberville is not pleased. Where is a coach to turn when conventional methods have failed? Baseball managers refer to this grim state of affairs as "time to flip the spread"—as in, you walk into the postgame clubhouse where your defeated charges are glumly chewing sandwiches from a table in the center of the room. While lighting into them for their lack of focus, intensity, cojones, all of the above, you *flip the spread*, punctuating your point with a shower of cold cuts and condiments.

"Flipping the spread" need not denote the upending of a victuals-laden card table. It is a metaphor for any outburst designed to shake a team out of its torpor; to bring it into the moment. In *Bull Durham*, skipper Joe Riggins, played by the late Trey Parker, empties a bat bag. Tuberville, for his part—aware that Auburn will lose if his defense continues to surrender 10 yards per play—momentarily channels Bob Knight.

Afterward, no one can remember a similar outburst from smiling, staid Coach Tub. "Never seen him so mad," offensive guard Tim Duckworth will tell AUTigers.com. Defensive end Quentin Groves confides in the *Decatur Daily*, "He said he'd never been so ashamed in his entire life. Anytime you shame the head man, that's big."

The magical halftime oration is often just another wheezing prop trotted out by baffled sportswriters who can't sort out the anarchy in front of them to save their lives but can easily wrap their minds around a transformative tongue-lashing.

But this one actually works. After a first half in which "guys were thinking too much instead of playing," by Tuberville's reckoning, the Tigers cut loose. It helps that Groves does not return to the field, having chosen to lend his uniform, apparently, to Jevon Kearse.

There is Groves-Kearse torpedoing in from the right, sacking Leak on Florida's first possession of the second half. Onto the field trot the Gators punt team, including highly regarded senior punter Eric Wilbur. Auburn fans of a certain age will soon be joyfully drawing out his surname, in imitation of the way Mr. Ed, the talking horse of early television, pronounced the name of his architect friend (Wi-i-l-l-l-bur-r-r!).

Wilbur (the punter) will later explain that in the moments before the snap, he was distracted by movement along the Auburn front, which prevented him from concentrating, which resulted in a fumble. Scrambling to his left after recovering the ball, he succumbs to a panic best described as Yepremianesque, attempting a left-footed, rugby-style kick that is blocked by Jerraud Powers, who also recovers the ball, then somersaults over the goal line. The Tigers now lead 18–17. The decibel level in Jordan-Hare is ten times louder than anything Auburn fans had mustered for the Razorbacks a week earlier.

Groves-Kearse sacks Leak on Florida's *next* third-and-long, pressures him into an incompletion on the third-and-long after that and then, on the ensuing third down, makes one of the plays on which the 2006 college football will turn.

On third-and-three from the Tigers' six-yard line, Leak scans the field, pump-fakes, then pulls his arm back. His arm has *just* resumed forward motion when Groves strikes like the great white in *Jaws*. The ball is on the turf, the blood is in the water. Tigers recover. After a tense confab, the zebras rule it a fumble. Meyer burns a time-out to get the play reviewed, but the call stands. Auburn ball. While the Tigers fail to score on that possession, they do gnaw six minutes off the fourth quarter. In the end, it won't matter, because Leak's bad night is about to get worse.

With three minutes and change left to play—an eternity!—the Gators trail by a point. They've got the ball on their own 29. They need 40 yards to get in field goal range. On first down, with Bubba Caldwell wide open on a go-route up the right sideline, Leak underthrows him by 15 yards. The pass is intercepted by Eric Brock, who has time, if he so chooses, to signal a fair catch.

Why the rushed, awful throw? The official play-by-play contains this clue: *QB hurry by Quentin Groves.*

The Tigers turn that takeaway into a field goal. They tack on a window-dressing touchdown on the game's final play. (A desperate Florida lateral is scooped by Patrick Lee, who scores on a 20-yard fumble return.) The final score is 27–17. Florida's defensive focus has paid off. Sort of. Auburn won without scoring a touchdown on offense.

AND SO THE fratricide continues, SEC teams knocking each other off—Tennessee over Georgia, Florida over Tennessee, Arkansas over Auburn, Auburn over Florida—until none, it seems certain, will be left to contend for the national title. It has long been the lament of SEC fans (and players and coaches, Tuberville in particular) that their league is unduly penalized by college football's lack of a playoff system. With its (almost) across-the-board speed and quality and depth, they argue, it is difficult if not impossible for anyone to emerge unscathed from their SEC schedule.

Standing at the lectern as a losing coach for the first time in 2006, Meyer sought no refuge behind that excuse: "This is a tough-ass conference. That's part of the deal."

It only gets tougher. Florida still has Georgia, South Carolina, and Florida State on its regular season schedule. With a bye coming up, the Gators will have two weeks to marinate in their current misery—and they do look miserable. The team will soon lose its best defensive tackle: Marcus Thomas will be tossed from the team after twice testing positive for marijuana. And there is the quarterback situation.

At critical times against Auburn, Leak was deer-in-the-headlights hopeless. He'd regressed three years in a single night. Will Meyer throw him under the bus? Of course he won't. *If you're looking for someone to point fingers, you've got the wrong guy.* But then, he doesn't need to. Over in the Tigers interview area, Muschamp, the Auburn defensive coordinator, is doing it for him. "When you affect this quarterback"—when you sack him and level him just after he throws and make sure that you land on him with all your weight, in other words—"he'll throw it to you. And that's what happened tonight."

Where Muschamp is serious and unsmiling, his boss makes no effort to tamp down his euphoria. Tuberville has just followed one of the more disappointing losses of his Auburn career with a top-shelf win. And now he has a question: "Where's my toilet paper? I'm going to Toomer's Corner."

# CHAPTER 10

# Decline . . .

October 14, Los Angeles —Those aren't boos raining down on the Trojans in their home stadium. The fans must yelling "BOOOty!" Right?

Okay, so they're booing. They're jeering their own team. Their own undefeated team—the team that has played for the national championship each of the past three seasons. Before you judge these Trojans fans, before you label them fickle and fair-weather, walk a mile in their Reef sandals. Try to see things through their designer shades. They've watched their guys pose with the Heisman three of the past four years. Their team has won 51 of its last 53 regular season games. Their threshold for offensive ineptitude is low.

**AP TOP 10**

1. *Ohio State*
2. *Michigan*
3. *USC*
4. *West Virginia*
5. *Texas*
6. *Louisville*
7. *Tennessee*
8. *Auburn*
9. *Florida*
10. *Notre Dame*

And it is being exceeded this evening at the Coliseum. On the same night Leak and the Gators are finding a way to lose at Auburn, 'SC quarterback John David Booty is having a Leak-like outing. The third-ranked Trojans are showing all the closing instincts of George Costanza at last call. Having jumped to a 21–0 lead over the beleaguered Sun Devils of Arizona State—a team that is 0 for its last 11 games in California; that has been tattooed in its two previous outings, against Cal and Oregon—the Trojans are now hanging on for dear life.

Booty does not help his own cause by committing two second-half turnovers—a fumble and what Carroll will describe as a "horrendous" interception—which lead to 14 Sun Devils points. After the visitors knot the score at 21, 'SC takes over on its own 31-yard line. What follows is possibly the team's most bumbling drive of the season, lowlighted by: (1) an offensive pass interference call on Fred Davis; (2) a tripping call on left guard Drew Radovich; (3) Booty missing Dwayne Jarrett by a zip code on second-and-37. As they jog off the field, the Trojans are booed.

Southern California wins this game by taking Booty out of it, essentially. After firing a 14-yard touchdown pass to Jarrett 2:30 into the second quarter, the junior had failed to lead the team past midfield on its next six possessions.

It is at this point in the Arizona State game that Carroll makes an executive decision. The Trojans are finished throwing for the night. Plan B? Run it down the other guys' throats. On its penultimate possession, the USC offense reprises Sherman's March, driving 74 yards on 14 plays—one of which is a pass—for the game-winning touchdown. Ten of those carries, and 64 of those yards, go to Chauncey Washington, who's overcome a bad knee, a bad hamstring, and bad grades to earn this brief, shining moment.

I SEE SHADES of LenDale White. On a scorching afternoon in the desert one year earlier, with Leinart woozy from the effects of a cheap shot—Arizona State linebacker Robert James hit him late, driving the crown of his helmet into Leinart's chin, then piledrove him into the ground—Carroll put the game in the hands of his tailbacks. Bush was his usual quicksilver self. But it was White who led the cavalry charge, pounding between the tackles for 165 yards and two touchdowns *in the second half*, as 'SC climbed out of an 18-point hole to win going away.

Perusing *Fight On!*, the recent history of Trojans football, I am pleased to see that the authors, Steve Bisheff and Loel Schrader, included White on their list of 'SC's 50 greatest players, ever. In his three-year career, they note, White rushed for 3,159 yards— exactly 10 less than Bush. And they quote former Trojans guard John Drake, who observed, "Reggie is our physical mismatch, but LenDale is the law."

Midway through its first season without either of those backs, USC's ground game has yet to reach critical mass. While Washington was deputized for that final scoring drive against ASU, he is not The Law. Having begun the season with a bad hammy, he'll finish it with a bum knee. The truth is, the Trojans are still casting about for that money back. C. J. Gable showed flashes against Arkansas, but was outshined by Emmanuel Moody, who supplanted him as the starter. Moody's 130-yard game against Arizona will hold up as the most productive day by a USC back this season. Any one of these guys might *become* The Law. But right now, they're a suggestion box.

Until 'SC puts the fear of God in its opponent with a rushing attack, teams will make Booty's life harder. (Coming off the practice field three days after being jeered at the Coliseum, he essentially agrees with the boo-birds. "If they're not happy" with the offense, he promises, "we're not happy with it either. They're not alone.")

The frustration of Trojan Nation has been a month in the making. The euphoria of the Arkansas blowout had led to the satisfaction of a handy win over Nebraska, even if the Cornhuskers did play like they were more concerned with not being embarrassed than they were with winning. Next up: Arizona.

SEPTEMBER 23, TUCSON —I'm breaking the rules at Arizona Stadium. I'm standing behind the USC bench, talking to freshman fullback Stanley Havili. The rent-a-cops all around us have been told that's a no-no, but we're down to garbage time in another Wildcats loss. They're thinking about how they're going to beat traffic on the way home. They can't be bothered.

We're under three minutes. The Arizona offense is on the field, going through still another three-and-out. USC is on its way to a 20–3 win, but the Trojans haven't exactly overwhelmed. Two weeks after No. 8 LSU tattooed Arizona 45–3 in Baton Rouge, No. 3 USC took a three-nothing halftime lead into the locker room against those same Mildcats. While the defense has been spectacular—Arizona will finish with minus-16 rushing yards—this offense is barely recognizable from a year ago. And things may get worse before they get better. Dwayne Jarrett, the best player on the team, separated his shoulder while making a third-quarter touchdown reception. Then, on the very next series, it was Havili's turn.

He'd taken a swing pass from Booty eight yards around the right end. Taken out hard by two Arizona defenders at the sideline, he landed awkwardly, got up limping, and never did make it back onto the field. Now, in the final minutes of a game 'SC has safely in hand, Havili is sitting on the trainer's padded workbench with his left leg in an immobilizer. A heckler behind us is yelling, "Hey, what's you guys' average salary?" My brief, unauthorized dialogue with Stanley is excerpted here:

Me: "What's the word, Stanley. Is it broken?"

Havili: "A little bit."

This reply brought to mind the scene from *There's Something About Mary*, where Pat Healy, the gumshoe played by Matt Dillon, is picked up at the airport by his friend Sully, who has brought along a large dog.

Healy: "Does he bite?"

Sully: "A little. Get in."

Even though Havili's left fibula is fractured only a little, it will be enough to keep him out for the rest of the season.

As it happened, Stanley and I had been discussing the cinema earlier in the week. On my Tuesday visit to 'SC's practice, I'd asked him if he was familiar with the movie *This Is Spinal Tap*. Considering that he was three when that "rockumentary" was released in 1984, and that he is a Mormon—one of nine children of a Salt Lake City bus driver—I wasn't surprised when he politely told me no, he'd never caught that flick. So he could not appreciate the parallel between USC's bad luck at fullback and the serial misfortune suffered by the drummers in that heavy metal band.

While no Trojan fullback had "spontaneously combusted" (the sad fate of Tap drummer Peter "James" Bond) or perished in a "bizarre gardening accident" (the grim end met by Bond's predecessor, John "Stumpy" Pepys), there had been undeniably bad juju at the position. Brandon Hancock had shredded his knee in preseason practice, and Ryan Powdrell had ended up on the Coliseum turf with his ankle dislocated and his foot pointing the wrong way.

Up next on drums, so to speak, was Havili, a 2005 Super Prep All-America out of Cottonwood (Utah) High. As he sat on the trainer's workbench in his immobilizer, the third 'SC fullback to suffer a season-ending injury, I thought it best not to remind him of our conversation earlier in the week.

On the 110-mile drive south, from Sky Harbor Airport to Tucson, a sultry-voiced woman on 96.1 KLPX is telling me what I already knew, that it is 82 degrees and beautiful. It is a day so gorgeous that nothing could ruin it—not the profusion of Arizona drivers unclear on the concept of *getting your ass out of the left lane if you want to drive 57 mph*; and not the deejay's decision, in the middle of an otherwise fulfilling 40-minute classic rock marathon, to play a song by REO Speedwagon.

On a rectangle of open space just north of the football stadium, the lion has lain down with the lamb. Sort of. You've got 'SC fans and Arizona fans, tailgating side by side. An Arizona alum walking past some guys in Booty Patrols T-shirts rakes the air with his "claws" while producing a feline growl which, frankly, needs a lot of work. In rapid succession I walk past a voluptuous, raven-haired undergraduate whose T-shirt says LOOKING FOR MR. RIGHT NOW, and a Donovan look-alike (Leitch, not McNabb) whose shirt says AN AWKWARD MORNING IS BETTER THAN A BORING NIGHT. I should introduce them.

Arizona had it going on in the 1990s, with Dick Tomey's "Desert Swarm" defense. The Wildcats won 10 games in 1993 and shut out Miami in the Fiesta Bowl. Five years later they won 12 games, skunked Nebraska in the Holiday Bowl, and finished the season ranked third in the country. Arizona hasn't been to a bowl since. The head coach here is Mike Stoops, a great guy whom I got to know when he was defensive coordinator at Oklahoma. This is his third season at Arizona, and the jury's still out. With the 2005 season going south on him, Stoops burned the redshirt of freshman quarterback Willie Tuitama, who led the team to wins over Oregon State and undefeated UCLA, salvaging the Wildcats' season and giving them hope for 2006. Arizona is 2-1 in Stoops's third season. Tuitama's prowess is the subject of a sign painted on a sheet draped over Gate 11: NO TROJAN IS BIG ENOUGH TO PROTECT YOUR BOOTY FROM OUR WILLIE.

The authors are implying, if I'm not mistaken, that Arizona is about to make USC its bitch. Unfortunately for the Wildcats, these games are decided by the players on the field, rather than by drunken frat boys with spray paint and filched linens. Arizona's defense is gnarly: Antoine Cason, who picks off Booty in the second quarter, might be the best cover corner I'll see this season. But the offense can't get out of it own way. The Wildcats net a sorry-ass 154 total yards on the night. And it is this, the performance of his defense, that the stubbornly upbeat Carroll chooses to emphasize after the game.

First, he leads a gaggle of writers halfway across the field, in order to be heard over the Spirit of Troy, which, having finished the alma mater, launches into "Tusk." During this 30-yard promenade, the AP's Andrew Bagnato can be overheard observing, "We've already gained more yards than the home team."

What Carroll says: "I love the fact that we're playing defense like this. We're gonna really be able to count on these guys to be a big factor."

What he means: *We're going to have to count on them, because with Jarrett out and Havili done, we're hosed on offense.*

"We haven't been in many games like this, and it was really fun."
*It's been 52 games since we scored 20 points or less.*

"I don't know [what he'd do about the fullback situation]. We'll figure it out. Right now I don't have a solution for it, and I don't want to talk about it."

*Right now I don't have a solution for it, and I don't want to talk about it.*

THE COYOTE UGLY win in Tucson was an augury of ugliness to come. On September 30 at Washington State, freshman safety Taylor Mays intercepted a pass in the end zone as time ran out at Washington State, preserving a 28–22 victory. A week later in the Coliseum, the Washington Huskies lined up with a chance to win the game on the final snap.

Which never came. Having stopped the clock after the previous play, the zebras fired it up again sooner than Washington quarterback Isaiah Stanback expected. As poor Isaiah stood over center calling signals, time expired. That strange anticlimax and the game's final score—26–20—obscured the fact that the Trojans offense put up one measly touchdown in the game. (The balance of 'SC points came courtesy of Mario Danelo, who kicked four field goals, plus a touchdown off a fake field goal: Nice throw, Mike McDonald!)

By the time those Trojans fans started booing their own team against Arizona State on October 14, the offense had been mediocre for a month. Yes, there were fans who wanted to see what Mark

Sanchez—Booty's backup—can do. Says Steve Sarkisian, who in addition to calling plays is the quarterback coach, "I think those were the same guys calling for Matt's head after the Cal game." Leinart threw three interceptions in 'SC's triple-overtime loss to Cal in 2003. That game, three years old, stands, astonishingly, as the Trojans' last regular season loss.

Sarkisian sees another parallel. Two of Leinart's interceptions in that defeat were forced throws to Mike Williams, a sensational power forward of a wide out whose name had been changed by Dwayne Jarrett to Mike Who? The same way Leinart had become overreliant on Williams, Sark suggested, Booty had been guilty of looking for No. 8, to the exclusion of his other targets. And now defensive coordinators were wise to him.

"He's going through a transition stage," Sarkisian goes on, climbing into Booty's head. Where it may have been easier, early in the season, "to get some of those primary throws out, now I have to get to number two, number three, number four." It's an immensely difficult step to take. "You figure it out the hard way."

Every year around Memorial Day, rangers at Yosemite National Park install cables on the east face of Half Dome, without which very few hikers can make it up the near-50-degree pitch to the summit. Such is the incline of Booty's learning curve right now. He is figuring it out the hard way, as Sarkisian said—and without cables. His go-to guys can't seem to stay on the field together. Jarrett separated his left shoulder against Arizona, didn't make the trip to Pullman, and was a nonfactor against Washington—the same game Smith wrenched an ankle, slowing him for the remainder of that contest, and sidelining him for much of the Arizona State game, the first of six contests missed by steady, veteran third receiver Chris McFoy, who fractured his left shoulder at Washington State.

How is the head man holding up? He looks more careworn than I remember. Informed of this after practice on October 17,

Carroll replies, "Careworn? What's careworn?" (It means the lines around his eyes are etched more deeply.)

He's got a bone to pick with the half-dozen scribes who scrum around him on the field. One of the beat guys wrote that Allen Bradford, the freshman safety-turned-tailback-turned fullback, had been lining up as a receiver. Carroll has never kept reporters out of practice. But part of the deal is that they agree to keep such wrinkles out of their stories. "I'm not paranoid about this stuff," he tells the scribes, "and I'm not trying to be a jerk about it, but something like this pisses me off, because I lose an edge."

I know Carroll isn't paranoid. I know from paranoid. The week I was doing a story on his New York Jets in 1997, Bill Parcells denied my request to speak with three assistant coaches, including the strength coach. Of course, you couldn't blame the Tuna for not wanting his strength coach talking to the press. A few careless remarks on, say, the benefits of plyometric training, and the next thing you know the season's down the drain.

I once had a notebook confiscated while standing on the practice field at Houston, during the reign of mad-scientist run-and-shoot guru John Jenkins, who strutted and fretted his hour on college football's stage back in the late 1980s, and then was heard no more. Some dickhead security guard said, "I'm not sure you're allowed to be diagrammin' plays," and disappeared with my notebook for 10 minutes. I worked hard not to be overly snide when he returned it. You've got to watch whom you smart-mouth in Texas. You don't know who's helping make America safer by carrying a concealed weapon.

Carroll's lecture is a reminder of how good the beat guys have it here. Most other teams I visit, practices are closed. Players are off-limits after Monday at Michigan, Tuesday elsewhere. Coaches will tell you they're just looking out for the welfare of these "student-athletes." Bullshit. They're doing it because they can. Most of the players I talk to on Monday and Tuesday would be more than happy to chat Thursday or Friday, but are forbidden by their head coach, whose unspoken message is: I own your ass, I will control whom you talk to and when you talk to them, besides which, I can't trust you not to say something stupid, so shut your mouth and go do some power cleans.

Carroll opens practices, lets his guys talk to the media most of the week (they're off-limits Friday). He opens the locker room after games. It's as if he believes the give-and-take might actually assist them in developing life skills that could benefit them down the road! What a sadly misguided notion. Imagine how much success he'd have if he only emulated the way Lloyd Carr does it at Michigan.

The postpractice klatch continues. Carroll is pumped about the way the team finished against Arizona State. "We don't have an inexperienced running game anymore." No matter how narrow the victories, he is jacked up to be undefeated at the bye. By the time they tee it up again, 11 days hence in Corvallis, "we will be as close to full strength as we've been, other than the fullback position."

The session ends on a slightly surreal note, with the head coach reminiscing about his cameo role in the 1973 Disney flick *The World's Greatest Athlete*. Carroll was a safety at Pacific when called on to play Jan-Michael Vincent's double in a football scene. Catching a carom in the far end zone, the future USC head coach zigzags frenetically 108 yards for a touchdown.

"It took forever" to get the scene, recalls Carroll, who has never really stopped zigzagging frenetically, and who was clearly *destined* to work in Los Angeles.

Walking back to Heritage Hall with him, I bring up a recent comment by ESPN's Kirk Herbstreit, who'd stirred outrage in the Kingdom of Troy with his recent proclamation that USC had been so unimpressive in its recent victories that it "should apologize" for winning.

"Yeah, we ought to apologize," says Carroll, a slight edge in his voice. "Can't wait to talk to Herbie again."

"He forgets," says Carroll of the ex–Buckeye quarterback. "Look at the season Ohio State won it all"—in 2002. "They won 13–7, 10–6, 14–9—they had seven games like that, and they won 14 that year. I hope we win 14 and I can say, 'Apologize for this.' "

Is it USC's fate to scratch and struggle and claw for wins this year? Halfway through the season, what is this team's identity?

"You figure it out," he replies. "That's your job." But the next time he opens his mouth, he ventures a response to my question. "I tell these guys all the time what we are. We're disciplined, we finish well, we're very poised in pressure situations, and we get it done in the end."

Take those final minutes against Arizona State. "We smoke it right down the field, take the lead, defense goes out, forces a punt. We run out the clock, we go home. The theme of last week was finishing—finishing the game, finishing the first half of the season 6-0, and we did it. F____n' A, we did it. Let's go have some fun on the bye!"

THE TROJANS WILL use the extra week to get healthy, to focus on making big plays on offense and creating turnovers on defense. They need to fight their way out of this little malaise before November 11. The date marks the start of a three-game gauntlet—Oregon, Cal, Notre Dame—that will define their season. By escaping against Arizona State, by sailing into the safe haven of their bye week with a perfect record, the Trojans now stand a very strong chance of being 8-0 when the Ducks come calling on the second Saturday in November. Two teams stand between them and that critical homestretch. One is Stanford, hands down the worst squad in the Pac-10. The other is 'SC's next opponent, Oregon State.

This game is not a gimme. The Trojans lost in Corvallis in 2000, the first of a string of Pac-10 defeats that cost woebegone Paul Hackett his job. And the Beavers gave 'SC a fright in 2004.

Playing in a fog so dense that radio announcers had to call the game from the sideline at Reser Stadium, Oregon State jumped to a 13–0 lead before fading and losing 28–20. It's unlikely that this year's Beavers squad will be the one that snaps 'SC's streak of 27 straight Pac-10 wins. Oregon State has already lost this season to Boise State, Cal, and Washington State. Its stud tailback, Yvenson Bernard, is on crutches. Fans have been booing head coach Mike Riley and quarterback Matt Moore. Take it from me. When you've been around the game as long as I have, you develop a sixth sense about these things. Frankly, this one has the makings of a blowout.

# CHAPTER 11

# Back in the Hunt

October 28, Jacksonville, Fla. — Rather than follow the Trojans to the Willamette Valley, let's head for someplace more cosmopolitan. It's hard to believe, as one admires the skyline of this glittering metropolis, that Jacksonville was originally named Cowford. (It sat at a narrows on the St. Johns River, where cattle often crossed.) Fearing such a bucolic handle might give folks the wrong impression of their urbane burg, the powers that be renamed the city for Andrew Jackson, the first military governor of the Florida Territory.

**BCS TOP 10**

*1. Ohio State*
*2. Michigan*
*3. USC*
*4. West Virginia*
*5. Auburn*
*6. Florida*
*7. Texas*
*8. Louisville*
*9. Notre Dame*
*10. California*

That would make Tom Coughlin the second military governor of this territory. It was Coughlin, a Parcells acolyte who coached the Jacksonville Jaguars from 1995 to 2002, who recently drove New York Giants superstar running back Tiki Barber into premature retirement. (Barber said he was worn down by Coughlin's excessively and gratuitously grueling regimen.) Before his fascist shtick lost its flavor on the bedpost overnight, Coughlin wrung excellent results from his charges, twice coaching the expansion Jags to the AFC Championship Game.

One of the best players in franchise history was ex-Trojan left tackle Tony Boselli, who suffered a high ankle sprain in 1997 that kept him out of four games. In late November, with Jacksonville in the thick of the divisional race, the team traveled to Cincinnati. As Boselli limped pathetically through warm-ups, backup tackle Jeff Novak watched him closely. "He could barely walk," Novak recalls. "I got ready to play."

In the locker room, Coughlin approached Boselli and asked him if he could go. Novak, sitting beside Boselli, listened in on their exchange.

"I don't know," he said. "I can't push off it. I can't explode off the ball. It hurts pretty bad."

"I need more than that," replied Coughlin, anxiously. "Give me a percentage. What percentage are you?"

"Maybe fifty," said Boselli, after a pause.

"Coughlin rubs his chin," says Novak. "He looks me right in the eye—I'm a hundred percent, I'm *raring* to play—and says to Tony, 'Do you think you can give me sixty?'"

"I can only give you fifty," said Boselli, not budging.

"Crap!" came the reply. "All right, Novak," said Coughlin, with a mixture of disgust and resignation. "You're starting."

Now that's coaching!

Coughlin was fired following three straight losing seasons—the Jaguars were able to restrain their celebrations, one trusts, until he'd left the building—and replaced by younger, hipper Jack Del Rio. Not yet 40, the ex–USC linebacker was more of a player's coach. In his first year, he put a tree stump in the dressing room, the better to remind the fellows of his hang-in-there motto: Keep Chopping. The axe and stump were removed after punter Chris Hanson inadvertently plunged the axe blade deep into his right leg, an injury that required emergency surgery, and caused him to miss the rest of the season. The answer to your question, perceptive reader, is: Yes! This *is* the same Chris Hanson who'd required hospitalization the previous year when he suffered first- and second-degree burns in a fondue mishap.

THOSE WHO WOULD dwell on Jacksonville's corrupt, racist past do her a disservice. For they paint an incomplete portrait of this up-and-coming city. After all, Jacksonville was also renowned for its violent crime and pungent aroma, a sulfurous, rotten egg funk bequeathed by paper mills and chemical plants. Also, Lynyrd Skynyrd hailed from here.

The city has undergone a municipal makeover, spurred in large part by football. A decade after the expansion Jaguars began play, the city hosted Super Bowl 39—Charlie Weis's final game in the NFL, the New England Patriots' 24–21 win over the Philadelphia Eagles. (So what if the city is woefully short of hotel rooms, Jags owner and shoe magnate Wayne Weaver had told his fellow owners: We'll dock a bunch of cruise ships on the St. Johns, and people can sleep there!)

Various companies have moved their headquarters to Jacksonville of late, including the CSX Corporation, whose headquarters at 500 Water Street stand directly across from the Jacksonville Landing, a riverfront dining and shopping complex that has helped revitalize the downtown area. On the night of October 29, 2005, a CSX video security camera recorded part of the fatal beating of Thomas Oliver Brown.

ONE WEEKEND EACH fall, in late October or early November, The Landing is transformed into a writhing, groping mosh pit of drunken humanity, a bacchanalia that is part and parcel of The World's Largest Outdoor Cocktail Party. That, until recently, was the moniker assigned to the annual Georgia-Florida game, an ancient rivalry so volatile that it must be contested at a neutral site. Since 1933, that venue has been Jacksonville, even though that city is a mere 73 miles from Gainesville, while Athens, Georgia lies 342 miles to the north.

Thomas Brown, 23, was a senior at Florida who'd spent the hours before his death watching Florida's 14–10 victory over the Bulldogs in a restaurant with some of his Beta Theta Pi brothers. After leaving the restaurant, he became separated from his friends, and was set upon by five attackers, at least one of whom was "looking for a fight," according to testimony given by another of the attackers. Brown was held down by three of his assailants while the other two beat him, according to authorities who reviewed the video. An autopsy revealed that he died of a massive brain hemorrhage, the result of a ruptured artery in his neck. It also pegged his blood alcohol level at .026—more than three times the legal limit, but well within the norm at The World's Largest Outdoor Cocktail Party.

Brown's death followed by one year the death of David Ferguson, a 19-year-old Florida sophomore who wandered from The Landing on the night of the game, apparently intoxicated, and whose body was found three days later. He'd fallen from the sixth story of a parking garage into a 40-foot crevice between the garage and an adjacent building.

Spurred to action by the attrition to its student body, Florida officials took a series of steps designed to dilute the school's party culture. Alcohol ads were pulled from the Gators' radio and TV sports programming; alcohol signage at Florida sporting events was dropped, as was "Drunk Bitch Friday," a weekly segment on the *Lex and Terry* show, a syndicated radio program that had been broadcast on WRUF in Gainesville.

Shortly after Brown's death, SEC commissioner Mike Slive got a letter from Jeremy Foley, the Florida athletic director, asking for his help downplaying the nickname of the Florida-Georgia game. Acknowledging that the networks "had nothing to do with creating this phrase," Foley noted in his letter, excerpted in *USA Today*, that both universities and the city of Jacksonville had "worked very hard to curb the alcohol abuse that is associated with this game and by labeling this game in this manner an inconsistent message is being sent to all fans, especially our respective students."

Slive responded by sending letters to TV executives, who were instructed to tell the talent: ixnay on the ocktail-Cay. After decades of meritorious service, the phrase "The World's Largest Outdoor Cocktail Party" was retired.

MOTORING SOUTH ON 1-95 on the eve of The Game Formerly Known as The World's Largest Outdoor Cocktail Party, or, The Saturnalia That Dare Not Speak Its Name, I am wondering if Slive's proscription will make any difference to the actual revelers on the ground. It had not curbed the rowdiness of the Bulldog fans at the Ruby Tuesday near the airport, where I'd just taken a solitary dinner. Sitting in my booth, drinking in the ambient sounds of the restaurant—adult men who interrupted their barking only long enough to shout "HOW 'BOUT THEM DAWGS?" (the question was rhetorical)—I was transported to late December 1986, to the Hall of Fame Bowl at Tampa Stadium. My younger brother Mark, as mentioned earlier, was a defensive tackle and long-snapper at Boston College. A good number of his seven siblings, including me, made it to Florida for the game, as did my parents. We were joined by my grandmother, the redoubtable Lennie Reeves, an imperious, white-haired octogenarian who had been to six of the world's seven continents but had never, until that night, attended a Division I football game. Her shoes, with their one-inch heels, were not ideal for the mile-long trek from the parking lot, which took us through a field muddied by recent rains. Steadying her was my grandfather, Norm—we called him Grand-WASP—with whom she'd won more than a few ballroom dancing contests on the transoceanic cruises they so loved.

She'd accompanied her husband to a few Ivy League tailgates. But this was different. There were no glee clubs or raccoon coats. There were only drunk, uncouth Southerners, all wearing red, many with dogs' paws painted on their faces. Had she missed some memo? At what point had it become acceptable in this country for perfect strangers, reeking of alcohol, to enter someone's personal space and bark like a dog at them?

We finally got to our seats and enjoyed a tense, close, well-played game featuring no long-snapping mishaps, thank Christ. The Eagles trailed until five seconds remained in the game, at which point Shawn Halloran, the quarterback who followed Doug Flutie at BC, threw a touchdown pass to Kelvin Martin, giving the underdogs a 27–24 victory. While her energy had flagged during the game, Lennie caught a second wind on the journey back to the car. Picking a line through the mud in her heels, she took pleasure in barking at subdued Bulldogs fans, to the mortification of Norm, who tried vainly to shush her.

On East Forsyth Street, I fall into a stream of pedestrians headed for The Landing. A Florida student jogs past in a pair of orange, high-topped Converses that I very much admire. A guy in front of me, sporting PacSun shorts and backward-facing ball-cap, is explaining to his compadre, "It's all for a game, bud. It's all for a game."

The last words written in my notebook that night are these: *Go, Jags, says the contrarian.*

That is when the heavens let go. The ensuing downpour drives us into alcoves and under awnings. It is a sustained torrent that soaks coiffures, plasters cotton shirts to nubile bosoms, and kills an untold number of buzzes. Some higher power, it seems, has gotten the memo from Slive. After huddling for 10 minutes in the lee of an office building on Bay Street, I walk back to my car, muttering the words I hear myself saying more and more these days: "I'm too old for this shit."

I have more success finding a party the next day. Walking through Parking Lot K en route to Alltel Stadium, I am drawn to an aging Dodge Ram van, in whose windshield blinks a neon-encased Georgia helmet, and on whose roof is moored a six-foot inflatable "Hairy Dawg"—kept firm and rigid by a gas-powered generator.

The van is owned by one John Short, a member of the Jacksonville Bulldog Club—"the largest Bulldog club in the country," he informs me. "A lot of people don't know that."

For a man whose Zuba pants are held up by strident red suspenders, a man wearing a foam Bulldogs helmet and a bone-shaped "Bite Me, Gators" bowtie, he is disconcertingly serious. That's because the subject is tailgating, which he takes quite seriously. He's owned this brown-and-cream sin bin since 1986. "It's only been used for tailgating. I always carry six cases of liquor, four tables—two we use for food—the flag and flag stands, all different kinds of signs, and Hairy, the blow-up dog."

He is 62 and sells insurance. Short isn't short: He goes six-foot-three or so. Nor is he particular about who is playing *inside* the stadium. "I have a similar setup for Jaguars games," he tells me. Compared to Sunday's revels, he allows, the tailgating at TGFKATWLOCP is on an altogether different plane. "I've been to the last twenty-seven of these," he tells me. "There's nothing quite like it."

His reputation extends far and wide in these circles. A series of spectacularly beautiful women drop by the tailgate to chat up Short and avail themselves of his Gator Killer Punch, an antifreeze-colored elixir comprised, he tells me, of "fourteen ingredients, including nine different liquors and liqueurs and a bottle of grain. It's so popular because you can't taste the alcohol."

Mike Guenther, sporting a Georgia-red pimp ensemble that Prince would find garish, leads a quartet of similarly outrageously dressed Bulldogs fans in a rendition of a song that asks (again, rhetorically):

> *Who's that comin' down the track?*
> *It's that MEAN MACHINE in red and black!*
> *Ain't nothin' finer in the land!*

A guy walks by in a T-shirt that says LEAK MY BALLS. For four straight years, Georgia fans have had a field day making vulgar puns on Leak's name. Their team has had far less success stopping him on the field. He'll finish his career 3-1 against the Dawgs.

Short would later invite me to the Bulldog Club barbecue after the game, to be held not far away, in a park on the banks of the St. Johns. "On the years we win," he says, "the club president gets thrown in the river," which, back in the old days, was "nothin' to look forward to, considering how polluted it was." The river's cleaner now, but it hasn't mattered lately. Florida has won all but two of the last 16 of these border wars.

"Nobody's been swimming in a while."

LAST WE SAW the Gators they were filing out of the visitors' locker room at Auburn, subdued, heartbroken, pissed. Leak, you will remember, seemed lost, shellshocked. Wide out Bubba Caldwell had sat in a classroom chair in a cramped interview area, looking straight ahead. Asked about his quarterback, Bubba trod a fine line between honesty and tact. "He played an all right game, but he made a couple of mistakes that cost us."

"Sometimes you don't make big plays."

"We expect a little more, but we don't blame him."

After the regular season, I asked Meyer how the team had responded to that loss. Had they quickly put it behind them?

The opposite, he told me. "They were devastated, crushed, unable to function for a while. And I was glad. I think a team that gets over a loss easily is not a very good team."

There was brave talk of how the guys still controlled their own destiny in the SEC, how they could still get to the conference championship game. But there was moping and self-pity. One of the team goals before the season was a national championship, and that had evanesced into the night air above Jordan-Hare. The winner of the Big Ten, whether it was Ohio State or Michigan, would have one of the spots in the national title game nailed down. Undefeated USC would probably grab the other, and even if they didn't, there were various undefeated Big East teams who'd be doing some serious bellyaching if a one-loss team got into the big game ahead of them. In the line of teams trying to get into a BCS bowl, the Gators would soon find themselves behind Rutgers, for crissakes. The Scarlet Knights were looking to go 7-0 with a win over Pittsburgh on October 21. Sure, there was a bunch of football still to be played. But some of the sizzle had gone out of the season for the Gators.

Like every smart, successful coach I've seen, from Mack Brown to Bob Stoops to Pete Carroll, Meyer had arrived in his new environs and embraced, rather than shunned or ignored, its traditions and icons.

Drawing on his bottomless reservoir of self-confidence, Meyer seemed genuinely unbothered by the legacy of Spurrier, the visor-abusing generalissimo who'd set the standard for football excellence in Gainesville. After winning the Heisman Trophy as the Gators quarterback in 1966, Spurrier kicked around for a decade in the NFL before finding his true calling as a coach. (One early indication of his genius: he got Duke into a bowl game.) At Florida he installed the so-called Fun and Gun, a pass-happy, cerebral scheme that required quarterbacks and receivers to get a presnap read of the defense, and gave him the opportunity, when they failed, to verbally accost them on television. It was prolific (the Gators scored 500 points four years running); it was successful (Spurrier won 120 games in his 12 seasons in Gainesville); and it was, blessedly, a departure from the Pleistocene-epoch offenses favored in that coldbed of innovation otherwise known as the SEC. In addition to winning the school's first national title, in 1996; in addition to coining the nickname by which Florida's Ben Hill Griffin Stadium is better known—The Swamp—Spurrier revolutionized football in the South.

In his two seasons on campus, Meyer has gone out of his way to acknowledge Spurrier's accomplishments, placing the Ol' Ball Coach on a level with such hallowed old ball coaches as Joe Paterno and Woody Hayes. "Damn right there's a shadow," Meyer exclaimed. "It's a big one, and it should be that way." Even as he accorded Spurrier his propers, Meyer made it clear that he was quite comfortable working in that shadow.

Which was a good thing, because in 2006, Spurrier became the sporting equivalent of the guy your wife used to date in college who ends up crashing in the guest room for three weeks. The man known as The Visor returned, MacArthur-like, for a pregame ceremony on September 2, commemorating the 10-year anniversary of the 1996 national title. (He'd coached his current team, the South Carolina Gamecocks, to victory the previous Thursday night.) He was back again, four Saturdays later (two days after the Gamecocks lost a heartbreaker to Auburn), to see his name added to the Ring of Honor, a form of secular deification the Gators bestow upon their best and brightest. And he would be back on November 11, when the Gators hosted South Carolina. Meyer could have been forgiven for asking the Fightin' Gator Marching Band to prepare a special song for Spurrier—the old Dan Hicks number, "How Can I Miss You When You Won't Go Away?"

With his team in the tank two days after its first loss of the season, Meyer found inspiration in one of Spurrier's greatest players. The 1996 club may have finished the season No. 1, but it was not undefeated. Laid low by a late-season loss to Florida State in Tallahassee, those Gators rallied to win the SEC and national titles. Before returning to campus for that 10-year anniversary to-do, former Gators quarterback Danny Wuerffel had been asked, during a teleconference, to summon his most lasting memory from that season.

He spoke of the gutshot feeling of losing to the Seminoles, and the empty, unmoored sensation that followed. He spoke of having "poured so much into something and there had been so much pressure and then it all sort of evaporated."

He recalled the criticism from without: "So much negativity coming from a lot of different directions."

And he remembered how the team overcame that negativity. Seniors like James Bates, Lawrence Wright, and Jeff Mitchell— Wuerffel was too modest to include himself—forbade the team from following the rest of Gator Nation out onto the ledge. Instead, they provided "a huge rallying of the morale to get ready for what was to come."

After a day or two of sulking and self-pity, the 1996 Gators focused on crushing Alabama in the SEC title game, which they did, behind a six-touchdown, Heisman-clinching performance by Wuerffel. To keep its national title hopes alive, Florida still needed to catch a series of breaks, and damned if it didn't. Texas upset No. 3 Nebraska in the Big 12 title game. Ohio State beat No. 2 Arizona State in the final seconds of the Rose Bowl. In the rematch, played in the Sugar Bowl, rather than in Tallahassee, the Gators annihilated Florida State 52–20, clinching the school's first national championship.

His team's ability "to reorient" after its sole defeat "was the key for us," Wuerffel had recalled in that teleconference. "It is one thing to be successful, but to have been knocked down and get back up is a pretty special thing."

The mental toughness he described was precisely what Florida needed now, in the wake of the Auburn loss. The guy who'd set up Wuerffel's preseason teleconference, Gators sports information director Steve McClain, recalled the quarterback's riffs on the resilience of the 1996 team. Struck by the parallels to the season in progress—a team with national title ambitions gets kicked in the teeth during the regular season—McClain dug up a recording of the teleconference. Meyer listened, and was blown away.

The following day, the players sat rapt while Wuerffel's message was played over the speakers in the meeting room. Pacing like a reverend, seldom raising his voice, Meyer wove the themes of Wuerffel's remarks into his address to the team:

"Some people win the Heisman Trophy, some don't."

"Some people get punched in the mouth and get back up. And some don't."

"Some people are champions, and some aren't."

Implicit in his words, a question: *What kind of people were they?*

At the end of the meeting, players were given wallet-sized, laminated cards bearing Wuerffel's "testimony." They would carry them for the rest of the season.

Those inspiring words do not translate, right away, into inspired football. When the game finally begins at Alltel Stadium, Florida and Georgia look almost as sloppy as some of the tailgaters still outside. Leak fumbles on the first play from scrimmage. While he does recover the ball and lead the team to a touchdown, eight plays and 63 yards later, the tone for an artless game has been set.

That touchdown, incidentally, was punched in on a 12-yard end-around to wide receiver Andre Caldwell, who strikes again five minutes into the second quarter. Going upstairs on the first play of a new possession, Leak lofts a 40-yard bomblet to Caldwell, who puts Florida up by two touchdowns.

A jacked-up Florida defense pads the lead on the first play of the second half, with velociraptor/defensive end Derrick Harvey stripping the ball from tailback Kregg Lumpkin, and defensive tackle Ray McDonald picking up the loose ball and rumbling nine yards for a touchdown on the reconstructed knees that will creak and groan with arthritis by the time he is 32. At which point he can reflect on the fact this his touchdown against Georgia in the 2006 Cocktail Party put the Gators up 21–nil. It looks like a blowout may be brewing, until Leak returns the favor, tossing a pick that the Bulldogs convert into their first touchdown of the day.

Any grumbling for Tebow is quieted with nine minutes left in the game by Tebow himself. The freshman fumbles on his own nine-yard line, a disastrous giveaway that allows the Bulldogs back in the game. After forcing a Florida punt with five minutes left on the clock, the Dawgs have the ball on their own 38. They lose six yards on three plays. How is this game even close? The Bulldogs punt, and actually hold the Gators on a third-and-short, defensive end Quentin Moses throwing Caldwell backward for a two-yard loss.

But a flag is down: inadvertent facemask by Moses. The five-yard penalty is enough to move the chains. Game, set, match.

At midfield I catch up with Caldwell, whose smile cuts the gathering darkness. Despite school policy forbidding interviews on the field after the game, he is happy to recount the first of his two touchdowns, a 12-yard run on a reverse. His teammates executed their blocks, leaving him just one man to beat. "One-on-one," continues Caldwell, who does not want for self-confidence, "I ain't gonna lose too many of those. Coming out here, putting up two TDs to help our team win," he adds, "I feel I got my swagger back." Funny, I hadn't noticed that his swagger had gone missing.

We wander down to the end zone, where the Fightin' Gator Marching Band strikes up the alma mater. Meyer has insisted that the players learn the words. Now I hear him tell the guys around him, "All right, gentlemen, get your helmets up." The stragglers hold their helmets over their heads.

Back in the stadium, Meyer is almost comically conflicted between irreconcilable compulsions: the desire to celebrate a gutsy if slovenly victory over a bitter rival, and the need to tick off all the areas in which the Gators want for improvement.

"We're not performing well," he says, donning the hair shirt. One the pillars of his offense—of everyone's offense, really—"is great ball security," yet each quarterback committed a gruesome, costly turnover. "And penalties are a problem."

Corrections will be made, he vows. Steps will be taken. When? Later that night, he says. And he means it. McClain tells me the assistants will be brainstorming at Meyer's house before the evening is out.

Aware, suddenly, that he does not sound like a winning coach—a coach whose team had just clinched the SEC East, assuring itself a spot in the conference championship—Meyer changes tack: "Enjoy the win, man," he says, as much to himself as anyone. "Especially against those guys, especially in this environment."

A faraway upset has given the Gators added incentive to start hitting on all cylinders. During the postgame press conference,

Meyer's obstinate refusal to acknowledge that piece of good fortune is agitating Tony Barnhart, the venerable *Atlanta Constitution-Journal* columnist, who practically sputters:

"The fact remains, your team is alive in the national title hunt!"

"Gotta get a first down," Meyer deadpans.

"That was the break you had to have in the BCS!" Barnhart persists.

"You saw the same offense I saw," rejoins the coach. "We gotta go beat Vanderbilt."


WHAT IS THIS break of which he speaks? I was getting around to that. Out on the field, earlier, as Bubba Caldwell announced the return of his prodigal swagger, he'd been forced to raise his voice to be heard over the roar of delight that greeted this announcement:

"Ladies and gentlemen, in a game just ending, USC 33, Oregon State . . . 35."

# CHAPTER 12

# . . . and Fall

November 4, Palo Alto, Calif. —Six days after the fact, the Trojans do not seem overly upset about their first Pac-10 loss in three years. Upsetting them, as they file into the gleaming, recently renovated Stanford Stadium, is the news that they will not be able to have their normal walk-through, on account of some workers' having just finished touching up the paint job on some of the yard lines. The paint hasn't dried yet, meaning there will be no Phat on Phat, the slow-motion touch football game contested by the linemen. There will be little of the roughhousing that helps break up the pregame tension. "What do you mean we can't go on the field?" demands one indignant defensive back. "Someone's going to pay for that."

This is Terrell Thomas, whose hair is pulled back in orderly rows, and whose feistiness stands out on a humdrum Friday after-

**BCS TOP 10**

1. *Ohio State*
2. *Michigan*
3. *West Virginia*
4. *Florida*
5. *Louisville*
6. *Auburn*
7. *Texas*
8. *USC*
9. *Notre Dame*
10. *California*

noon, and on a 'SC roster long on talent but not so long on veteran leadership.

This is the theory propounded by my colleague Dan Weber, the 'SC beat writer for the *Riverside Press-Enterprise*. With nothing coming easy for these Trojans—the loss at Oregon State, remember, was preceded by three single-digit wins—many diagnoses have been set forth for what the hell ails these guys; why a team with twice the talent of anyone on its schedule goes through long stretches of games unable to get out of its own way. Weber makes the point that, for whatever reason, this team does not boast a group of outspoken elder statesmen—a point to which we shall return.

THE TRIP NORTH was welcomed by Carroll, and not just because Stanford represents the lowest-hanging fruit on the schedule. (The hopeless Cardinal is winless in eight games, has been out-scored 276–83, and is coached by Pete's old friend, Walt Harris, who will be fired shortly after the season.) Bay Area trips are a homecoming for Carroll, who has been visiting The Farm, as this spectacular campus is known, since his days as a three-sport star at Redwood High in Marin County, a 45-minute drive (with light traffic) up the Peninsula and over the Golden Gate Bridge. Standing on the edge of the field, where we are careful not to step on any wet paint, Carroll points to a distant spot from which, he says, he once watched UCLA's Gary Beban carve up the home team. "I sat way up high, a million miles from the field," he recalls, "and after a while you didn't even care about the game. But it's really cool to be here."

I ask him how he got down here from Marin: 101 or 280?

"I'm a 280 guy," he says. "Come on. It's the most beautiful highway in the world." (Weis, I honestly believe, would take the 101. It's more direct.)

Hard-pressed to come up with anything charitable to say about the Stanford football team, Carroll seems almost relieved to be

**WRONG TEAM:** After stripping Billy Pittman in the first half, and denying Texas a certain score, Ohio State linebacker James Laurinaitis intercepted Colt McCoy's first pass of the second half, setting up a field goal that put the Buckeyes up by 10 in their 24–7 victory in the Brawl in the Royal. *(Bill Frakes/SI)*

**SCARY MOMENT:** On the final play of his college career, Trojans fullback Ryan Powdrell dislocates his left ankle against Nebraska. USC's lack of an experienced fullback probably cost the Trojans a shot at the national title. *(John W. McDonough/SI)*

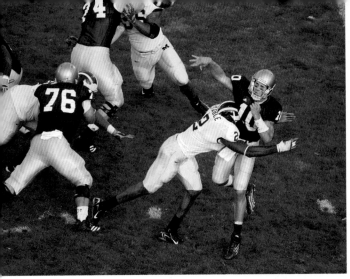

LI'L HELP? Quinn was sacked three times and pressured—flushed, clobbered, or otherwise harassed—on at least a dozen other occasions against Michigan. Darius Walker's helpful assessment: "We've gotta understand who we're blocking." (Bill Frakes/SI)

IT'S A BIRD, IT'S A PLANE, IT'S Auburn linebacker Tray Blackmon, who would later recover Chris Leak's critical and controversial fourth-quarter fumble—a huge play in Florida's sole loss of the season. (Bill Frakes/ SI)

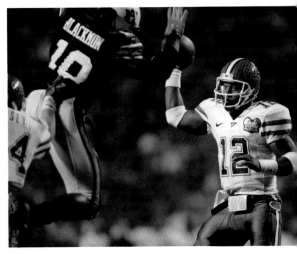

OVERRATED: The No. 2–ranked Irish were out of this one early. Notre Dame trailed Michigan 34–7 in the first half, and didn't get a first down until four minutes into the second quarter, which explains the long faces in the student section. (David E. Klutho/SI)

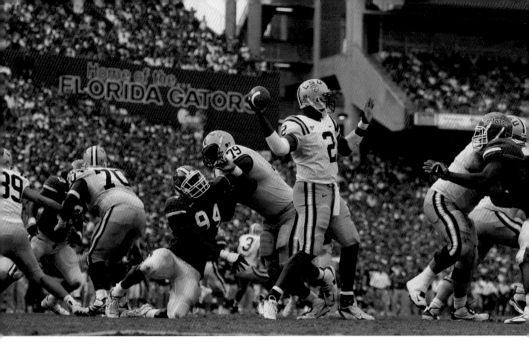

**LONG DAY IN THE SWAMP:** The future No. 1 pick in the NFL draft was made to look ordinary by an ornery Florida defense. On a day dominated by the heroics of Tim Tebow, LSU's JaMarcus Russell threw three picks, and had a momentum-killing fumble on the goal line in LSU's 23–10 loss at Florida. *(Bob Rosato/SI)*

**THE BACCHANAL THAT DARE NOT SPEAK ITS NAME:** Tailgaters outside Alltel Stadium before the Georgia-Florida game don't seem overly concerned with the SEC's request that people cease and desist from referring to this game as the World's Largest Outdoor Cocktail Party. In fact, they'd drink to that. *(Bill Frakes/SI)*

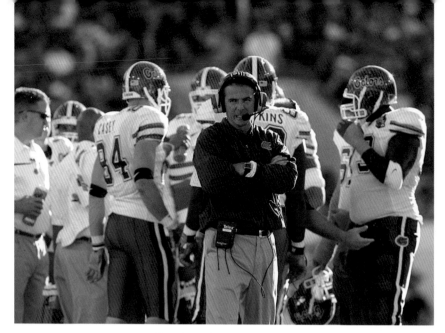

**BEWARE THE GLARE:** Meyer fixes his subjects with a gaze so direct, so penetrating, that it is capable of introducing doubt in the mind of an umpire; melting the heart of a recruit's mother; of stirring obedience and urgency in his players. *(Bob Rosato/SI)*

**NOR THE BATTLE TO THE STRONG:** After distributing stones to his teammates on the eve of the game—to bring to mind David and Goliath—Oregon State's Sammie Strougher took good care of the rock. His 70-yard punt return for a TD gave the Beavers a 30–10 lead early in the third quarter. *(Peter Read Miller/SI)*

**ON THE BRIGHT SIDE:** Trojans wideout Steve Smith, often overshadowed by Jarrett, was incandescent in the Oregon State loss. His line: 11 catches, 258 yards, 2 touchdowns. *(Peter Read Miller/SI)*

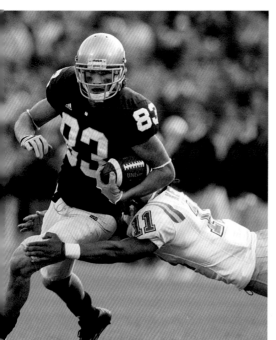

**IS THAT POLO YOU'RE WEARING?** After an uncharacteristically quiet day, Jeff Samardzija showed up when it mattered against UCLA. Here he breaks the tackle of safety Dennis Keyes to score Notre Dame's last-minute, game-winning touchdown. *(Simon Bruty/SI)*

**ALLELUIA!:** In a battle of the Big East unbeatens, Rutgers rallied for a last-second, 28–25 victory over Louisville. Freshman wideout Kenny Britt, whose 67-yard catch helped the Knights come back from a nine-point halftime deficit, celebrates the school's biggest win in 137 years with a few of his friends. *(David Bergman/CORBIS)*

MOMENT OF SILENCE: The day after Bo Schembechler's death, 105,708 fans at Ohio Stadium stood in silent tribute to him, described over the p.a. by the Buckeyes' announcer as "a legend and an icon . . . an alumnus and a friend." *(Bob Rosato/SI)*

HAND HIM THE HEISMAN: Against the nation's tenth-ranked defense, Smith completed 21 of 26 passes for 241 yards and three touchdowns—in the first two quarters. The Buckeyes senior had the trophy sewn up by halftime. *(Bob Rosato/SI)*

IS THIS FAIR? The 6'5" Jarrett elevates over 5'11" Mike Richardson for the second of his three touchdowns against Notre Dame. Richardson, a cornerback, was similarly helpless to prevent Jarrett's soaring, one-handed snag later in the game. *(Robert Beck/SI)*

**FINAL VISIT:** Dwayne Jarrett defeats Leon Hall's one-on-one coverage to score a 62-yard touchdown, his second in two Trojans possessions. It was the 41st and final touchdown in his three-year career at USC. *(Robert Beck/SI)*

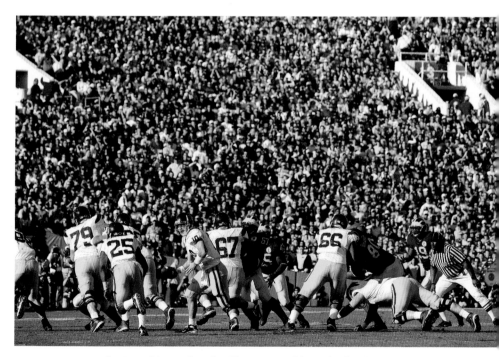

**WHY BOTHER?** John David Booty hands off to C. J. Gable in the first half of the Rose Bowl, in which USC rushed for all of 48 yards. Early in the second half, the Trojans abandoned the run, putting the game squarely on Booty's shoulders. *(Robert Beck/SI)*

**WATCH YOUR BACK:** After beating tackle Alex Boone like a rented mule, Jarvis Moss sacks and strips Troy Smith late in the second half, setting up the Gators' fourth TD. *(Robert Beck/SI)*

**GRAND FINALE:** Chris Leak was masterful on his last night in a Florida uniform. Distributing the ball to six different receivers, the title-game MVP completed 25 of his 36 passes for a touchdown and no interceptions. *(John Biever/SI)*

**I'M BUYING:** Zabransky's faked pass on the Fiesta Bowl–winning Statue of Liberty play had Sooners defensive end C. J. Ah You (99) leaning in the wrong direction. After "futzing around" for a long moment, tailback Ian Johnson took Z's surreptitious handoff and won the game. *(Collegiate Images/BCS)*

able to sing the praises of its new home, this shimmering state-of-the-art seven-week-old venue, erected on the site of the old, 85,000-seat Stanford Stadium. Carroll salutes the "drive and tremendous vision" of the architects, administrators, and laborers who pulled it off. "Very, very impressive," he marvels, looking around, and he is right. Before the Cardinal faithful had exited the doomed old bowl after Stanford's loss to Notre Dame last November, bulldozers had begun gouging out its sod. The new, 50,000-seat version, with its wider, cushier seats, improved sightlines, and modernized and more numerous lavatories opened on September 16. The ribbon cutting was followed by the sight of Navy slicing its way through the home team in a 37–9 victory, which discouraging result came on the heels of Stanford's even more discouraging one-point loss to San Jose State.

Among the stadium's new amenities are a pair of Brobdingnagian, high-resolution scoreboards, one of which is replaying over and over, at a greatly hopped-up speed, a recording of the stadium's death and rebirth, its razing and reconstruction: the exhausting labors of 10 months compressed into a minute.

I find myself mesmerized by the time-lapse video: night following day following night; bleachers imploding; Matchbox bulldozers frantically maneuvering; and a new, improved arena springing to life. It calls to mind the cheap devices used by movie directors to denote the passage of time: sped-up clocks; pages torn off a calendar. It calls to mind—with Carroll nearby—the temporal nature of dynasties. I think of George C. Scott's voiceover at the end of *Patton*, when he speaks of the triumphant Roman general who returns to the city at the head of a victory parade. All the while a slave whispers in the ear of the conquering hero, "Sic transit gloria mundi." *Thus passes the glory of the world.*

Are we present at the decline of the Trojan empire?

The ~~emperor~~ head coach is weary of such suggestions; weary of discussing the Oregon State loss. It wasn't a lack of veteran leadership; wasn't lethargy coming out of a bye week; wasn't John David Booty's low release point. It was the inspired, error-free play of some pretty damned good players in Corvallis and a series of self-inflicted 'SC wounds.

"We dropped the ball on the ground three times," he says. "That's the reality of it."

We're not having this discussion, in other words, if his guys take care of the damn rock.

SAMMIE STROUGHTER TOOK care of the rock. Six days earlier, in Oregon State's Reser Stadium, he'd hung on to it while making eight catches for 127 yards, and throughout the 70-yard punt return for a touchdown, which gave the Beavers a 30–10 lead midway through the third quarter.

And Sammie Stroughter took care of the rocks. On the eve of the game, on the heels of a chapel service in which the story of David and Goliath was invoked, Stroughter had produced a plastic grocery bag of rocks. Whereas David took five smooth stones from a nearby stream, according to the Book of Samuel, Stroughter got his from H. D. Weddell, a team chaplain. No matter. In addition to providing an irresistible lead to columnists, those rocks served as a reminder to his teammates that the race is not always to the swift, nor the battle to the strong.

This was not supposed to be a close game. This was supposed to be Exhibit 37 in the case of Pissed-Off Beavers Fans vs. Oregon State Head Coach Mike Riley, who'd presided over a disheartening 2-3 start, including home losses to Boise State (a defeat that wouldn't look so bad by the season's end) and Washington State. During the latter loss, senior quarterback Matt Moore—a transfer from UCLA—was booed by his fellow students, some of whom prepared signs advocating for redshirt freshman Sean Canfield.

Riley empathized. A coach's son and former star quarterback at Corvallis High, he played for Bear Bryant at Alabama in the early 1970s. Now in the fourth season of his second tour of duty as the

Beavers head coach, he's won 22 games against 19 defeats. Since the beginning of the 2005 season, however, he is 7-9, and the buzz around town is that this favorite son is in his final season.

Riley stuck with Moore, who came out slinging on OSU's first possession. He hit Stroughter for 22 yards, backup tailback Clinton Polk for eight, wide out Anthony Wheat-Brown for 18, Stroughter for 13 more. On third-and-goal from 'SC's one-yard line, he rolled right on a run-pass option, tucked the ball, and hook-slid across the plane, taking a forearm to the face for his efforts. The Beavers did not look remotely intimidated.

But their lead appeared to be short-lived as Booty coolly carved up Oregon State's dee, driving to the nine-yard line before being seized with the first of the day's brain cramps. Forcing the ball to Jarrett on first-and-goal, he was picked off by Bryan Payton, who returned the interception to the far 48-yard line before Booty knocked him out of bounds.

With his team trailing 10–7 early in the second quarter, Booty muffed the exchange with center Ryan Kalil, a giveaway quickly converted into an Alexis Serna field goal. Then it was Chauncey's turn to give until it hurt.

On the second play of 'SC's ensuing possession, Chauncey Washington put the ball on the ground. The fumble was recovered by safety Alan Darlin, who later informed reporters that he played the game with one of Stroughter's stones tucked into his girdle pads. Four plays later, Serna booted his third field goal of the half, his second in 63 seconds. This one, a bomb from 53 yards out, gave the Beavers a 16–7 lead.

Despite playing dumber than Stroughter's bag of rocks, 'SC only trailed 16–10 at the half. They'd climbed out of deeper holes. Carroll and his staff were the coaches known for their canny adjustments at intermission. Yet there was Moore on the Beavers' first possession of the third quarter, doing another Benihana number on the Trojans secondary, dropping a gorgeous throw into the outstretched arms of a diving (and well-covered) Stroughter for a 36-yard chunk, then sealing the deal with a perfectly placed pass to the back of the end zone, where only Joe Newton, his tight end, could reach it.

The Trojans knew all about Stroughter: The junior flyboy had already taken two punts to the house this season, one against Eastern Washington, another against Boise State. No Trojan was more familiar with his singular burst than Dallas Sartz, who graduated from Granite Bay (California) High two years ahead of Stroughter. The two were members of the Grizzlies 4 x 100-meter relay team in 2002, Sartz's senior year. They'd chatted by phone a few weeks earlier. Now with just eight minutes to play in the third quarter, Stroughter backpedaled under a booming punt from Greg Woidneck. Barreling down on him was Sartz, hoping to knock his friend's block off.

Using the linebacker's speed against him, Stroughter cut deftly to the inside, feeling the breeze as his former teammate flew past, then engaging his afterburners. Stroughter was in full flight at the 50 when he cut back to the outside, eluding the diving Brian Cushing, the last Trojan to have a decent shot at him. So clean was the return that Stroughter actually throttled down inside the fifteen-yard line as the crowd of 44-plus thousand at Reser Stadium went berserk.

One of the reasons Oregon State had been a 12-point dog in its own stadium was that its stud tailback, Yvenson Bernard, spent the week on crutches with a badly sprained ankle. His replacement was Clinton Polk, an unproven juco transfer who came into the game with all of 29 touches on his résumé. He would now be called upon to make his first career start against the No. 3 team in the country. So calm and copacetic was Polk about this prospect that he could be seen throwing up on the sideline after the first series. But he settled down and played his ass off, rushing for a hundred yards on 22 carries; catching a handful of passes. He picked up blitzes. He recovered an onside kick. Most important: *He held on to the rock.*

Which was more than you could say for his 'SC counterpart. On the first play from scrimmage following Stroughter's punt return, Washington coughed it up again, his second fumble in six touches. The Beavers recovered; Serna booted his fourth and final field goal. With 4:51 left in the third quarter, the most dominant team of the decade trailed unranked Oregon State 33–10.

IT WAS MY privilege, in the spring of 2006, to attend my first Masters at Augusta, Georgia. As a utility guy in *SI*'s golf coverage, I was assigned a feature on David Duval, the Oakley-armored enigma who in the space of five years had gone from the world's No. 1 player to a guy struggling to make the cut. But he'd been showing flashes. I watched him on the range, I followed him through three practice rounds, and the guy was striping the ball. As soon as it mattered on Thursday morning, he had no clue, duck-hooking his opening drive off a loblolly pine and setting the tone for a first-round 84 that served as a primer on Augusta's varied plant life.

The next morning Duval hooked his drive into some azaleas on No. 2, en route to a quintuple-bogey 10. That's right. A Laurel and Hardy. Instead of picking up his ball and going home—at that point he stood a dispiriting 19 over through 20 holes—Duval did something completely unexpected: He turned back the clock and started playing like the Duval of old, hitting fairways, dive-bombing pins, and burying putts. He birdied numbers 3, 7, 12, 14, 15, and 17. On a day no one had a higher front-nine score than Duval's 43, no one bettered his back-nine 32.

I thought of that bipolar round while watching a replay of USC's furious rally against the Beavers. As it had for Duval, arriving at rock bottom seemed to exercise some liberating effect on Booty; freed him to cross some unseen transom. His first three passes following Serna's final field goal went for 33 yards, 25 yards, and 17 yards. While that drive died on the 10-yard line—Booty threw incomplete on fourth down—it served notice that 'SC still had life.

First to crack under the weight of the Trojans' inevitable surge was Kyle Loomis, a true freshman punter who muffed a fine snap, handing Booty a 16-yard field to work with. Four plays later, he'd narrowed the gap to 16 with a four-yard touchdown strike to his tight end, Fred Davis.

Three minutes later Booty looked off the safety, pump-faked to his right, then hit a streaking Steve Smith in a seam in the Beavers' zone coverage. Following that 37-yard touchdown, there was Washington—squeezing the ball as if he were a Secret Service agent and it contained the nuclear codes—bulling in for the two-point conversion. With more than 12 minutes to play, the Trojans had closed to within eight points.

But the Trojans could not score on their next two series. When Booty completed a 32-yarder to Jarrett on the first play of 'SC's final possession, Riley instructed his offensive coordinator to prepare a package for overtime. But the Beavers stiffened. With just under two minutes to play, 'SC was looking at a third-and-11 at midfield. So it was a *bad* time for Kalil, the center, to false-start. But on third-and-16, Booty calmly picked up 14 with a pass to Smith, to whom he returned on the following play. On a career afternoon on which he caught 11 passes for 258 yards, the senior had no finer moment than this balletic, contorted sideline grab that moved the chains on the ensuing fourth-and-two. On second-and-goal from the two, Booty went back to Smith, firing a short TD pass that closed the margin to 33–31 with seven seconds remaining. The comeback was all but complete.

It would never be completed. The play selected for the two-point conversion was a pass to Jarrett—lining up left, he ran a quick square-out and never really got open—which, in my view, showed a poverty of imagination. It also showed how far Oregon State had come in two years, since the Beavers gagged up that lead against LSU. This was a team that would win eight of its last nine games; a well-coached unit with quality, character players like Jeff Van Orsow, a deceptively quick defensive end who bullrushed All-American left tackle Sam Baker, then thrust his right arm to the sky, where it stayed after he slapped Booty's final pass of the day to the ground.

As at Notre Dame Stadium the previous October, a tsunami of students swept over the field. As at Notre Dame, they were shooed off the turf, the game clock not having expired. Unlike at Notre Dame, the Trojans had used up all the magic at their disposal. Once Polk recovered the onside kick, the field was mobbed again, and stayed mobbed. Oregon State hadn't knocked off a team with so lofty a ranking since 1967, when O.J. Simpson and the No. 1 Trojans went down 3–0 on this same field. The delirious Beavers fans were proxies for the fans of all the one-loss teams—Auburn, Florida, Texas—whose chance to reach the BCS title game had just been resurrected.

Standing in a stadium on the other side of the continent, where 85,000 SEC fans roared their delight at the news of USC's misfortune, it seemed the whole world took pleasure in the Trojans' pain. Call it SChadenfreude.

AND WHO COULD blame them? Such is my thinking on the evening of November 3. Following the Trojans' truncated Stanford walk-through, I motor north to San Francisco, in time for the 'SC pep rally at Union Square. The site is well chosen for the visitors from SoCal: it will take place at the base of a 95-foot-high fluted column commemorating a long-ago ass kicking. On May 1, 1898, a plaque informs us, the forces of Admiral Dewey's forces "attacked and destroyed the Spanish fleet of ten warships" in Manila Bay, "and held the city in subjugation until the arrival of troops from America." This monument to martial prowess is slightly anomalous in the heart of this famously peace-loving city. As are the tanned, cardinal-and-gold-clad, Republican-leaning invaders now taking over the Square, drawing curious, and occasionally hostile glances from San Franciscans trying to get to the nearby BART station.

Around seven-fifteen, the cardinal trickle of musicians down Powell, across Post, and into the Square becomes a steady flow, then a torrent. Band members arrive en masse. Night has fallen, but, like Jake and Elwood Blues, they're wearing sunglasses. Ambient light from surrounding stores—Macy's, Saks, Niketown—is briefly eclipsed for me by the Goliathan figure of David Baker, the commissioner of the Arena Football League, who appears on the sidewalk, pulls me into the Westin St. Francis, and buys me a drink. The commish is also the father of 'SC's most talented offensive lineman, left tackle Sam Baker, who goes 6'5", 305, but still looks up to his old man. The former UC-Irvine basketball center has four inches and 50 pounds on his youngest son. Whereas Sam is the strong, silent type, parting with answers as if he were donating organs, Baker pere is 'SC's MVP (Most Voluble Parent).

I first met the commish while reporting an AFL feature in the mid-1990s. He shared the story of one revenue-starved team that had allowed a local "spa merchant" to set up a hot tub in the arena. Contest winners were invited to watch the game while soaking with several bikini-clad lovelies. One night, during a rare, *televised* AFL contest—this was before ESPN bought a stake in the league— an errant pass found its way into the hot tub, upon whose occupants the camera lingered. "Boy," fretted Baker, who at the time was cultivating a partnership with NFL commissioner Paul Tagliabue, "I hope Tags is watching the hockey game."

I'm interested in his take on the loss in Corvallis. During that three-week span of offensive futility, he thinks guys "were playing so tight, were so afraid to make a mistake," that they were less than the sum of their parts. Finding themselves in a three-touchdown hole, he says, somehow relaxed them. "It was kind of like they broke the chains."

Is USC's reign dead? "I don't know," he admits. "I do know that after last Saturday, those guys know what it means not to quit."

That their season was so recently blemished has not exactly chastened the rowdy 'SC fans now thronging Union Square, where the Song Girls are high-kicking like Rockettes, the Spirit of Troy is brassily announcing the school's arrival, and the microphone has been hijacked by a 60-something "yell leader"—a gentleman in suspenders who is now threatening to lead the crowd in something called "the Southern California spellout!"

"This becomes territorial," he declaims, and I think of my dog, ever intent on marking his territory. "This becomes about WHO WE ARE, and that they KNOW WE ARE HERE." Dude, I am thinking, "they" are already aware of your presence. By your strident cardinal-and-gold garb, by your eagerness to ride our cable cars, by your short pants in November, we shall know ye.

"And so I say to you, how do we do that? You know how we do that." Then why ask, sir? "We do it with a Southern California Spellout! That's our signature, that tells people who we are. It lets them know what we believe in, what we stand for. And we stand for—not for Stanford!"—he pauses, giving the crowd a couple beats to appreciate his nifty wordplay—"we stand for GREAT-NESS and we stand for THE AMERICAN WAY."

Sooooo, if I didn't go to, or don't cheer for 'SC, I am diverging from the American Way? Good to know.

The Spellout goes poorly. When the crowd responds anemically, Spellout Guy cuts it short. "No, no, no, no. We're going to start again, at the risk of people thinking we stunk."

Just when you think the Spellout is over, Spellout Guy notes that with the Cal Bears hosting UCLA tomorrow, there are a fair number of Bruins "oozing around. . . . State education being what it is, we have to tell 'em what we just spelled!"

Now *there's* a plan. Call attention to the academic gulf between your alma mater and UCLA and Cal. After all, USC professor George Olah did win a Nobel Prize for chemistry in 1994. Does UCLA have any Nobel laureates? They have three, you say? And that's 17 shy of Cal-Berkeley's 20? Hmmm. Maybe Spellout Guy should stick to his strengths. He spells very well.

. . . .

MY MILD ANNOYANCE with the Trojans is a quibble, a mere baga-telle beside the animosity percolating in Adam Cohen this evening. It wasn't so much that the Stanford football team is trailing by five touchdowns with six minutes to play (backup quarterback Mark Sanchez is about to increase the visitors' lead to 42–0). Not only has Stanford not won a game this year, they've only led in a single game—that one-point loss to San Jose State. It's not so much the Trojan players Cohen despises as it is the shades wearing, direction ignoring, song repeating members of the school's marching band. A senior trombonist, Cohen is also the president of the Leland Stanford Junior University Marching Band. When he talks about the Spirit of Troy, Cohen is unable to disguise his contempt.

"Cal is the rival," he is telling me as Sanchez throws a 22-yard rope to wide-out-of-the-future Travon Patterson. "But USC is the enemy."

Asked if there is friction between the bands, he does not mince words: "We hate the USC band. They go where they're not supposed to go, after they've been asked not to go there. They play when they're not supposed to be playing. They play over us, they play when there are guys injured on the field."

Our conversation is interrupted by a frantic, necktied drum major, distinguishable by his cardinal-tinted Mohawk haircut and the apparatus strapped to his back—is it? I believe it *is* a jet pack, or a convincing facsimile—who shouts, "MINOR CHORD!" The band responds as one, everyone blasting on his or her instrument a minor chord.

What's up with that, I ask, and Cohen enlightens me. The Spirit of Troy has a relatively small repertoire of songs it prefers to play over and over. And over and over. The song that drives the Stanford Band around the bend is "Escalation"—"The one that sounds like a military death march," says Cohen. Since the Spirit of Troy plays it in a major chord, the Stanford Band takes pleasure in stepping on "Escalation" by playing a minor chord, "or any note that sounds terrible," during its performance.

A few rows closer to the field, the Stanford musicians have a counting prop, with which they keep track of the number of times the Spirit of Troy plays "Escalation." "It was 37 at halftime. It's gotta be around 70 now," says Cohen, rolling his eyes. "I can't imagine doing *anything* 70 times. But then, we have a complete opposite philosophy. We try to be different and entertaining, like a rock band."

They recently behaved like a rock band. Last July, a dozen or so LSJUMBers trashed the "Band Shak," the temporary trailer that had been their headquarters. There had been a misunderstanding: The band was moving into its posh *new* quarters, and thought the Shak was going to be destroyed anyway. They were just getting a jump on the demolition.

Instead, they stood accused of vandalism, and found themselves placed on something called "indefinite provisional status" by vice provost of student affairs Greg Boardman, who clearly has a copy of Dean Wormer's playbook. It was Wormer, of course, who put the Deltas on "double-secret probation" in *Animal House*. Just as he asked, "Who dropped a whole truckload of Fizzies into the swim meet? Who delivered the medical school cadavers to the alumni dinner?" – it is not difficult to envision Vice Provost Boardman demanding to know:

- Who formed two lines outside the courthouse during the O.J. Simpson trial, forcing attorneys returning from their lunch break to walk a gauntlet of musicians covering The Tubes' "White Punks on Dope" and The Zombies' "She's Not There"?
- Who drove a White Bronco around the track at halftime of that year's USC game?
- Who was banned from the Oregon campus after its halftime performance mocking the plight of the endangered spotted owl? ("Mr. Spotted Owl!" declaimed a student narrator. "Your environment has been destroyed, your home is now a roll of Brawny, and your family has flown

the coop. What are you going to do? Me, I'm going to Disneyland.")

- Who offended Mormons by lampooning polygamy during halftime of the BYU game, when the band's assistant manager pretended to "marry" five members of the dance team, while the band announcer celebrated marriage as a sacred bond "between a man and a woman . . . and a woman . . . and a woman . . . and a woman."

- Whose drum major provoked outrage at Notre Dame by dressing as a nun, with full wimple and habit, then proceeding to direct the band with a crucifix? (He was tackled from behind by an outraged woman—possibly Opus Dei—who promised, "You're going to Hell for this!")

- And whose announcer offended Jewish spectators at a game against San Jose State by using the expression, "No chuppah, no schtuppa"?

And that list doesn't even include the LSJUMB's finest moment: its premature foray onto the gridiron with four seconds remaining in the 1982 Big Game, as the Bears lateraled their way down the field, first through the Cardinal kickoff team, then through members of the Stanford band, and finally, into sports history.

My feeling is, if the Stanford band breaks some glass and bruises some feelings once in a while—okay, every time they set foot on the field—so what? They're college students. That's part of their job. Tonight's halftime show is a less interesting spectacle—indeed, college football is a less interesting sport—with the Stanford band on Vice Provost Boardman's version of double-secret probation. I look forward to the day when the VP sees fit to lift the band's "provisional status." Until that time, the band might consider hosting what Douglas C. Niedermeyer described, with revulsion, as "a Roman Toga pary." Maybe they could get the VP's wife to attend.

. . . .

As IT HAS for so many teams in recent years, a trip to The Farm proves just the tonic for what ails 'SC. The game is decided early in the second quarter, when the Trojans put up two touchdowns *in the span of five seconds.* Unsettled, perhaps, by giving up a 21-yard touchdown pass to Jarrett with 13:19 left in the half, Stanford cornerback Wopamo Osaisai fumbles the ensuing kickoff—the ball stripped out by linebacker Keith Rivers. The Trojans recover, and Booty hits Smith for a seven-yard TD on the next play, making the score 21–0—a reasonably safe lead over a squad that has scored four touchdowns in its last six games. This one is over early.

It was the converse of the fiasco in Corvallis. USC takes care of the ball on offense and takes it away on defense—which Carroll will pinpoint as the most important development of the night. The Trojans' fourth touchdown is a 71-yard scoop-and-score by Terrell Thomas, the cornerback who'd been put out by the disruption of Friday's walk-through. The redshirt junior from Rancho Cucamonga also has a sack and a pick. By turning in the finest game of his career, Thomas covers a check he'd written with his mouth the night before.

To the surprise of everyone, he'd stood during the defensive meeting and given a speech as stirring as it was unexpected. He talked about the standards that had been set by previous Trojan defenses (not, presumably, the one Vince Young saw), and how he and his teammates needed to meet them more consistently. "We can't just show up in the third quarter when our backs are against the wall," he admonished. "We gotta show up from the get-go."

Thomas's decision to stand and be heard came a few hours after Weber, the beat writer (and an ex–football coach at Kentucky's Covington Catholic High), had put forth his theory on why the 2006 Trojans were less than the sum of their parts.

Casting his gaze back to the summer of 2002, when he was assigned the Trojans beat, Weber recalled stopping by the campus one July afternoon. What he saw was the team working out in sweltering heat "under the clear direction and leadership of Carson Palmer and Troy Polamalu"—great players who took the team on their shoulders and set a standard for leadership that would later be matched by an honor roll of Trojans Weber quickly ticked off: There was Matt Grootegoed, Lofa Tatupu, Matt Leinart, Reggie Bush ("An unbelievable practice player for someone so talented," Weber marvels). There was Mike Williams ("Really"), Shaun Cody, Mike Patterson ("Just his presence"), Kenechi Udeze, Brandon Hancock, David Kirtman, Matt Cassel, Will Poole, Jacob Rogers, Keary Colbert ("Maybe the best leader of them all and the one Pete always singled out as the most likely football coach in the bunch"). You had Justin Fargas ("He practiced *so* hard"), Ryan Killeen, Deuce Lutui ("His senior season"), and Fred Matua.

Weber's point in calling that formidable roll: There was so much leadership ahead of the 2006 Trojans "there wasn't much chance for it to develop in this most recent group." He excepted Kalil, "who exerted his mostly to the close circle of offensive linemen."

Those issues, it turns out, are being addressed. That very night, Terrell Thomas got permission from Nick Holt, the defensive coordinator, to address the defense. Having stood, Thomas then went out and delivered.

Booty represents another possible breakthrough. Against the Cardinal he is clean and efficient, like a seasoned hit man. He completes 12 of 23 passes for 203 yards. He throws for three touchdowns and no picks. His numbers could have been double those, but Carroll has no desire to hang 70 points on an old friend. I ask Booty in the postgame locker room if he made some kind of quantum leap during his sensational second half against the Beavers, if he went to some place, some level, he'd never before reached. It was in defeat, ironically, that he played at last like a worthy heir to Leinart and Palmer.

"We lost, and it was terrible," he tells me. "But coming out of that loss we saw a lot of things that built character. It was a reminder that you gotta work hard, 'cause any week, you can get beat. Just 'cause you're 'SC doesn't mean you're gonna win games."

That's the thing with Booty: Ask the guy about himself, he comes back at you with a bunch of collective pronouns. Okay, JD, let's try this again: How did *your* play during the comeback affect *you*? Is *your* confidence level at an all-time high? Please answer in the first person, making frequent use of the pronoun "*I*."

While he proves incapable of that latter request, he does let on that some good came of the loss: "Obviously you hate to be in that situation, 'cause you're down, and you end up losing. But you know, showing everybody what our offense—and what I'm capable of doing . . . "—Note breakthrough use of "*I*"—"that was big. And even though we're down, we make a heck of a comeback. That's remarkable in itself."

Cushing the elephant-backer is still getting dressed 10 feet away. The team has always had nights like this, performances like this, in it. "But something had been holding us back, like a barrier or something," he muses. "We broke through it last week—too late, but we broke through. Now we just have to bring that attitude every game."

This is the metaphor I keep hearing: the Trojans have cast off their chains, have cut the surly bonds of mediocrity, and are now free, as their head coach says, "to be who we are." This emancipation has taken place just in time for the three-game homestretch—Oregon, Cal, Notre Dame—that will determine the success or failure of the season. Walking toward the team bus with Holt, I ask him how close this team is to playing like the sum of its parts, or better. To him the answer is obvious. "We're *this* close," he answers. "We're right there. It's right around the corner."

# CHAPTER 13

# Grand Theft

**BCS TOP 10**

1. *Ohio State*
2. *USC*
3. *Michigan*
4. *Auburn*
5. *West Virginia*
6. *Florida*
7. *Louisville*
8. *Notre Dame*
9. *Texas*
10. *California*

October 21, South Bend, Ind. —They are sharper than your average stadium usher, these yellow-jacketed Notre Dame Stadium employees. This guy may be a moonlighting cop. He's been onto me since I got here.

I'm on the sideline an hour or so before kickoff against the UCLA Bruins. I'm watching Weis walk the stretch line, shaking players' hands, imparting encouragement and, for all I know, sarcasm. His famous heft calls to mind that of a pope, or one of the Bourbon kings. In an article earlier this season, I chronicled his distinctive flatfooted stride, a kind of semi-waddle. Then I found out why he walks that way. In his book *No Excuses*, Weis writes about how he nearly died from a botched gastric bypass operation in 2002, and about the subsequent nerve damage he incurred, which has cost him some of the feeling in both feet.

Dangling on a string attached to one of my belt loops is a photo pass that gives me permission to be here, rather than up in the press box, where I belong. Domer security doesn't need to know that I'd borrowed the pass from an *SI* photographer who somehow ended up with an extra.

Yet Domer security *does* know. This guy's been eyeballing me for a while. So when he approaches, five or so minutes before kickoff, I realize the jig is up. Politely but firmly, he notes my lack of a camera or any photo equipment whatsoever. He starts explaining that it gets awfully crowded on the sideline, but I don't let him finish.

I was just about to head up to the press box, I assure him. As he escorts me to the steps, I inform him that I've been kicked out of better places.

"Oh yeah?" he says, coming right back at me. "Name one."

CHECKMATE, BROTHER. WHERE else would you want to be on a mid-October afternoon? For a venue that holds 80,795 souls this stadium is uncannily *intimate.* Everything, everyone seems close enough to reach out and touch. Even the Goodyear blimp—no weak-ass, knockoff Snoopy blimps for the Irish!—seems within range of a Geoff Price punt.

John Updike famously described Fenway Park as a place where everything "seems in curiously sharp focus, like the inside of one of those peeping-type Easter eggs." I've never looked into one of those. But I have . . . rather, I *know people* who, in their carefree twenties, before they had children and real jobs, might have experimented with psilocybin mushrooms, and spoke afterward of looking out at a world of heightened, intense colors—not unlike what I am experiencing today. The gold in the Fighting Irish helmets—rendered more resplendent by actual 24K gold flakes mixed into the paint sprayed onto them by student managers—has never been more luminous. Colors are popping, from the green of the turf (which is actually Kentucky bluegrass, but never mind), to the blue tartan of the Irish Guard, a kind of Praetorian cordon that marches ahead of the band, to the yellow of the fall mums in the planters that create a little buffer zone between the fans and the field.

AFTER THE MIRACLE in the Monsoon in East Lansing, the Irish cruised to home wins over Purdue and Stanford, then into a bye week. The break arrived, serendipitously, at the midpoint of a 12-game season. It gave Weis a chance, as he put it, "to actually lay on the couch and watch [UCLA's] game. . . . It's always interesting to be like the rest of the free world and be able to watch a game and listen to commentary, the different things they say."

Translation: It's always interesting to listen to the commentary and find out how little they know. *I swear to God, these guys are all the same: If they don't know what the hell a defense is they call it cover two.*

Weis was talking about his off weekend—his wife, Maura, gave him a to-do list that involved a considerable chunk of time spent in the family horse barn—on the Tuesday before the UCLA game. Even though I'm certain such work is beneath him, I savor a mental picture of Weis mucking out stalls.

This was early in his Tuesday press conference, five days before the UCLA game. Weis is very good after games. Win or lose, he's as candid as he can be, and always good for a couple belly laughs. His Sunday afternoon presser is an illuminating dissection of the previous day's game. But his intellect is never more fully on display than during the Tuesday press conference, where he discusses the upcoming opponent, his remarks ranging all over its roster, from starters to backups, from the straightforward to the arcane. He goes into astonishing detail, seldom glancing at the index cards leaning against the microphone stand in front of him. Tuesdays with Charlie are enlightening for what they reveal about the other team, and what they reveal about Charlie.

"At tight end," he was telling us, "it looks like they suffered a serious injury to Ryan Moya, their starter"—during that UCLA-

Oregon game he watched on his couch. He ticks off the name of the Bruins' second-string tight end, Logan Paulsen; the third-stringer ("J. J. Hair is the most experienced guy"); and, leaving no stone-handed reserve unturned, the fourth-stringer. ("The one guy I think we my see some this week is Snead, who is a former defensive end.")

Weis is college football's Eye of Sauron: all who set foot on the field come under his pitiless gaze. Frailty, weakness, hesitation: it is all duly noted. Listen to Weis's riff on backup quarterback Patrick Cowan, thrust by injury into the starting role two games ago: "Cowan, who was their backup quarterback, now the starter, is also their holder. You have to be concerned with that. [Riley] Jondle, their long snapper, has been doing it for four years. He's pretty good."

After a detailed briefing on the Bruins offense, Weis moved to the other side of the ball, where UCLA had made startling improvements. The team that finished the 2005 season ranked 112th in total defense had moved up to ninth. Until Oregon gashed them for 256 rushing yards—the Ducks won at home, 30–20—the Bruins were ranked second in the nation against the run. First-year defensive coordinator DeWayne Walker has made a huge difference. Wiry, bespectacled, and well traveled, he'd apprenticed under such defensive eminences as Pete Carroll, Bill Belichick, and Gregg Williams, the Washington Redskins well-regarded dee coordinator. In his first year as a coordinator, Walker was making it clear that he has mastered the dark arts of his profession.

His most effective weapons are defensive ends Justin Hickman and Bruce Davis, bookend bad-asses who will finish the season with a combined 25 sacks. These guys had been creating some *serious* havoc. Weis, meanwhile, would be starting a true freshman at right tackle in Sam Young. It made sense that Davis and Hickman would have his full attention. "These guys," he concluded, "are very productive pains in the butt."

He noted that first-string linebacker Christian Taylor did not start against Oregon, but came in on the second series. Was he injured? In Walker's doghouse? Inquiries would be made. He remarked on the scant playing time logged against Oregon by Eric McNeal, a linebacker who had been a fixture in UCLA's nickel defense. Weis vows to find out "what the situation is with McNeal."

How do you get to be head coach at Notre Dame? You lie awake nights wondering why Eric McNeal got dropped from UCLA's nickel package against Oregon. I get the impression Weis would notice if the UCLA band showed up without its regular triangle player.

Notre Dame and UCLA will be forever linked by an immortal moment. It occurred, of course, on a basketball court, when the Bill Walton–led Bruins took an 88-game winning streak into the Athletic and Convocation Center on January 19, 1974. UCLA led 70–59 with three and a half minutes to play. But Dwight Clay's fallaway jumper with 29 seconds remaining capped a 12–0 Irish run, and the streak died in South Bend.

This is but the third time the schools have met on the gridiron; the first since 1964. It feels odd to me, an unnatural juxtaposition of football cultures, an incursion against Notre Dame's hallowed rivalry with USC. That feeling will go away as soon as the hitting starts.

SPEAKING OF INCURSIONS, it is the night before the game, and I am striding under cover of darkness across the so-called God Quad—the rectangle that includes the Basilica of the Sacred Heart and Notre Dame's adminstration building, better known by its distinguishing feature, the Golden Dome. It is 11:45 p.m. I should be asleep in my bed at the Jameson Inn, or, more plausibly, having a late-evening malt beverage at the Linebacker Lounge across the street from my hotel. Instead I have joined my old friend John Walters, an ex–*SI* writer who left us to join NBC.com. We have decided to experience something called "Drum Circle," which takes place at midnight at the foot of the Dome.

A crowd has formed a tight circle at the base of the steps to the ad building. A little after midnight, the throng is parted by flashlight-wielding authorities who make a path for the stars of this show: the percussionists in the Notre Dame Marching Band. Looking neither left nor right, they file into the circle and launch into what I am later told is a cover of "Encounter the Ultimate," which, as you probably do not need to be told, is the theme from *Mortal Kombat: Annihilation*. Then we get some Metallica. The cymbalists in particular are going off, spinning like dervishes, playing patty-cake with their instruments. Drummers arch backward, bow forward. Things are getting a little frenzied down here. These percussionists are clearly feeding off the crowd's energy. They are rock stars for a night. Band geeks no more.

A tall, senior xylophonist named Alexandra Hanson later fills me in. Drum circle "isn't so much a rehearsal as it is a chance to get the students pumped up, and get ourselves pumped up."

"Get loud, get crazy, and if you don't know the cheers," shouts a guy with a snare drum who seems to be in charge—the Alpha Drummer—"watch somebody who does."

Crowded 10-deep around the circle, packed onto the steps of the ad building, the students start to rock out, possibly in spite of themselves. Awash in all this percussion, it is nearly impossible to remain still. Very few do. I cannot help but glance up at the gilded statue of Our Lady atop the Dome, her arms slightly raised and spread, and wonder what she is making of this borderline pagan rite.

My favorite cheer is one that comes complete with a specific set of semaphores. After urging the team to "BEAT THE BRUINS!" the cheer builds inexorably—"Yeah! Oh Yeah! Oh Yeah! WHOOOOO!"—to a finale that can only be described as, well, *climactic*, during which the students use their hands to make circles over their heads, like a baseball umpire signaling a home run. (Shades of "Paradise by the Dashboard Light"?) To summarize: While sharpening their exhortations for the next day's contest, these devout young Catholics are mimicking—quite inadvertently, I am certain—what Justin Timberlake calls "LoveSounds."

I have faith that Our Lady, spotlit overhead, will prevent the chaste young adults around me from hearing the cheer quite the same way.

BEFORE GETTING THE thumb from that vigilant, contrarian usher, I'm standing on the sideline with Brian Murphy, no relation, an ex-newspaperman and a fellow Bay Area resident. Despite his virtuosity as a scribe, Murph jumped when KNBR, our local sports station, offered him a morning drive-time gig.

This is his first time in the stadium. Like all Notre Dame virgins, he is inspired—awestruck, even—by the spectacle. "We come from the nation of California," he shouts in my ear, on account of The Solid Gold Sound, as UCLA's marching band is known, filing past. "But *this*"—with a sweeping gesture he takes in band, crowd, blimp—"this is the real America."

Who are you, I ask him, John Cougar Mellencamp? You want to wake up here in February, be my guest. But I see his point. Right now it's 60 and sunny in the heartland. Our hangovers are fading, the game's about to begin. All's right with the world.

Then, we see him. Out in front of the UCLA band, an off-putting sight. Instead of drum major with a preposterous, plumed hat ripped from the pages of Dr. Seuss; instead of a baton-twirling coed wearing something form fitting and sparkly, The Solid Gold Sound is led by . . . a juggler. A guy frantically throwing balls up and catching them. Obviously this is someone's attempt to be "fresh." Today, in the House That Rockne Built, it falls flat.

"Christ," says Murph. "They've got Rudy and Rockne and the Gipper. They've got the Four Horsemen and a leprechaun. We got a f____n' juggler. We're gonna get rolled."

. . . .

HE IS WRONG about that, as becomes clear after a few series. The two teams are well matched. Darius Walker rips off a 10-yard run on his first touch. He is just coming out of a nifty, counterclockwise spin on the next play when strong safety Chris Horton—whom DeWayne Walker calls "my thug in the run game"—hits him so hard that the running back's next of kin can probably feel it. The ball pops out, the Bruins recover. Justin Medlock's 42-yard field goal is good . . . but doesn't count. False start, UCLA. Medlock yanks the 47-yarder wide left. At the time, it doesn't seem like that big a big deal.

Confident in his defense, UCLA head coach Karl Dorrell goes for it on fourth-and-one on his own 44. The call is predictable: quarterback sneak. Defensive tackle Derek Landri destroys the center, and Cowan gets nothing. Irish ball. Taking advantage of the short field, Quinn gets Notre Dame in the end zone eight plays later. The touchdown comes on a two-yard lob to Samardzija, who is belted as he makes the catch, but hangs on. He produces zero yards for the rest of the half. This is not shaping up to be one of his better games.

That's due, in large part, to the fact that Quinn barely has time to blink before Hickman and Davis are in his grill. Especially Hickman. For much of the day, the 6'2", 265-pound senior is lined up over Young, the youngster. Reading the media guide, I see that Hickman lists as his biggest football thrill the three sacks he got against Snow Junior College in his one season as a juco player in Arizona. He'll finish today with three sacks of Quinn, two pressures, and another four tackles behind the line of scrimmage. Maybe they can update his "biggest thrill" in the online version of the guide.

A disgusted Weis calls time-out after consecutive plays net zilch on Notre Dame's first possession of the second quarter. The discussion on the sideline becomes irrelevant when Hickman throws the scrambling Quinn for a 16-yard sack. The next Irish possession is, if possible, even sorrier, and is here chronicled in my always comprehensive notes ("inc." is short for incomplete):

*false start, 85 – duh*
*inc, dropped.*
*run for very little*
*inc.*
*world's worst punt*

Price, the punter, has been splendid each time I've seen him this season. But the 22-yard excrescence that glances off the side of his foot on this fourth-and-13 gives UCLA the ball on the ND 39-yard line. On third down, Cowan throws an underneath pass to a Coke machine with limbs named William Snead, who turns up-field, arranges for a couple Domers to bounce off him, and rumbles 36 yards for the go-ahead touchdown. It is Snead's first catch of the season. The guy is listed as a defensive end. Where have I heard his name before? Oh yeah. He's the fourth-stringer Weis told us Tuesday to keep an eye on. *The one guy I think we may see some this week is Snead.*

Notre Dame trails 14–10 at the half, and has a serious battle on its hands. Quinn is getting tenderized as if this were Michigan all over again, and the running game is nonexistent.

The good news? Aside from giving up two long passes, the Irish defense is playing well. That's about it for the good news.

Notre Dame continues to spin gold into straw in the third quarter. A promising scenario—first-and-goal at the Bruins five—is transformed, following Davis's second sack of the afternoon, into fourth-and-goal at the 15. The Irish settle for a field goal. Beaten like a rented mule on the sack is right guard Bob Morton. When it rains, it pours.

Medlock answers with a 29-yarder midway through the fourth. The score is 17–13 when Notre Dame takes over on its own 27-yard line with just under four minutes to play. If the Irish don't get points on this possession, they're cooked. They will be losing more than just a game. They will be losing, in all likelihood, a shot at a BCS bowl. The season that began with such promise will be judged a disappointment. The five games left on the schedule will turn into a dispiriting trudge to some depressing bowl in the low-rent district of the postseason.

Quinn finds Samardzija for a 16-yard gain on first-and-10. About time. Where the hell has this guy been for two quarters? David Grimes, the will-o'-the-wisp wide out having a breakout game, gathers in a pair of nine-yard passes. The first gets the team past midfield. The second, on third-and-10, leaves the Irish *just* shy of the first-down marker. A 52-yard field goal attempt being a nonstarter in Weis's mind, the coach calls for a sneak on fourth-and-one. And Quinn is stuffed. And that, ladies and gentleman, is your ball game.

Really. It should have been the ball game. How is it not the ball game?

Clock management isn't sexy, but it keeps the Irish alive on this afternoon, which by now had turned overcast and ominous. When Quinn failed to gain on fourth-and-one and UCLA took over on downs, what did Weis do? He burned the first of his three time-outs. Before the Bruins ran a single play. What's up with that? Well, there are 2:20 left to play. New rules installed this season to speed up games dictate that, even on a change of possession, the clock starts before the ball is snapped. By calling time, the Irish prevent Cowan from bleeding 25 seconds off the clock. The time-out also gives Weis a chance to gather the defense around him, and foretell the future: "Fellas, here is what's going to happen: They're going to run three times. . . . We're going to call a time-out after the first play, we're going to call a timeout after the second play, and after the third play get off the ground as quick as you possibly can, to save us as much time as you can." Here's what happens:

First-and-10: Chris Markey rushes for no gain on first down. Notre Dame calls timeout. Clock down to 2:15.

Second-and-10: Markey fights for three. Notre Dame calls timeout. Clock down to 2:09.

Third-and-seven: Markey loses two. The Irish have no more timeouts.

(Looking back on the moment, Weis will point out that "you'll see our guys not only making a tackle, but you'll see Zibby and those guys pulling everyone up to get back to the huddle as their running back is lying on the ground faking an injury.")

Fourth-and-nine: The Bruins take a delay of game on fourth down, burning as much clock as they can.

Fourth-and-14: Irish narrowly avoid catastrophe when Casey Cullen, a former walk-on defensive end, is flagged for defensive holding, a 10-yard penalty that would've handed the Bruins a first down—and victory—had they not just taken the delay of game.

Fourth-and-four: Aaron Perez's 59-yard punt goes through the end zone. Touchback. On six snaps, the Bruins have burned 78 seconds. Quinn will have 62 seconds to work with. A crowd of 80,795, Notre Dame's 190th consecutive sellout, nervously awaits the denouement.

Well, make that a crowd of 80,794. At least one Notre Dame supporter has left the building, unable to abide the tension.

Robin Quinn took her leave at halftime. Even though she's much better at coping with game-day nerves than in Brady's first two years—"It's like I would get the flu every Saturday," she says—she finds it difficult to sit still, to be with people. She runs errands, fills the gas tank in her son's car, tidies the house he shares with free safety Chinedum Ndukwe. That way, even if the team doesn't come out on top, the day hasn't been a total wash. *I cleaned out your refrigerator. It was getting a little disgusting.* With the Irish on the cusp of defeat against UCLA, Robin found herself, naturally, in a car wash.

Up to this point in the game, Quinn has completed exactly one pass of longer than 13 yards to his wide receivers. As he takes the shotgun snap and drops back, you see Davis on his blind side, hurdling the blocking back like Edwin Moses and drawing a bead on Quinn, who feels the pressure, scrambles right, and fires a dart to Samardzija, who steps out of bounds 21 yards upfield.

What jumps out at you on the next play, a 14-yard pass to Grimes, is how much time Quinn has. He actually has several seconds to bounce on the balls of his feet and survey the field, which, on this long day at the office for the Irish hogs, feels like several eternities. That's because, after terrorizing Notre Dame for 59 minutes, Bruins defensive coordinator DeWayne Walker has suddenly become conservative. That's right: The Bruins have gone to their "prevent" defense. They only rush four.

Three receivers line up left. John Carlson, the tight end, draws the short straw. He'll stay in and block. Samardzija is split a dozen yards outside him; Rhema McKnight is way the hell over by the sideline. Protection is adequate, which, today, is a luxury. Lined up left this time, you see Davis rag-dolling Darius Walker, but Walker only allows himself to be rag-dolled *away* from Quinn, who picks out a receiver and, after a textbook exhibition of his quick, powerful release . . . decides not to get rid of the ball quite yet.

It's a crucial moment. Samardzija is running a crossing pattern, left to right, 15 yards beyond the line of scrimmage. Cornerback Trey Brown has tight coverage, until the wide out reaches the middle of the field, where Brown is supposed to hand him off to linebacker Christian Taylor. But Quinn's pump fake freezes the Bruins—fouls up the handoff, as it were. Following the flight of the pass Quinn didn't throw, Taylor takes a step in the wrong direction, giving Samardzija what he lives for: separation. Signaling with his left arm—*I'm open*—he catches Quinn's eye and, a moment later, the ball.

In a single fluid motion at the Bruins' 28-yard line, Samardzija makes the catch and turns upfield, high-stepping out of the arms of the lunging Taylor. At the 15 he cuts inside free safety Dennis Keyes, who has overpursued and now attempts what one disgusted UCLA alum will later describe as "a Polo tackle." ("A Polo tackle," he explains, "is when you just kind of brush up against the guy who's running by you long enough to say, 'I love your cologne. Is that Polo?' ")

The Polo tackle knocks Samardzija off balance. But he recovers, and is sailing for the end zone as Horton and Brown, the safety and corner, close like Stinger missiles.

. . . .

MEANWHILE, IN A suds-engulfed vehicle in the Hi Speed Auto Wash several miles away, a 40-something woman has apparently lost her mind. "Luckily, I could hear the game on the radio," says Robin, who, recalling the moment, performs a creditable Don Criqui impersonation: "Quinn goes back to pass . . . *complete to Samardzija!*"

As Shark outruns those last defenders, Robin is losing it in the car. "The guy who runs the place must have thought I was suffering from claustrophobia, and having a breakdown," she figures. Emancipated from the car wash, she cracks open the windows and drives honking and shouting at complete strangers down Edison Avenue.

Had decorum not prevented him from doing so, Fighting Irish athletic director Kevin White might've joined Mrs. Quinn. Between now and their showdown at USC, the Irish have four opponents: North Carolina and the service academies. If they lose one of those, they don't deserve a BCS bowl bid. If they lose to the Trojans, they'll still be 10-2, and will very likely pull down a BCS invite. For Notre Dame, the payout at those five top-shelf games is a cool $4.5 million. (That's because they're an independent. Teams that are members of a conference get $17 million, which they must then share with their socialist league-mates.) After the BCS bowls, there's a fairly precipitous drop to less remunerative games: your Brut Sun Bowl, your Gaylord Hotels Music City Bowl, your Bell Helicopter Armed Forces and Pioneer PureVision Las Vegas Bowls—some of which pay so little that, after flying the team and the band and the cheerleaders out, then ponying up for their food and lodging, you're lucky to lose less than a hundred grand.

What it boils down to, in stark economic turns, is that Quinn's pass to Samardzija was worth a cool $4 million for the university. Not that the place is hurting for cash. (Its endowment, last I checked, was $ 3.7 billion.) But four mill is four mill.

Morton, the likeable right guard, hangs out in the interview area for as long as we need him, cheerfully recounting the
carnage.

"On that one play where Hickman split you [and the tackle] and
got a sack," asks one reporter, pen poised over his notebook—"what
happened on that play?"

"He split us," Morton replied, speaking slowly, for the writer's
benefit, "and got a sack."

In my notes, along with his quotes, I jot a question: *Why is this
man smiling?* He was part of a line that surrendered five sacks,
paved the way for 41 net yards rushing, and generally made Davis
and Hickman look like Carl Eller and Deacon Jones. "As much as
I'm not going to enjoy watching film tomorrow," declares the red-
headed senior, "I had more fun playing this game than I have in
five years at Notre Dame." He goes on to celebrate the skill and
sportsmanship of the Bruins front four, whom he describes as "the
classiest group I've ever played against."

Morton is smiling because he sees the situation clearly. This
team has an altogether different personality from the one pro-
jected for it as recently as August. Against quality defenses, this
offense struggles. It struggles to run, it struggles to protect its
marquee quarterback. Uncomfortable a fit though it may be at this
storied university with its own TV network and its cake deal with
the BCS, Notre Dame has a new, blue-collar identity. The 2006
Fighting Irish are the plucky underdogs for whom nothing comes
easy. They may have played like crud for 59 minutes today, but
they pulled it out. For the first time in 14 years and only the third
time in school history, Notre Dame won a game with a touchdown
in the final 30 seconds. Morton is damned if he's not going to
enjoy it.

In the Bruins' room I seek out Hickman to congratulate him
on a brilliant game. He is at once gracious, disgusted, inconsol-
able. I ask him what the hell he ate for breakfast. "The guy I was
going up against was a true freshman," he says. "Can't get blocked
by a true freshman." Nor was he.

"We were stronger," he goes on. "We were holding the line and pushing them back. We gave it away on the last drive."

Walker, the defensive coordinator, is second-guessing himself. After three plays in "prevent," he says, he was going to start bringing the house again; was going to go back to what had worked so well all afternoon. But it was on that third play that Quinn pump-faked, and saw Samardzija. . . .

So the Irish improve to 6-1, UCLA falls to 4-3. I wonder, after such a bitter loss, if the Bruins make like the Michigan State Spartans now and proceed directly into the tank. I wonder what team I will see when they take field at the Rose Bowl six weeks from now, against USC.

WHAT I DO not wonder is where I'll be the night of November 2. I'll be on my sofa with an adult beverage in hand and the boob tube tuned to ESPN. If my children ask, I'll explain that "Daddy's working."

Notwithstanding the title of this tome, Thursday night has begun to accrue a certain cache in college football circles. This has everything to do with the emergence of a conference best known, in previous years, for basketball. The Big East is blowing up.

On Thursday, November 2, third-ranked West Virginia visited No. 5 Louisville, a game of unbeatens that eclipsed, in terms of offensive brilliance and national title implications, anything that happened on the following Saturday. The Cardinals hoped to use this game as palate cleanser after choking up a 24–7, fourth-quarter lead against the Mountaineers a year ago, then losing in the third OT.

"Hopefully we don't go to a triple overtime game," remarked head coach Bobby Petrino. "It might be hard on the heart."

Junior quarterback Brian Brohm would be taking the field against West Virginia seven weeks after surgery to repair a torn ligament in his right thumb. While he'd displayed true grit, returning to action just a month after his operation, he hasn't been as sharp as he was, pre-injury. If Louisville is to keep pace with the nation's No. 1 rushing attack—the peerless duo of tailback Steve Slaton and quarterback Pat White will gash defenses for nearly 3,000 yards this season—Brohm will need to find his old form.

Witnessing Slaton's otherworldly burst, his ability to set up blocks and break linebacker's ankles with his cuts, it's useful to remember that he was an afterthought in the West Virginia's 2005 recruiting class. After tearing up the Philadelphia Catholic League for Conwell-Egan in Levittown, Pennsylvania, he accepted a scholarship from Maryland. But in a spasm of bad judgment reminiscent of Boston Red Sox owner Harry Frazee's decision to sell Babe Ruth to the Yankees, Terrapins head man Ralph Friedgen yanked the offer during Slaton's senior season.

So Slaton accepted a full ride to West Virginia, where he was overshadowed by another incoming tailback—one Jason Gwaltney, who'd turned up his nose at USC and Ohio State to play in Morgantown.

Midway through that season, Slaton was a household name, and Gwaltney was thinking about transferring. (He since has.) In his second game as a starter, Slaton scored a school-record six touchdowns—all in the second half—in that triple overtime, come-from-behind, rend-the-still-beating-heart-from-your-chest-and-fling-it-in-the-dust win over the Cardinals.

The rematch, in Lousville's Papa John's Cardinal Stadium, is being billed as the biggest game ever played in the Bluegrass State—bigger, even, than the annual showdowns between Louisville prep powerhouses Trinity and St. Xavier, which regularly draw 35,000 spectators. The Trinity Shamrocks are quarterbacked this season by one Nick Petrino, who threw for 369 yards and five touchdowns in a recent win over Ballard High. Nick's dad, Bobby, coaches the Cardinals; his starting quarterback, Brohm, is himself a former Shamrock.

The Mountaineers are only down 16–14 at halftime, but something's wrong with Slaton: he's taken a helmet to his left elbow that makes it tougher for him to secure the ball. He coughs up the rock on consecutive touches in the third quarter. Linebacker Malik Jackson returns the second of those fumbles 13 yards for a score. Five plays later a dreadlocked freshman named Trent Guy scores the first touchdown of his college career on a 40-yard punt return. West Virginia is suddenly in a 16-point hole, and the black-clad mob at Papa John's is off the hook.

There will be no come-from-behind victory for the visitors on this night. Brohm is crisp and pinpoint, looking off safeties, threading passes through narrow apertures, carving up the Mountaineers for 354 yards and a touchdown in a frantic, 44–34 victory. West Virginia may be out of the hunt for the national title—if a one-loss team makes it to Glendale, it won't be from this arriviste conference—but Louisville is right in the mix. With this win, they earn a bump up to No. 3 in the BCS poll. USC's got a loss. Everyone in the SEC's got a loss. The Cardinals might just end up in the BCS title game. First things first, however. For Louisville, the road to Glendale goes through Piscataway.

THEY WERE so bad for so long, it's flat-out strange to see Rutgers ranked.

But there they are, 8–0 and 15th in the AP poll. Six years after he left Miami at the height of a Hurricanes mini-dynasty—a career move that looked ill advised for a long time—Greg Schiano is the toast of the Garden State. The Scarlet Knights have turned a corner, learned how to finish games; how to keep swinging a figurative ax.

Schiano, like Jacksonville Jaguars head man Jack Del Rio a devotee of lumberjack metaphors, bestows the "Ax Award" after each game on the Rutgers player who has best embodied the mantra "Keep chopping." For me, that expression echoes the ancient Zen saying, "Chop wood, carry water."

Whether the goal is mindfulness or the Meineke Car Care Bowl (which has a Big East tie-in and would dearly love to host the

Scarlet Knights), Rutgers is on its way. Top-notch college football has returned to "the banks of the Old Raritan."

So go the lyrics of the Rutgers alma mater, composed by Howard Fullerton in 1873—a full four years after his university made history fielding a team that clashed with Princeton in the first-ever college football game. (Rutgers won, 6–4, despite the admonition of an umbrella-waving professor who shouted at players, "You will come to no Christian end!")

One hundred thirty-seven years later, the Scarlet Knights will finally play a game of comparable magnitude. In the Big East's second battle of ranked unbeatens in seven days, No. 3 Louisville visits Rutgers Stadium tonight. Ticket-seeking students camped out in a shantytown dubbed "Schianoville." For the first time in its history, a ranked Rutgers team will face a ranked opponent.

UNTIL THE FOURTH week of this season, when the Knights debuted at No. 23 in the AP poll, the team had been ranked for precisely six weeks of its 137-year history. Rutgers's most renowned victory remained its first. While it's overly facile to say that it's been downhill for the Knights since 1873, it's not so far from the mark. A sampler of the school's more recent futility: from 1991 to 2004, Rutgers was 18-75-1 in Big East play. (They failed to win a single conference game from 2000 to '03). This is a Rutgers program whose 64–6 loss to Miami in 2000 was, compared to its 80–7 loss in Morgantown a year later, a taut, suspenseful affair. This is a team that has dropped games, in recent seasons, to Villanova, Buffalo (by 23), and New Hampshire.

"We didn't know how to win," fifth-year senior Brian Leonard told *SI*. Leonard is a fullback from Gouverneur, New York, who raised his father's eyebrows by choosing the Knights over Notre Dame. "We just didn't have the confidence and the leadership. We do now."

While the 6'2", 235-pound fifth-year senior started the season as a Heisman Trophy candidate—perhaps you saw him on that

Leonard-for-Heisman billboard in Times Square—these days he is merely working for one. Tailback Ray Rice will finish the season with 1,794 rushing yards and 20 touchdowns. (Leonard will be the first fullback taken in the NFL draft.)

So, does Rutgers have a prayer against the UofL?


OF COURSE IT does. Schiano has been waiting for six years to coach in a game like this: the opportunity to knock off a top-five team on national TV. (For the second straight week, the Game of Week is on Thursday night.) This is not the Mountaineers defense Brohm will be trying to solve. Schiano, whose previous gig was as defensive coordinator at Miami, doubles as his own defensive coordinator at Rutgers: his guys are made of sterner stuff than anyone Louisville has seen this season. The Knights are ranked second in the nation in pass defense (West Virginia is 66th), scoring defense, and total defense. They've got an undersized but active front seven that hopes to get in Brohm's face early and often.

Brohm does not seem overly concerned by any of this while leading Cardinals to a 25–7 lead midway through the second quarter. Hell, Middle Tennessee State gave Louisville a better game than this. If Rutgers is going to claw its way back into this game, Mike Teel is going to have make a few plays.

Teel is the Knights' redshirt sophomore quarterback whose most impressive statistic is his record. Dating back to his days at Don Bosco Prep, he's 33-1 as a starter. Schiano is bringing him along slowly: seven times this season, Teel has thrown for 145 yards or fewer. He needs to connect on some long passes against Louisville to create some space for Rice.

That's exactly what happens late in the second quarter. Teel finds Kordell Young on a short crossing route. Young blazes up the soft middle of the Lousiville zone for 39 yards. With the Cards still catching their breath, Rice takes a pitch left, beats three defenders to the edge, and goes 18 yards for the touchdown that brings the Knights to within nine.

That was the margin at halftime, when the home team was granted some special dispensation. That, at least, was the impression I got, watching ESPN's broadcast from my living room in northern California. Rutgers, it seemed, was allowed to field 15 defensive players for the entire second half. How else do they shut out an offense averaging nearly 500 yards a game? There was middle 'backer Quint Frierson, sticking ball carrier George Stripling for a three-yard loss; Frierson again splitting a six-yard sack of Brohm with Eric Foster. There was defensive tackle Ramel Meekins, an ex-walk-on built like a bank safe, sacking Brohm, then talking to him, shouting something uncharitable into his ear hole.

In his defense, I would say Meekins was merely following the example of Jeff Brohm, the Cardinals quarterback coach, who vented his frustration by haranguing his little brother after every punt, every three-and-out. He's dressing down his brother, I explained to my 10-year-old son, because he doesn't have time to yell at every single offensive lineman.

Teel will only connect on eight of his 21 passes tonight. But he makes the completions count. With just under five minutes to play in the third quarter, he slightly overthrows wideout Kenny Britt on a crosser. A true freshman who seemed to be suffering from a case of alligator arms in the first half—an unwillingness to fully extend for passes that promised to get him blown up—he goes airborne for this one, and isn't brought down for 67 yards. Rice finishes for him, slicing four yards up the middle to bring the home team within three.

Meekins continues to make Brohm's life miserable with a sack and a hurry on Louisville's next possession. After two Cardinal punts, a Rutgers drive stalls at Lousiville's 29-yard line. Jeremy (Judge) Ito grooves a 46-yard field goal to tie the game.

From unexpected angles, the Scarlet Knight defenders keep coming, beating blocks, forcing Brohm to pull down the ball and run with it, then tattooing him. The Cardinals must punt again with five minutes and change left in the game, and Rutgers takes over on its own nine-yard-line. Of his 131 yards rushing on the night, Rice gouges out 42 on this possession. Yet the most inspired call of the drive is a screen pass to Leonard, who moves the chains with a 26-yard gain on third-and-six. Rice follows with a bruising, 20-yard run well into Ito's field-goal range. Four plays later, with 21 seconds on the clock, the Judge lines up a 33-yard attempt . . . and misses! It sails wide left. But there's a flag on the play. A Cardinal cornerback jumped offside. Given a second chance to be a hero, Ito cashes in. Brohm is sacked on Louisiville's final snap—appropriately—and the blimp shot shows a green field overrun with scarlet. Flanked by state troopers, Schiano stands with his arms folded, awaiting Petrino's handshake. He's made a conscious decision, it's clear, to present a dignified mien to the world. His plan is complicated when his players drench him with Gatorade.

Around him: about what you would expect from students celebrating the biggest win in school history. Complete bedlam. Unalloyed joy. Jersey girls and guys waving white towels, holding signs that say It's "R" Time and Football Was Born Here.

The producer throws it to sideline reporter, who is standing with Rice, and tells us she can "feel the goose bumps" on his arm. I don't think she's exaggerating. I have goose bumps myself. "I'm ready to cry right now," Rice warns her. "I don't know how to hold it back." But he gets through a few shouted questions, giving all the credit to his teammates, dedicating the victory to "everybody in New Jersey, everybody that believed in us."

When the interview is over you can hear him shout, "Where's my mother?" Janet Rice materializes from the throng to hug her boy. This beautiful snapshot brings down the curtain on one of the defining moments of this season, a vignette made more magical by the fact that it happened here, on the banks of the old Raritan, where college football was born.

# CHAPTER 14

# Judgment Day

November 17, Columbus, Ohio — The question is not why Bo Schembechler had to die today of all days, 27 hours before kickoff of the most important, consequential edition of a rivalry he personally resuscitated. The question is, How did the man live as long as did? My theory: stubbornness—the same obstinacy that prevented him from overhauling a smash-mouth, ground-bound offense even after losing his first five Rose Bowls to Pac-10 teams better versed in that futuristic stratagem known as the passing game.

**BCS TOP 10**

1. *Ohio State*
2. *Michigan*
3. *USC*
4. *Florida*
5. *Notre Dame*
6. *Rutgers*
7. *Arkansas*
8. *West Virginia*
9. *Wisconsin*
10. *Louisville*

The cardiac arrest that that took him this morning, at the age of 77, came 37 years after his first heart attack, two decades after his second. He endured two quadruple bypasses, suffered from diabetes, and had a pacemaker installed the month before he finally exited this vale. While pushing his wheelchair during that particular hospital stay, a nurse asked the old coach for his weight.

"I'm 205 pounds of hardened blue steel," came the reply. Spoken like a legend.

I had one brief audience with Schembechler, and I earned it. Among the many talents of Michigan associate athletic director Bruce Madej is his ability to remain affable, sympathetic, and understanding while shooting you directly to hell on all of your interview requests. Such was the case on September 15, 1989—the day before Michigan opened at home against No. 1–ranked Notre Dame. Of course Schembechler would not have time to answer even a single question from me, Madej reported, with his ever-present smile. The coach had dispensed his wisdom to the media as recently as Monday. How could he be expected to make time for *SI* with the game a scant 24 hours away?

Of course I understand, I assured him, not understanding in the least. Where is he now?

He was just finishing up production meetings with ABC. And so, without permission, or much of a game plan, I made my way over to that part of the complex where the great man was sharing his insights with the talking heads who would call the next day's game. Pretending to be lost, I started sticking my head into rooms. When I saw Keith Jackson, I knew I was getting warm. The production meeting was at an end; Schembechler was standing. I strode up to him and introduced myself as *SI*'s new college football writer. He was at once polite and distracted, shaking my hand, nodding, and already looking over my shoulder as I expressed my frustration at not being able to schedule an interview. He was already walking away as he informed me that he had some meetings to get to.


MY HUNCH, AFTERWARD, was that those meetings did not focus on kickoff coverage. The next day, Notre Dame's Rocket Ismail returned a pair of kickoffs for touchdowns, twice producing a surreal quiet in the Big House, which contained roughly 106,000 people, and single-handedly accounting for Notre Dame's 24–19 victory. The Wolverines would not lose again until they met USC in the Rose Bowl.

Ismail's extraterrestrial afternoon in Ann Arbor came two decades after Schembechler's first season as Michigan's head coach. The program was at a low ebb. The previous November, Ohio State had hung half a hundred on its bitterest rival in a 50–14 beatdown. To reach the half-century mark, Woody Hayes went for two after the Buckeyes' final touchdown. Asked afterward why he felt the need to go for two, he is said to have replied, "Because I couldn't go for three." (Leading 55–0 late in the 1946 game, Michigan lined up to kick a field goal; Woodrow may have been avenging that decision.)

During his six years as an Ohio State assistant earlier in his career, Schembechler had befriended Hayes. So Woody was stung by his protégé's decision, in 1969, not only to consort with the enemy, but to lead them. That was the year Schembechler became head coach at Michigan, a school Hayes despised so much that he refused to buy gas in the state; refused even to speak its name, referring to it only as "that school up north."

With the team buses cruising up Route 23 on the final Friday of the 1969 regular season, bound for "that school," it seemed certain that the Buckeyes were rolling toward their second straight national title. Sportswriters of the day could not resist labeling them college football's Greatest Team Ever. They had five first-team All-Americans and went into Michigan Stadium riding a 22-game winning streak.

Loaded though they were, they didn't have a monopoly on great players. Lining up at tackle for Michigan was the immense and immensely talented Dan Dierdorf, who had cringed upon learning that Schembechler would be his new head coach. As Dierdorf explained in 2000, to a luncheon audience at his College Football Hall of Fame induction, the two had a history.

The year before Dierdorf headed off to Ann Arbor, a visitor came calling on him at Glenwood High in Canton, Ohio. It was a recruiter from Miami of Ohio—the head coach, in fact. Guy by the name of Schembechler. With a scholarship offer from Michigan in his back pocket, Dierdorf saw no reason to take the meeting. Figuring "I'm never going to see him again," Dierdorf recalled, he "went out the back door."

The following year, Schembechler was named head coach at Michigan. Hoping his rudeness had been forgotten, Dierdorf approached the new headman, his hand outstretched. "Coach Schembechler," he effused, "how you doing?"

"He sticks his hand out," recounts Dierdorf, "and his hand goes right past my hand and he grabs me right in the stomach. He looks me in the eye and says, 'You're fat, you're mine, and I never forget.'"

It was a presumably leaner Dierdorf who started on the 1969 team that took a 7-2 record into The Game. Having destroyed the Wolverines the previous year, the Buckeyes were favored by 17.

They lost by 12. In a watershed victory that awakened the Wolverines from their long slumber, vest-pocket cornerback Barry Pierson intercepted three passes and returned a punt 60 yards, to the Buckeye three-yard line. Following a thunderous block by Dierdorf, quarterback Don Moorehead plunged in for the touchdown that gave the Wolverines a nine-point lead. The Buckeyes did not score again, throwing six interceptions in a 24–12 loss that could only have deepened Hayes's mistrust of the forward pass.

For the revitalizing effect it had on the moribund Michigan program, that victory is widely considered the greatest in school history. It ushered in the Ten-Year War, as it is called in the heartland, a decade in which the Ohio State–Michigan rivalry, always intense, turned white hot. Pupil got the best of mentor during that era: Schembechler went 5-4-1 against his former boss. Four times between 1970 and '75, both squads came into the game in the AP's top five.

Six weeks after that seminal victory over the Buckeyes, the Wolverines traveled to the Rose Bowl. On the eve of the game, a 10–3 loss to USC, Schembechler suffered his first heart attack. He was only 40. That trip prefigured the trouble Schembechler would have—with bowl games and his ticker—for decades to come.

I HAD RETURNED to Ann Arbor in early November for a feature on Schembechler's friend and (indirect) successor, Lloyd Carr. Immediately after receiving the assignment on a Friday, I commenced carpet-bombing the Wolverines' sports information office with phone messages and e-mails. I knew that Carr would be off-limits as of the following Monday afternoon, after submitting to reporters' questions at his weekly, sound bite–free press conference. Would it be possible, I asked Michigan sports info, to get some face time with His Eminence—even if it was only 10 or 15 minutes—for the four-page feature we would be running in our weekly magazine, with its estimated readership of 18 or so million.

Sports information director Dave Ablauf returned my call on Saturday. The answer was . . . maybe. They'd get back to me as soon as they had word from Lloyd. By late Sunday morning, I'd heard nothing. But if I was going to be in Ann Arbor for Monday's press conferences—Monday is the only day Michigan makes players available to the media, though they are often not players anyone wants to talk to—I would need to leave soon for the airport. So I did.

I was standing in a security line at SFO, and had just been selected for special screening when my phone went off. I immediately recognized the upbeat voice of Bruce Madej, who cheerfully announced, "Yeah, hey, Lloyd doesn't want to do it! Nothing personal. He just doesn't feel like the focus should be on him."

So I flew to Detroit, drove to Ann Arbor, and took dutiful notes at Carr's arid press conference, after which I followed him into a corridor at Crisler Arena, shook his hand, and scavenged a scene I ended up using for my lead. I talked to current and former players. I talked to guys who'd coached with him and against him. (While it might have been helpful to speak with some of the coaches on his actual staff, those men were, understandably, off-limits, kickoff against always dangerous Indiana being a mere 120 hours away.) I talked to Michigan athletic director Bill Martin and to one of Carr's daughters-in-law. And I talked to some of the Michigan beat writers and columnists. I probably shouldn't admit that, but they were insightful and generous, and they saved my ass.

The one person I *really* wanted to talk to was Schembechler, who'd gotten out of coaching after the 1989 season, who still had an office in the football complex that bore his name. That should not be a problem, Ablauf told me that Monday, and again the following Wednesday. After that, he started to hedge his bets. When I saw him Saturday, in the press box at Indiana's Memorial Stadium, he told me that Bo would be holding a press conference on Monday.

My deadline was Sunday morning. Bo and I never did talk.

I had spoken with Gerald Ford. This was in the fall of 2003. Ford, an ex–Wolverines center, shared his recollections of Ohio State games gone by. I interviewed George W. Bush, before and after mountain biking with him on his ranch in Crawford, Texas. That was in the summer of 2005, a few weeks before Katrina, and a few weeks after I'd met John Kerry at the Tour de France. We had a nice chat. The following year I spoke to Bill Clinton for a story on Lance Armstrong. Bono called a few days later, for the same story.

To summarize: I can talk to U.S. Presidents, I can get Bono on the phone from frikkin' Rio de Janeiro (he did put me on hold at one point to take a call from Brazilian president "Lula" Da Silva), but I can't get five minutes on the phone with a Michigan head coach.

Fortunately, I'm not bitter about it.


SCHEMBECHLER WAS A pistol at that Monday press conference. That was the word. He showed up for Tuesday's football practice, sitting on a stool, the *Ann Arbor News* would later report, because he had trouble standing. He canceled a Thursday meeting with his heart specialist in order to address the team. Later that afternoon he taped a segment for an upcoming HBO special on The Game. That night he had dinner at the Chop House in Ann Arbor.

On the last morning of his life, while driving to the studios of a local TV station, Schembechler did a 12-minute spot with a local AM station, during which he "sounded intense, sounded ready, sounded like Bo," one of the hosts would later recall.

Apparently he *was* ready. After arriving at WXYZ-TV in Southfield to tape his weekly show, Schembechler excused himself to go to the restroom, which is where a colleague found him, face-down and unconscious, shortly after 9:00 a.m. He was pronounced dead at 11:42 a.m.

He and Hayes, who preceded him in death by 19 years, had turned this game into The Game. No matchup of Buckeyes and Wolverines had ever been bigger, more saturated with significance than the 2006 edition, a One versus Two matchup doubling as the Big Ten title game and a play-in to the national championship. And that was *before* the single most beloved figure in the 127-year history of Michigan football died the day before the game. Now this most bilious and beer-drenched of border wars would be over-laid with grief on one side and, at the very least, grudging respect on the other. The passing of Bo gave new meaning to a Saturday ESPN had dubbed "Judgment Day."

I GET THE news at O'Hare. I'm connecting to Columbus. I've got messages on my phone from three different editors. The Web site needs something, pronto. I compose a quick, short obit that I hope will strike an appropriately elegiac note. (In retrospect, I probably should have just focused on spelling all the words correctly.) My hope, I told readers, is that Schembechler's death will inject a note of mourning and introspection into the otherwise Jägermeister-fueled, F-bomb-laced atmosphere that has come to define this an-cient grudge, particularly when it's contested in Columbus. Perhaps there will be less mayhem, vandalism, and arson than on the night of the win over Texas.

On the short hop to Port Columbus International Airport (the international flights are as cunningly hidden as the "Port"), I am listening to the woman in the row behind me. She is a Michigan fan, and rightly concerned about her physical well-being. "I've got the chick factor going for me," she is telling her neighbor, "so I'm hoping that prevents me from being accosted."

In my jacket pocket is a folded piece of paper – a printed-out Ticketmaster pass to tonight's "Hate Michigan Rally" at the Newport Music Hall on North High Street. I wonder if the Rally has been canceled, considering that its headline performers are the self-described "best damn punk band in the land," a quartet of guys who dress up like Woody Hayes and call themselves the Dead Schembechlers.

The death of Schembechler notwithstanding, the Dead Schembechlers have decided that the show must go on. At a hastily called press conference earlier that afternoon, lead singer Bo Biafra, best known for such half-sung, half-screamed numbers as "Bomb Ann Arbor Now" and "I Wipe My Ass with Wolverine Fur," showed the world a softer, more caring side. With fellow musicians Bo Vicious (bass), Bo Scabies (drums), and Bo Thunders standing in solidarity behind him, Biafra extended the band's "deepest sympathies and heartfelt prayers to the Schembechler family." That evening's show, he announced, would be its final appearance as the Dead Schembechlers. Proceeds would be donated to a charity "of the Schembechler family's choosing."

He is rather less decorous and conciliatory when he appears on stage around 11 that night, by which time I have worked my way through most of a pail-sized draft beer, and realized that if I wanted to blend in, I should have worn a backward-facing Buckeyes ballcap, James Laurinaitis jersey, and a necklace strung with actual buckeye nuts. The band took its sweet time coming out on stage— possibly because it was waiting for the fog machine to produce more than a sorry little shin-high curtain of mist. What Stonehenge was to Spinal Tap, artificial fog is to the Dead Schembechlers. Finally, with Bo Scabies laying down a steady backbeat, Bo Biafra welcomes us to the 2006 Hate Michigan Rally, then makes it official, "This will be our last show ever as the Dead Schembechlers." They are taking this drastic step, he goes on, "to honor a man who went astray."

It's a fine line, and Bo Biafra walks it with aplomb, according the deceased his propers while continuing to dump on Michigan in general. As Buckeye Nation knows, Schembechler was an Ohio State guy before he took the job at the "school up north." Even though "he became the face of the evil football empire," Biafra thunders, "we will always salute Schembechler the man and former Buckeye."

Eulogy delivered, the lead singer reminds us how lucky we are: "You can say you saw the Dead Schembechlers on the eve of the greatest victory in the history of this rivalry. . . . All kidding aside," he says, and I lift pen to notebook, preparing to chronicle some heartfelt sentiment, "if you walk away from here with just one thought, let it be this." That is the band's cue to launch violently into "Michigan Stadium Is a Pile of Shit," after which Biafra poses a question to the people in the mosh pit: "You kids aren't *tired* here, are you?"

As a prelude to "Chad Henne Is a Motherf____g Joke," Bo Biafra notes caustically that security forbids those in the mosh pit from crowd surfing.

"You can't surf, but this [expletive] can," he said, tossing into the crowd a life-sized inflatable Chad Henne doll. "Be gentle, now."

The Bos are decked out in white dress shirts, neckties, Woody spectacles, and the headgear favored by the late legend: black ballcap adorned with the block *O*. "Because so many ladies have requested it," Biafra announces midway through the set, "we're going to remove our jackets." As Hayes used negative reinforcement to get the most out his players, Biafra continues to harangue the audience, to get the most from it. "We ain't playing the f_____ VFW Post, so let's hear it for a song called 'I Hate Michigan!' "

Coming out of "M Means Moron," Bo Biafra pats himself on the back: "I'd like to take a moment to say how great we sound tonight." And, I must admit, I agree with him. These guys are ripping it up. Their show is raw but the band is tight. The songs are fast, furious, and very, very funny. In a dark way. As the set goes on, more and more people are bopping and hopping in the pit; Bo Biafra can stop shaming them. After the guys tear through "I'm Not Gay (But I Wanna F___ Brutus Buckeye")—a daring selection, I think, in this red state—and "Wide Left: The Ballad of Mike Lantry," I am calling it a night, taking my leave of this rocking venue, when I hear Bo Biafra boil the beauty of college football down to 11 words:

"Who ever thought we would all love to hate so much?"


"I DON'T HATE anybody. I don't hate anything. I think 'hate' is too strong a word. I might dislike someone's ways, but I don't hate anybody."

This was Troy Smith, five days before The Game, responding to a reporter who asked him if he "hated Michigan as a kid."

Explaining that he had a lot to think about, what with reading the defense and making calls at the line and getting through his progression, "the quarterback has to be calmest guy, the most cool guy out there on the field."

But you can do that while despising the opponent, correct? "Another thing that helps me . . . is the respect I have for my opponent. [I don't] try to put them in a situation where they're below or beneath me. They prepare just like we do. I have respect for everyone I go against."

Surely a human wrecking-ball like Quinn Pitcock, the Buckeyes' sensational defensive tackle and a native of Piqua, Ohio, could be counted on to spew some bile. How about it, Quinn?

"Someone please tell me when all this started," says the senior.

"There's no true hate. I've been up there. I go on riding trips and stuff like that."

That's right, the 295-pound Pitcock is an aficionado of dirt bikes, which raises a series of questions which must be put off for another day. "I have friends there," he continues. All the hate speech, he says, "is just one of those football things everybody likes to get hyped up about."

I made it a point to talk to wide receiver Anthony Gonzalez, a philosophy major with a 4.0 GPA who may be the smartest player on the field tomorrow. Feeling the need to change the subject after Gonzalez gently admonished me for having never read any Plato ("You've never read Plato? You've *got* to read the *Republic*"), I asked after his father.

Eduardo Gonzalez emigrated from Cuba and was offered a football scholarship to Michigan in the late 1960s. He was a stud running back for the Wolverines, but suffered a career-ending injury in his second season. "After that, it was a struggle just to pay for school," the son explained. "Back in those days, when you got injured, they took your scholarship away."

Did he leave on bad terms with Bo? I ask, looking to stir the pot a little.

"My dad?" replied Gonzo, taken aback. "He has great things to say about Bo. *Great* things."

Sigh. Paraphrasing the Blackeyed Peas: Where is the hate?

Outside the walls of the football complex, fans of the respective teams—Ohioans, in particular—are in closer touch with their abhorrence, their detestation, their extreme dislike of the supporters of the other side. It was for this reason that, in the days before the game, Michigan associate vice president and dean of students Sue Eklund sent an e-mail to the student body, warning of the dangers of traveling to Columbus. It was a memo modeled after one of those State Department–issued travel advisories for people thinking of going to Kyrgyzstan, or the Democratic Republic of Congo.

"We know that it can be uncomfortable being in an opposing

team's environment," Dean Eklund wrote. "We would like to offer a few suggestions in order to help you stay safe and have a positive experience this weekend:

- Try carpooling to the game; if possible, drive a car with non-Michigan license plates.
- Keep your Michigan gear to a minimum, or wait until you are inside the stadium to display it.
- Stay with a group.
- Stay low-key; don't draw unnecessary attention to yourself.
- If verbally harassed by opposing fans, don't take the bait.
- Avoid High Street in Columbus."

The memo closes with the suggestion to call 9-1-1 "if at any time you feel unsafe," and mentions that a detachment of "U-M campus police will also will be available in Columbus to support our fans."

Do Colorado fans remove their license plates before driving to Lincoln? Are Oregon fans afraid to wear Duck attire around Corvallis? Does Stanford bring *its own private militia* to Cal? I think not.

Game day. I don't bother asking my friends in the Buckeyes sports information office for parking passes anymore. It gives them too much pleasure to refuse me. I find a spot a mile or so from Ohio Stadium, way the hell out by the Expo Center, and start walking west. There are already a lot of parties in progress, a lot of furniture on lawns, where later, it will tempt arsonists. It's still two hours before kickoff, but a lot of these kids are already inebriated, and not in an Algonquin Round Table kind of way. It is a measure of the level of debauchery that I am surprised not in the least by the sight of the Girls Gone Wild bus, parked on High Street. I approach five Columbus city cops, standing outside Charley's Steakery. I ask if they think the death of Bo will tamp down some of the rowdiness; if a few sofas that might otherwise have been torched, might be spared.

"With this crowd?" says one of the officers. "Take a wild guess."

As if on cue, a young woman with a F__ MICHIGAN T-shirt approaches the officer, her arms outspread. "Can I get a picture with you?"

He is pleased to oblige.

"Once the sun goes down," another cop tells me, "we lose our best friend."

AFTER A MOMENT of silence, the overwhelmingly Buckeye-friendly crowd of 105,708 remains standing for a gracious tribute: With footage of the blue-capped Schembechler playing on the scoreboard, the PA announcer spoke of the loss of "a legend and an icon . . . an alumnus and a friend."

The desire to pay their respects to this "icon" has wrongfooted some Buckeyes fans, who are in the habit of decanting anti-Wolverines bile this time of year. They are further quieted by the crisp, seven-play, 80-yard drive directed by Henne on the game's opening possession. The junior passed on four of his first six snaps—our first clue that even though Bo's spirit hovered over it, this game might not be an homage to him.

During the Ten-Year War, with Woody and Bo glaring daggers at one another across the field, The Game featured all of eight touchdown passes. Today we will see six. The Heisman Trophy won't be awarded for another five weeks. But it will be sewn up this afternoon. The Troy Smith Show is about to begin.

Ohio State answers with a touchdown drive of its own, covering 69 yards in 14 plays. Twelve of those are pass plays (on one, Smith is sacked). The drive nearly stalls on third-and-16. On second down, Smith is leveled by beastly rush end LaMarr Woodley, after which they engage in a spirited exchange of views. Smith's next statement is nonverbal, as he snaps off a 27-yard rope to Roy Hall, a studly, physical wide out whose modest contributions to the passing game have been overshadowed this season by Ginn,

Gonzalez, and the Brians: sophomores Brian Hartline and Brian Robiskie. With Tressel's game plan calling for multiple four- and five-receiver sets today—would Woody even recognize this as football?—everyone will get touches. Smith's touchdown pass, seven snaps later, is a one-yard bullet to a ridiculously wide-open Hall.

Now it's back to the ground, with Smith taking the ball around right end for six yards on Ohio State's first possession of the second quarter. On second down, freshman running back Chris (Beanie) Wells goes in motion, left to right. He's coughed the ball up four times this season, but Tressel has stuck with him. Now Smith takes a shotgun snap and hands to Wells, who is looking for daylight around left end but finds himself in the arms of outside 'backer Shawn Crable, who has badly beaten the tight end with an inside move, but is now so stunned by his good fortune that he fails to wrap up Wells. The freshman spins inside, up the gut of the defense, high-stepping into the secondary, outracing corner-backs Leon Hall and Trent Morgan to the end zone. The Wolverines have allowed 29.9 rushing yards per game this season. A freshman just zoomed for 52 and a touchdown.

The Buckeyes continue to attack Michigan's strength on their next drive. Pittman pounds for four over left guard; slashes for nine around right end. Wells, the short-yardage back, dives for two on second-and-one.

My mistake. He *would've* picked up the first, if Smith hadn't retrieved the ball from his belly, then looked downfield. With the casual air of a guy playing catch on the sideline, he flicks a 39-yard touchdown pass to Ginn, who has used the play fake and his own superhero's burst to get behind Leon Hall, whose reputation as the Big Ten's best cover corner is of no assistance to him at this moment. Ginn elevates to make the grab, then tumbles into the end zone, putting the Bucks up by two touchdowns with just over six minutes in the half.

That throw and catch brings to mind a moment from last night. "Ted Ginn Did Everythin' " is the Dead Schembechlers' frenetic and only slightly hyperbolic paean to No. 7. The song's lyrics pose questions that its title answers:

> *Who fought off giant asteroids to keep the earth from dyin'?*
> *Who led the troops in World War 2 & then saved Private*
>    *Ryan?*
> *Ted Ginn! Ted Ginn! Ted Ginn did everythin'!*

It hardly mattered, as the Buckeyes rolled their record to 11-0 this season, that Ginn had not *really* done everything. For the third straight season, he has been sensational. He just hasn't been sensational in the jack-of-all trades manner that was predicted for him.

Remember, Ginn played quarterback, receiver, and defensive back, and returned kicks for the Glenville Tarblooders. He came to Columbus in the wake of two-threat Chris Gamble, and there was talk of his playing offense, defense, and on special teams. He got a half-dozen snaps at quarterback in the Alamo Bowl—the Bucks were down to a single quarterback, remember—ratcheting up expectations which, in hindsight, seem preposterous.

At the tail end of what will be his final college season, talk of his taking snaps at defensive back has long been empty chatter. While he did throw a 33-yard touchdown pass to backup tight end Rory Nichol against Indiana, we've seen none of the once-ballyhooed Shot-Ginn formation. Teams wised up and stopped kicking to him (he has one punt return for a score this season).

The biggest reason Ginn isn't doing everything is that Tressel doesn't need him to. These Buckeyes are absolutely loaded. You've got Pittman in the backfield being pushed by superfrosh Wells. And you've got four stud receivers aside from Ginn, all of whom are beneficiaries of the special attention he gets.

"Sometimes we'll line up with four wide receivers," he will tell me after the game, "and I'll look at the defense and there's three guys looking at me. I can point out plays where guys have been so scared of me trying to beat 'em deep that they forgot about Gonzo."

Not that Gonzalez needs help getting open. Michigan has closed to within a touchdown when the Buckeyes get the ball back with two minutes and change left in the half. Working in hurry-up mode, Smith throws on eight straight plays, completing seven, three to Gonzo. On a second-and-six at the Wolverines' eight-yard line, the Bucks come out with five wides. Sniffing around for the mismatch, Smith looks right and sees a linebacker lined up over Gonzalez in the slot. That would be Chris Graham, who adjusts his coverage at the last second, edging inside, taking away the crossing route. Uh, make that *trying* to take away the crossing route.

Gonzo runs right at him, feinting right then pushing off *hard* to his left, flashing open in the middle. Smith's pass finds him at the goal line a millisecond before strong safety Jamar Addams, whose hard, clean shot fails to part Gonzalez from the ball. His eighth touchdown of the season puts the Bucks up 28–14.

It is hard to know at halftime which to find more astounding: Smith's numbers—he is 21 of 26 for 241 yards and three touchdowns—or the fact that he is amassing them against Michigan, which came into the contest allowing opponents 12.1 points and 231 yards per game. The Buckeyes have 320 yards through 30 minutes. More profoundly out of character for the Wolverines, touted by some as the finest run defense college football has seen in the last half century, is the 79 yards they've surrendered on the ground. Surely Ron English, the ballyhooed first-year coordinator, will get that fixed during the intermission.

And you know they're coming back. The team that spent this season watching scenes from *Cinderella Man* lifts itself off the canvas—with a spot of assistance from the home team. Belatedly channeling Bo, the Wolverines finally get the ground game going, mounting a five-play scoring drive early in the third quarter. The drive covers 60 yards: Mike Hart gets 59 of them, and the touchdown.

Feeling infallible, perhaps, following his first-half performance, Smith throws toward a triple-covered Gonzalez: the pass is deflected, then picked off by Alan Branch, the sensational junior defensive tackle. Four plays later, kicker Garrett Rivas nails a 39-yard field goal, making the score 28–24.

High anxiety now pervades the Horseshoe, and the maize block *M* on Carr's cap stands for Momentum. Michigan has come out swinging in the second half. But when it most needs a stop to preserve that Momentum, the Michigan dee gives up its longest play of the season. On second-and-one, with the Wolverines looking for a play-action pass—Ginn burned them earlier on this down and distance—Pittman lines up in the "I" formation. Fullback Stan White takes out the defensive tackle. Next guy through is pulling guard Steve Rehring, a 6'8", 329-pound redshirt sophomore who notices, upon hitting the hole, that "it was already wide enough for four of me to fit in, so I knew Pitt was going to get through."

Pittman's 56-yard touchdown pushes the lead back into double digits. But the 2006 Wolverines are like Schembechler, who stuck around for 36 years after his first heart attack. They will not go gentle into that good night.

A botched snap results in a fumble that is covered by Branch, whose second takeaway gives the Wolverines their shortest field of the night. Hart punches it in three plays later. Forty seconds into the fourth quarter, the score is 35–31. The Wolverines are full of life.

The Buckeyes have survived a third fumble when they get the ball back with 10:38 left to play. Needing desperately to pad their lead and eat some clock, they do both. After Smith dashes nine yards around right end to give the Bucks a first down at their 28-yard line, Michigan burns a time-out. On the Ohio State sideline, Tressel decides it is time to heed Bebe's advice.

Every three months or so, Tressel will tell me after the game, "I get a nice letter from an older lady from Akron. Her name is Bebe." In her most recent missive, Bebe warned the coach about a premonition she'd had. In 60 years of following the Buckeyes, she's seen Michigan use the Statue of Liberty play to great effect. She warned Tressel that they might pull it out this year.

Which got the coach thinking. At Thursday's staff meeting, he threw out a suggestion: "What if we got the Statue of Liberty in this week?"

The Statue of Liberty is a musty old sleight-of-hard in which the quarterback fakes a pass, then hands the ball to a running back. On first-and-10 at his own 28-yard line, Smith whirls to his left and fires a pass into the flat . . . but where is the ball? It's been plucked from the quarterback's hand by Pittman, who sprints 26 yards around right end. When the story behind that play-call appears in *SI* the following week, Bebe will get calls from five different states. The *Akron Beacon-Journal*'s Marla Ridenour tracks down "Buckeye Bebe" Webner, 79, and writes a delightful little feature. Bebe, it turns out, had sent Tressel's mother, Eloise, a pair of Buckeye earrings shortly after her son landed the Ohio State job. She worried, you see, that Eloise would only have Youngstown State earrings. (Do they make Penguin earrings?)

The two arranged to meet, but Eloise died in August 2001, before her son's first Ohio State game. "That's when Webner decided to begin writing Tressel," wrote Ridenour, "mainly to thank him for beating Michigan. She still has the four or five notes he sent in reply."

She'll be wanting to drop him another note. Six plays after Pittman's long run, the Wolverines are guilty of a personal foul— a helmet-to-helmet hit on Smith at the right sideline—that is equal measures dumb and devastating. The roughing-the-passer call on Crable gives the Buckeyes a new set of downs. Three snaps later Smith throws his fourth TD pass of the night, a 13-yarder to Robiskie, the flanker from Chagrin Falls, Ohio, who strikes a storklike pose while making sure he gets one foot down in the end zone. The play is reviewed: he did.

The Wolverines answer with a desperation score. They trail 42–39 with 2:18—there's still hope!—but Ginn gobbles up the onside kick. Three Pittman runs kill the rest of the clock.

. . . .

MAURICE CLARETT WAS the hero the last time I covered The Game in Columbus. Craig Krenzel was borne to midfield on the shoulders of delirious fans, and police pepper-sprayed an unruly mob in one of the end zones. Even though I was at least 20 yards away, my eyes began to water up and sting, and I thought: Hey, this stuff really works.

No pepper spray this time, but the scene, to me, is scarier. I'm swept to midfield, where I find myself stuck in a logjam of heaving, unreasonable humanity. I start thinking about British soccer riots, and actually feel a twinge of panic. Breathing deeply, I work my painstaking way toward the near sideline, then to the south end zone. The crowd has thinned a bit when I run into Brutus Buckeye. I once attended a mascot camp in Blacksburg, Virginia. I know they're not allowed to speak while they're in character. That doesn't stop me from telling Brutus, "Hey, I was at a concert last night, and this guy was singing about you." He knows what I'm talking about.

With the win, the Buckeyes earn a trip to the BCS National Championship Game, to be held seven weeks hence—that's not a typo—in Glendale, Arizona. They claim their first outright Big Ten title in 24 years. Smith locks up the Heisman Trophy, and Tressel's record against Michigan improves to 5-1. This makes me feel a little sorry for Carr, a good coach and a good man who now stands before the press, his long face even longer than usual, explaining why he declined to deliver a win-one-for-the-Gipper speech—to use the passing of his friend and mentor "as a motivational deal. That would have been to dishonor him," says Carr, a notorious stoic who is now nearly overcome with emotion. Instead, he told the Wolverines that the best way to honor Schembechler was "to play in a way that would have made him proud."

On my way downstairs from the Ohio State interview room—the locker room is closed, naturally, because that's how Woody did it—I push through a set of double doors on the second floor, which is off-limits to such rabble as this reporter. Here, players, coaches, and their families congregate after the game. I stroll around, I say hi to Ginn, with whom I have a running joke about the *SI* cover jinx. (The Buckeyes lost to Texas in 2005 after Ginn appeared in full flight on the front of the magazine.) Ted, I said, I'll do what I can to make sure you're not on this week's cover.

Big smile. "Now, you don't need to go and do *that*." (Smith will grace our cover that week, on the run, eyes downfield, leaning into a throw, the very essence of field generalship.) Behind Ted Ginn, I spy Ted Ginn Sr., whom I hadn't seen since visiting him at home in Cleveland 14 months earlier. I can't imagine the pride he must be feeling. Seven of his former players are on the roster; three of them start. One of them is his namesake, who has just played his final game in the Horseshoe (though only the Ginns know that), and will go down as one of the most electrifying players in the history of Buckeye football. Another, who is not his son but who calls him "Dad," just put a stranglehold on the Heisman.

As we walk back toward the field, he talks about the journeys of those two teammates. "There was a time when Troy and Ted were considered throwaways," he recalls. "But we stayed with them, got them to believe, then got some other people to believe." Among those people was Tressel, who stands exposed tonight as the pen-pal to septuagenarian widows, and whom Ginn credits with nothing less than "helping save Troy's life."

It isn't exactly a one-way street. The Bucks are 12–0 and Glendale-bound. Shaking Ginn's hand, I tell him I'll see him in the desert. The mob has dispersed from the field, leaving behind a potpourri of refuse, cups, programs, wrappers, and discarded copies of tonight's special-edition *Columbus Dispatch*, with its blaring headline: ONE MORE TO GO!

## CHAPTER 15

# With Our Bare Hands

**N**ovember 25, Los Angeles —Knute Rockne died before his time, at the age of 53. The man who put Notre Dame on the map was one of eight people on a Fokker F-10 Trimotor that crashed on March 31, 1931, in a wheat field near Bazaar, Kansas. There were no survivors. An investigation revealed that "fatigue cracks" in one of the wings— Trimotors were made of a "wood laminate"—caused it to tear off the plane in midflight.

**BCS TOP 10**

1. *Ohio State*
2. *Michigan*
3. *USC*
4. *Florida*
5. *Notre Dame*
6. *Arkansas*
7. *West Virginia*
8. *Wisconsin*
9. *Louisville*
10. *LSU*

This week the Fighting Irish travel to USC for the 77th edition of the nation's most storied and sublime intersectional rivalry. The sad irony of the series is that, by helping to bring it about, Rockne set in motion the events that led to his own demise. A legend in his own time, Rockne was not immune to the allure of Hollywood, and the attraction was mutual. When it fell from the sky, Flight 599 was en route from Kansas City to Los Angeles, where the coach was to have signed a contract to appear in a movie called *The Spirit of Notre Dame.*

How did ND-'SC get its start? As the editor of the *Shinbone Express* tells Jimmy Stewart in *The Man Who Shot Liberty Valance*, "When the legend becomes fact, print the legend." In that spirit, allow me to first share the legend of how the rivalry was midwifed. Six years before he died, Rockne shared a train ride—from Lincoln, Nebraska, to Chicago—with one Gwynn Wilson, a representative of the USC Athletic Department. Wilson had been sent by his superiors to sell Rockne on a two-game series with the Trojans. But the Irish where already traveling so much in those days that they'd earned the mercenary moniker "Rockne's Ramblers." The answer was no.

But, wouldn't you know, Wilson's wife was in the parlor car, taking tea with Bonnie Rockne. The Fighting Irish had received a rude reception from the Cornhuskers in Nebraska. Mrs. Wilson spoke of the hospitality and golden sunlight awaiting visitors to Southern California. After Rockne went back to his berth and got an earful from his wife, he returned to where Wilson was seated and asked, matter-of-factly, "Now what did you say about a home-and-home series?"

While the timely intercession of Bonnie Rockne remains a treasured part of the lore of this series, her role appears to have been exaggerated. In his 1993 book *Shake Down the Thunder,* which relied on a previously undiscovered cache of Rockne's personal and athletic correspondence, author Murray Sperber provides convincing evidence that the Notre Dame–USC series got the green light only after a delegation of Trojans officials arrived in South Bend with a cash offer the Irish could not refuse—"such a fluttering guarantee," Rockne wrote to a friend, "that they could not turn it down."

Regardless of its provenance, this annual game has bloomed into a peerless cross-country classic. Much is made of the obvious, external differences: the flash of Hollywood versus the sturdy values of the heartland; the golden light of the Pacific sunset versus the light reflected off the Golden Dome. But the truth is, the two schools have a fair amount in common. Both are conservative at their core, Notre Dame more so, but not by much. Both are private schools that have made significant strides in recent decades upgrading their academic reputations. And this rivalry would never have been born, or survived so long, if the principals did not share a fearlessness, a "bring 'em on" ethos that underlies their scheduling philosophy (Notre Dame's weakness for the service academies notwithstanding). Like Tony Montana in *Scarface*, they got *ballss*.

This is what lifts Domers versus Trojans above the common run of college football border wars and conference-mandated showdowns. No one is forcing them to do it. In a landscape littered with "buy games" like Penn State versus Buffalo and Nebraska versus Nicholls State, Notre Dame versus Southern California serves as an example of what college football could be. The risk has paid off for both sides; each has used the other to burnish its legend.

With apologies to *Harper's* (and a nod to NDNation.com, where I found the superb essay from which many of these figures were mined), a Trojan-Domer index:

Number of times ND has beaten 'SC: 42
ND's rank, in number of victories over Trojans, among 'SC's all-
    time opponents: 1
Number of 'SC wins over ND: 31
'SC's rank, in number of victories over ND, among ND's all-time
    opponents: 1
Number of undefeated ND seasons spoiled by 'SC: 3
Number of undefeated 'SC seasons spoiled by ND: 2
Number of Heisman winners to play in the game: 14
ND Heisman winners: 7
'SC Heisman winners: 7
Number of times the national champion (AP or UPI) has played
    in this game: 14

Number of times ND beat USC between 1966 and 1982: 3
Number of times, in those three seasons, ND went on to win the
    national title: 3

"There's so much bitterness between Ohio State and Michigan
because they rub up against each other," says Holtz, who spent a
year on Woody Hayes's staff in Columbus. "They're in the same
conference; Michigan recruits heavily in Ohio. And the game usually determines the Big Ten championship."

The animosity is ratcheted down between Notre Dame and
USC, in Holtz's view, "because you don't live next door to 'em, you
don't interact that much with Southern California alums." Holtz,
who went 9-1-1 against the Trojans—the loss not coming until his
final season in South Bend—subjected his players every year to a
quiz on the lore of the rivalry. "It's a tradition of great players,
great coaches, and great games," Holtz told me. "I wanted guys to
know how fortunate they were to play in it."

Surely it was with more affection than malice that Carroll
opened his November 21 press conference with this apology:
"Sorry I'm a little late. I was reading Charlie's press conference
quotes."

Following Notre Dame's 41–9 win over Army (would it be in
poor taste to call it a "cakewalk"?), Weis was asked if he'd sneaked
a peek at any USC film ahead of time. The ironclad rules governing the secret union of American football coaches dictate that
there is only one acceptable answer. To say "yes" in this case is to
admit that you are guilty of "looking ahead," of failing to "take
each game one at a time."

Yes, replied Weis, trampling convention and precedent. "I've
watched every game, every play: offense, defense, special teams."
He catches himself. "No, I have not watched every play on special
teams."

Looking at the seven opponents on Notre Dame's schedule
after Michigan State—a septet dubbed "The Munificent Seven"

by NBC.com's John Walters—you can see where Weis might have found the odd hour here and there, to sneak away for an assignation with some cut-ups of the Trojans' goal-line package. Of Purdue, Stanford, UCLA, North Carolina, and the service academies, only the Bruins put much of a scare in the Irish. Notre Dame will bring a 10-1 record and a No. 6 ranking to L.A.

Asked to characterize his relationship with Carroll, Weis said, "Pete and I, we knew each other. We're friendly, but not friends."

It may not be personal between Weis and Carroll. But is it personal between Carroll and Weis?

Carroll hasn't told me that; I've simply inferred it. I could be wrong. Maybe his heart is full of affection for the Robot Genius, as Domers refer to their big-brained head coach. Maybe Carroll wasn't rolling his eyes at the bouquets cast at Weis's feet during the big guy's first season at Notre Dame; at the breathless descriptions of his offensive acumen.

Come to think of it, it probably doesn't stick in Carroll's craw, doesn't gnaw at him in the least that, two years after he was fired as head coach of the Patriots, Bill Belichick guided them to the first of three Super Bowls they would win in a four-year span. Belichick's offensive coordinator during that span, the man credited with molding Tom Brady, the former sixth-round pick, into the icily efficient, serial–Super Bowl MVP? The Robot Genius, naturally.

Carroll, remember, is the guy who has elevated competition to a religion. So it would make sense that he'd want to stick it to Weis every chance he got.

In addition to being a collision of grand football traditions, Notre Dame versus USC is a clash of starkly opposed coaching philosophies. On this side, you have Weis, the Son of Tuna, a Parcells disciple who writes admiringly of his old boss's methods in *No Excuses*:

"Bill's coaching philosophy with the players was to pressure them hard—stay on them, never relax, never let up. Even when things went well he would still tell his assistant coaches to keep the pressure on. Players never knew where they stood with Bill, and that was exactly how he wanted it. He wanted them uneasy."

Never relax? The way Carroll sees it, you're screwed if you don't relax. How else are you going to get to that place where mind and body are in harmony; where fears and doubts are quieted and you are free to rip it up on the field?

Or, as Tim Gallwey might put it, how are you going to quiet the "constant 'thinking' activity of Self 1, the ego mind, which causes interference with the natural capabilities of Self 2"?

Gallwey, one of Carroll's favorite writers, is the author of *The Inner Game of Tennis*, a 30-year-old guide on how to stop trying too hard and get out of your own way. Four days before the Notre Dame game, Carroll turns a question on his linebacking corps into a manifesto on the greatness inherent in every individual (with particular emphasis on those individuals who have accepted football scholarships to USC): "We're always trying to find things that individual players do in a special manner. Then we try to fit it in and allow them to demonstrate what's unique about their nature and their style. . . . We try to use them in ways that best express their ability. I think it took us a while to really start to display and exhibit the true nature that this group has."

IT TURNS OUT that the true nature of these linebackers, and this defense, is to take over games. On November 11 against the Oregon Ducks, the Trojans defense took the ball away twice, deep in Ducks territory, setting up the offense's second and third touchdowns in a 35–10 laugher. Oregon had come into the Coliseum ranked 21st in the country and averaging 35 points per game. The Ducks left wondering whether No. 96 for the Trojans had been Lawrence Jackson or Lawrence Taylor.

The Trojan known as LoJack began the season with some serious buzz. A redshirt junior defensive end, Jackson was coming off a 10-sack season. The Trojans sports info office was touting him as an All-America candidate. That talk faded as Jackson was held sackless through eight games. Yes, he was being double- and triple-teamed. But part of his statistical slump, he told me after the season, stemmed from the fact that he was trying too hard, being too tough on himself when he didn't produce.

Finally, he picked up Gallwey's book, which Carroll had given him him weeks earlier. Having absorbed some of the author's message about "learning to relax" and "trusting himself," he went out and turned Oregon's vaunted Quack Attack into Duck *confit*, racking up three sacks and 10 tackles. It's amazing what you can do when you get out of your own way.

The good news for USC had begun on November 9. In the most historic game in Piscataway since 1869, when Rutgers defeated Princeton 6–4 in the first college football game ever played, the Scarlet Knights upended No. 3 Lousville, 28–25. The anarchy on the field at Rutgers Stadium following Jeremy Ito's game-winning field goal prefigured the rankings chaos to follow, as two more Top 5 teams went down in flames on Saturday. No. 5 Auburn was ambushed by Georgia. That night, in glittering, cosmopolitan Manhattan, Kansas, Texas quarterback Colt McCoy, who'd been flat out ripping it up since that loss to Ohio State, injured his right shoulder on the Longhorns' first series against Kansas State. Without the Real McCoy, Texas bowed to Kansas State, 45–42.

The seventh-ranked Trojans went sailing back up to No. 3, the same slot they'd occupied before traveling to Corvallis two weeks earlier. It was as if the Oregon State loss had been magically erased.

USC kept right on rolling, coolly dispatching the Cal Bears on November 18, a win that assured Carroll's squad an unprecedented fifth straight Pac-10 championship. Suffering through a conspicuously quiet night was Bears wide out DeSean Jackson, a Long Beach Poly High product who'd signed with Cal after backing out of his verbal commitment to the Trojans on letter-of-intent day in 2005. Jackson, who had described himself as "the closest thing to Reggie Bush," would finish with a season-low two catches for an un-Bush-like 41 yards. DeSean, known as MeSean by 'SC partisans still chapped by his 11th-hour defection, is never quite the same safety after safely Kevin Ellison nearly beheads him on a crossing route early in the first quarter.

USC's 23–9 victory, coupled with Michigan's loss in the Horseshoe three time zones away, makes it likely—not a slam dunk, but likely—that the Trojans will move up to No. 2 in the BCS standings, if not this week, then next.

When the BCS rankings are released the following Monday, the Trojans are still stuck at No. 3, a whisker behind Michigan. But the Wolverines' regular season is over. USC can leapfrog them with a win over the Irish.

I am standing at Goux's Gate a few minutes before 4:00 p.m. the day after Thanksgiving. I want to see the ritual. I want to witness the laying on of hands.

To set foot on Howard Jones Football Field, where the team practices, Trojans pass through Goux's Gate. It is unheard of for a player to pass through the Gate without "tapping in"—touching the concrete mantel under which they pass. To the right of the sturdy double doors is a bronze relief of Goux, the late, great Trojan assistant coach. (From a tonsorial standpoint the artist has done him no favors: Goux's hair looks like Jimmy Johnson's.)

Here comes Ken Norton down the walkway from Heritage Hall. The linebackers coach is in conversation with Rocky Seto, who coaches the secondary. Very soon after, Carroll comes bounding down the lane. Before "tapping in," he stands in front of the bust, then runs his hands over Goux's face. I've never asked him why. It's clearly a private little ritual. Plus, the reason seems obvious. For good luck, good karma, to tap into Marv's passion and intensity.

Goux came to life for me earlier this week in a way he hadn't before. David Baker, the Arena Football League commissioner and father of the Trojans' best lineman, passed along an e-mail he'd received from a Goux-era Trojan who recalled a speech Goux delivered at Notre Dame Stadium on the eve of a game. While addressing the squad, Goux apparently wandered the field, inspecting the turf, repeatedly crying out, as if in a stage production, "Where is it? Where is it?"

Finally, he stopped and announced tearfully, "This is the spot. This is where they got me.

"I was clipped from behind right here," he continued, pointing at the offending patch of Kentucky bluegrass. Then he ordered the team to gather 'round: "Now listen to me. Notre Dame ended my dream as a player. They ended it right here where we stand together. I'll never be able to forget it or change it. I can, however, bring a football team here every other year with the best players the world has ever seen. A football team that is a great big family, whose only living, breathing desire is to be allowed by God one more opportunity to hit a Notre Dame football player as hard as humanly possible.

"Tomorrow we wake as one. Tomorrow we take the body. Tomorrow we are devastating, play after play, every man until the final whistle. If I see any man look up at the scoreboard, I'll kill him. To hell with the score—we came here for more than that. Tomorrow we take a program's heart and tear it to pieces with our bare hands."

FORTY-FIVE MINUTES BEFORE kickoff I watch Kevin Braun, the Leprechaun, take a deep breath and emerge from the tunnel at the west end of the Coliseum. In the space of 30 feet he strides into his character, transforming himself from a nice kid from Lancaster County, Pennsylvania, into a head-bobbing, arm-waving, Trojan-antagonizing bantam rooster, inviting the hostile crowd of nearly 92,000 to go ahead, give him their best shot. And they do. He is booed, and a guy hanging over the railing shouts, "Don't hurt the midget!"

It bugs some 'SC fans that when he wins the toss, Carroll likes to put his defense on the field first. It bugs them now. Brady Quinn goes right after cornerback Terrell Thomas on the game's first play: Rhema McKnight outleaps the cornerback for a 38-yard gain up the left sideline. When the drive stalls at the 'SC 29-yard line, I ask of no one in particular in the press box, "Does Notre Dame have anyone who can hit a 46-yard field goal?" Five Notre Dame beat writers answer as one: "No." Quinn overthrows McKnight to end the drive.

Booty can't find an open receiver and throws to his outlet, tailback C. J. Gable, who seems to be staking a claim to the tailback job late in the season, and who picks up 21 yards to midfield. On third down Fred Davis appears wide open in the soft middle of the Irish defense. Despite hard pressure from Abiamiri, Booty gets it to him for a pickup of 11. On first-and-goal at the nine, Booty drills Jarrett with a touchdown pass. Ndukwe, the Irish safety, has excellent coverage. It doesn't matter.

McKnight drops a look-in pass on third-and-five. Price's short, wobbly punt is fielded by Desmond Reed at his own 31-yard line. Reed, a 5'9" tailback and kick returner from San Gabriel, has been having a quiet season. It's remarkable that he's having a season at all. There was general mirth when the Irish took the field at Notre Dame Stadium for their walk-through the previous October. The bluegrass was conspicuously, almost ridiculously long— four inches, by some estimates. Coincidence or gamesmanship? As the *L.A. Times* later pointed out, a reporter at a press conference in early 2005 had noted USC's team speed, then asked Weis to comment on his own squad's overall speed.

"I think the grass needs to be longer," he replied, to general guffaws. "Next question."

When Reed turned and planted his right foot to field a kickoff in the second quarter of that storied 2005 game, the ligaments exploded. As he would later tell the *L.A. Times*, "The grass was real long and mushy, that's why I think my foot got stuck. . . . My knee had nowhere to go."

In addition to tearing ligaments, Reed stretched the peroneal nerve, according to the *Times*, leaving him with a condition called a "drop foot"—his right foot drags slightly when he walks. Despite Herculean rehabilitation, Reed's return remained up in the air through the summer. I noted during an August scrimmage that he had lost half a step but none of his moxie. When a pass intended for him fell incomplete in the end zone, Reed reached around to the referee's back pocket and threw the zebra's yellow flag. In brief chats with him, I have been struck by his utter lack of self-pity.

Thirteen and a half months after he suffered that devastating injury, it's impossible not to be happy for Reed as he takes Price's punt up the right sideline, cuts niftily to his left at midfield, and delivers a 43-yard return, setting up Booty's second touchdown pass to Jarrett. Mario Danelo is tacking on the extra point as I jot in my notebook, *Payback's a bitch.*

Facing a fourth-and-one at the 10-yard line, leading 14–3, Carroll turns up his nose at the field goal. Gable gashes the Irish for nine yards; Zbikowski grabs the freshman's facemask while taking him down. On second-and-goal at the one, Kalil stoves in the Irish front and Booty scores on the sneak.

It is on Notre Dame's next possession that Quinn makes the play that Carroll will find more galling than any other in this game. Dropping back to pass, he steps up in the pocket, pulls the ball down, and shows a surprising burst for a 6'4", 230-pounder, sprinting 60 yards up the left sideline before being taken down hard by Taylor Mays, the freshman safety. Quinn looks gimpy getting back to the huddle; he's suffered a slight cartilage tear in his knee, but this won't come out until after the season. The longest rush of his career is squandered when a freight-train hit by Keith Rivers relieves Darius Walker of both the ball and his senses. As Walker lies groggily on the turf, Trojans tackle Fili Moala recovers the fumble.

The Irish show spine. After their defense holds, linebacker Steve Quinn, no relation to the quarterback, slices through 'SC's protection to block Woidneck's punt. Quinn smothers the ball at the seven—precisely where Walker fumbled it away. It takes Brady

Quinn one play, a crisp little play-action pass to tight end Marcus Freeman, to get the Irish in the end zone. Okay. It's a game again. 21–10.

Having threatened to turn this into one of those Willingham-era thrashings, the Trojans are allowing the Irish to hang around. Taking note, as Michigan had, of Zbikowski's tendency to be juuust a bit too aggressive in run support, Booty's been luring him to the line with play fakes, then throwing into the vacant area behind him. Now, looking for more of those cheap yards, the quarterback targets Steve Smith on a skinny post. This time, Mike Richardson is on the case. The Irish corner peels off Smith and steps in front of the pass for his third interception in two games.

Booty is picked off on his next throw, as well, a screen pass to the tight end that is plucked from the air by dreadlocked defensive tackle Trevor Laws, who read the play all the way.

The game turns on what happens—or fails to happen—after those turnovers. Following the first interception, the offense of the No. 6 team in the nation, quarterbacked by the guy who will be the second quarterback taken in the upcoming NFL draft, gains seven yards on three plays, and punts. Following the second interception: three plays, four yards, punt.

Right now Southern California has the best defense in the country.

BEFORE TROY SMITH put up spectacular numbers against that proud Michigan defense, there had been talk that Quinn could make a run at the Heisman with a monster game in the Coliseum. There were precedents: Carson Palmer and Matt Leinart had used Notre Dame defenses as trampolines for their successful Heisman campaigns. Irish fans held out hope going into this game that turnabout might be fair play.

If Smith had the trophy locked up at halftime of the Michigan game, Quinn was officially out of the running at halftime against 'SC. He completed eight of 23 passes in the first half, for 109 yards and a touchdown. As one USC coach will declaim, à la the *Seinfeld* Soup Nazi, "No Heisman for you!"

THE GAME WILL end at 8:37 p.m., but it is over, in my mind, about an hour or so earlier, after the ninth play of 'SC's first drive of the second half. Booty's got his mojo back: he's completed passes to his tight end, Davis, and to third receiver Chris McFoy. Gable and Washington are getting nice chunks—five yards, six yards, five yards—on the ground. On first down at the Notre Dame 25-yard line, ball at the left hash mark, his back to the Peristyle, Booty drops backs, looks to his left, and, finding no one, heaves the ball across the field, toward the right sideline. I assume he is throwing it away to avoid a sack until a startled roar arises from that side of the stadium and consumes the Coliseum. His body parallel to the ground, like Superman, Jarrett has snatched the ball out of the air with his left hand, managing to drag his feet in the field of play while sailing out of bounds.

Consider that this pass had come from the far hash mark. Having traveled roughly 40 yards, it is coming in hot, and Jarrett spears it in full flight. Asked afterward to discuss this otherwordly feat, Jarrett explains, simply, "It's nothing new. It's just me being me."

He's right. Isn't new. It's the sort of magic that had spoiled Trojans fans during three years of Leinart and White and Bush. When Jarrett comes down with that circus catch, it feels like those days are back. It feels like Notre Dame is done. Zbikowski mugs Jarrett on the next play, a first-and-goal at the Irish six, and is called for interference. I read this question into the disgusted expression on his face: *How the hell else are we supposed to stop this guy?*

Washington's two-yard plunge on the next play puts the Trojans up, 28–10. Notre Dame answers with a 10-play touchdown drive, but the Irish defense can't buy a key stop in the second half. With 8:30 left in the game and the Trojans sitting on a 31–17 lead, Booty has a safety valve receiver wide open in the flat for an easy 10-yard gain on the next series—a sure thing. Instead he fires toward the receiver flashing open on a post pattern. That would be Jarrett, who makes the catch, spins, stiff-arms a defender, and accelerates into the end zone for a 43-yard touchdown, his third of the game. Nagging injuries and an inconsistent 'SC offense had depressed the junior's NFL stock earlier in the season, but he is making some money tonight.

The good news for Notre Dame is that they grind 14 plays for another touchdown. The bad news is, it's . . . taking them . . . much too long . . . to score. With 3:39 to play, they trail 37–24. We all know what's coming next—the whole gang of us standing under the goalposts behind the east end zone: me, John Walters, SI.com's Stewart Mandel, and USC alum (and former sports information intern) Will Ferrell.

Notre Dame's onside kick works to perfection. For the home team. The Irish load up the left side, but Cushing comes knifing in, snatches the ball out of the air on the first hop, and shows serious wheels motoring the other way for a 42-yard touchdown. The Coliseum boils over as the Bergen Flash, as Carroll calls him, pads the lead. No one is more jacked up than Ferrell, who jumps up and down while thrusting both arms to the sky. As he celebrates, his sweater rides up, baring his midriff—the same underbelly exposed by Ferrell's bearded passive-aggressive Gene Frenkle, who "explored the studio space" with a cowbell in one of the best *Saturday Night Live* skits ever.

WEIS'S FIRST WORDS to Carroll after the game: "Nice butt-kicking." He slaps hands with Ellison, the safety, shakes hands with Pat Ruel, the offensive line coach. Thomas Williams, the linebacker who's been pressed into emergency service as a full-back, has a hug for Charlie, who recruited him hard out of Vacaville (California) High. Weis is in no rush to get off the field, and I realize he's looking for someone. He's searching for his fellow Garden Stater, Jarrett, who, even by Jarrett's standards, had a monstrous night. Finally they find each other and share a hug, during which Weis would have been forgiven for whispering, "Take it from a guy with four Super Bowl rings—you belong in the League. Go now!"

ESPN analyst and ex-'SC quarterback Sean Salisbury is on the field with his son, Dylan, whom Weis makes it a point to greet.

"Hang in there, buddy," says the older Salisbury.

"Hey, I'm fine," Weis replies. "Don't worry about me."

In the long term, there is no need. Once Weis gets a few more of his recruiting classes into school, the Irish will start winning these marquee games. In the short term, there will be hiccups. Notre Dame will return just ten starters next season—four on offense, and Brady Quinn isn't one of them. When the two coaches run into each other a second time, Carroll asks Weis—out of genuine concern, I'm certain—"What are you guys gonna do next year?"


IT NOW FEELS predetermined, as close as you can get to a sure thing. The Trojans are going to Glendale. They've played for the national title in each of the past three seasons, and now, like swallows to San Juan Capistrano, they're going back. It's what this program does.

Kiffin, the offensive coordinator, is a bit of a wet blanket in victory. "We've still got work to do," he tells me in a near-empty locker room. "We're not a great offense. If we were, we wouldn't have turned the ball over twice.

"I mean, we're getting better," he adds. "But I'll tell you this: Last year's team would've scored 60 on these guys."

Weeks later, I would take inventory, combing through notes and transcripts, looking for evidence of hubris, of Trojans looking past their next opponent to the postseason.

I find the opposite. To a man, the Trojans refused to lift their gaze from the following week's opponent. There was nose tackle Sedrick Ellis on the field after the win, a 6'1", 295-pound Cassandra, steering reporters away from the subject of the BCS. "We definitely made a statement," he allowed, when asked if the Trojans deserve to be bumped to No. 2. "But that wasn't the goal. Remember, we have UCLA next week."

He was unconsciously echoing Carroll, who bristled later while recounting an exchange with Weis, who told him, "Good luck in the national championship."

"Charlie, you know I don't care about that," came Carroll's reply. "We play UCLA next week."

# CHAPTER 16

# You're Going to Need Some Help Today

**D**ecember 2, Pasadena, Calif. —An anecdote left over from my last visit to Notre Dame will serve us nicely here: Recall, if you will, my friend Brian Murphy, the radio personality and UCLA alum who had such an adverse reaction to the juggler. On October 20—the day before Brady Quinn slid a shiv between UCLA's ribs with that last-minute touchdown pass—Murph and some of his Bruins goombahs were strolling the campus, soaking up the

**BCS TOP 10**

*1. Ohio State*

*2. USC*

*3. Michigan*

*4. Florida*

*5. LSU*

*6. Louisville*

*7. Wisconsin*

*8. Boise State*

*9. Arkansas*

*10. Notre Dame*

ambience of what is sometimes called the Catholic Disneyland. It was a peak foliage weekend; the guys were tossing around a mini football, smiling at students and subway alumni.

Eager to visit the famous Grotto but clueless as to its where-abouts, they stopped a pair of passing priests. "They were walking along, hands clasped behind their backs, probably discussing the-ology," recalls Murph, who promptly interrupted them. "Excuse us," he said. "We're visiting from California. Could you direct us to the Grotto?"

It was the older priest, silver-haired, with a twinkle in his eye, who answered. When he did, Murph recalls, it was in a brogue "straight out of County Clare."

"So then, yew lads are lookin' fer the Grotto, eh? Well, 'tis no problem ta find it from hee-ur. Ye'll take this right, go fifty yards down the walk, then ta the right, ye'll find the lovely Grotto."

It was so perfect, such a quintessentially Notre Dame moment, Murph recalls, "My first thought was, this guy has got to be an out-of-work Chicago actor imported by the university for the weekend to give directions to tourists."

The Californians had thanked the padre and were walking away when he called after them, "So yew boys are from UCLA then? Well, yer prayers'll be heard, but not answered. The Lord'll be too busy granting Notre Dame the vict'ry.

"Yer chances would be greatly improved," he added, "if yer coach were still named Terry DonaHUE."

Before he became a vaguely grating talking head on football broadcasts; before he bombed as general manager for the 49ers— "We have a lot of stars, just no one you've ever heard of," he declared on his way out the door, and he was half-right—Terry Donahue was a damn good head coach for UCLA. Like hair bands and David Lynch, he peaked in the 1980s, during which decade his Bruins won three Rose Bowls. Donahue's teams won or shared five Pac-10 titles; he more than held his own against the Trojans. To UCLA fans, he represents the good old days.

The post-Donahue era has been marked by long stretches of mediocrity interspersed with briefer periods of excellence that end, invariably, with stunning late-season Enron-like collapses. The most recent of those came the previous November, when third-year head coach Karl Dorrell took his undefeated club to Arizona. The Bruins were 8-0, and ranked fifth in the BCS poll.

The Wildcats, 2-6 and playing for pride, took them apart, 52–14. Two weeks later, USC gained 679 yards of total offense in a 66–19 emasculation of their cross-town rivals.

The last-minute choke job against the Irish five weeks earlier had been out of character for UCLA, in that it contributed to a *mid*-season collapse, rather than the team's customary late-season implosion. The loss in South Bend was the second in a four-game skid that threatened to cost Dorrell his job. Coming off the last of those defeats, a two-touchdown loss at Cal, he hatched a plan to stanch the bleeding. With three games left in the season, Dorrell has sold the squad on a "mini-season." With a strong finish, they could cleanse the taste of that four-game losing streak; could become bowl-eligible; they could—this part was left unsaid—spare their coach the inconvenience of having to find a Realtor and get a whole bunch of new resumes printed up.

Sitting in my nightstand is a slender volume by John C. Maxwell called *The 21 Indispensable Qualities of a Leader*, of which my wife, after perusing the table of contents, estimated that I possess "three, maybe two." The book was assigned reading for UCLA players, who took part in something called Football 101 after the 2004 season. Football 101 was a Dorrell-mandated series of meetings and assignments designed to improve communication, "to give players and coaches a chance to connect," he told me. His hope was that, once they'd "connected," the members of the team could develop a trust and belief in one another that had been lacking in his first two seasons.

Dorrell is an ex–Bruins wide receiver who was thrown into the deep end when he got the UCLA job following the 2002 season, at the age of 39. A highly regarded assistant—his most recent stop had been as receivers coach for the Denver Broncos—he had no head-coaching experience. His transition was often turbulent. It was left to him to figure out everything from where he was supposed to stand on the sidelines to how best to deal with college students.

The Bruins were 6-0 when I visited Dorrell in his office midway through the 2005 season, but living dangerously, cheating death with dramatic comebacks. "Have we been perfect? No," he allowed. "But it's great to strive for perfection." The Bruins were working toward the contest, he said "when everything just clicks. I call it The Elusive Day."

The Elusive Day eluded UCLA in 2005 on account of the semipermeable membrane otherwise known as its defense, which gave up 35 or more points in six of its last eight games. Dorrell knew how to handle that. The 14th Quality of an Indispensable Leader is "Problem Solving" (a heading quickly followed by the Maxwellian profundity, "You Can't Let Your Problems Be a Problem"). We learn in this chapter that "effective leaders" are willing to "accept the truth." It has long been a strength of Dorrell's that when things are going poorly, he has been willing to look in the mirror and accept the cold, hard truth that the fault lies . . . with one or more of his assistants, whom he summarily fires.

Taking the fall in the wake of the 2005 season was defensive coordinator Larry Kerr. His replacement, DeWayne Walker, knew his way around SoCal. Walker played his high school ball right up the street from the Rose Bowl at John Muir High in Pasadena. Nomadic even by the peripatetic standards of the profession, Walker made stops at five different colleges before catching on with Carroll, then head coach of the Patriots, in 1988. When Carroll was fired, Belichick kept Walker on, but not for long. After he took the 'SC job in 2001, Carroll's first hire was Walker, who stuck around for all of one season before bouncing back to the NFL. When Dorrell hired him away from the Washington Redskins, one of the qualities that made Walker attractive was the fact that he knew, better than anyone on the Bruins staff, the inner workings of Carroll's mind. The Bruins had yet to beat 'SC in this millennium, and Dorrell was getting a little desperate.

I'M WALKING TO the media gate of the Rose Bowl when a surfer dude in board shorts pedals past. He's a 30-something guy—possibly late 20s, but not aging well—in a white cut-off T-shirt whose hand-lettered legend reads, BOTH TEAMS ARE WINNERS.

Certainly the scenery at the game known by some as the Silicone Bowl is extraordinary. The Rose Bowl is a world-class venue, lined with palm trees, ringed by the spectacular San Gabriel Mountains, all under a cloudless sky today. While taking a lap around the field before kickoff, I regret not having applied sunscreen. It is December 2.

Amidst the student managers and rent-a-cops on the 'SC sideline is a student with a superhero's build. "Dude," I ask him, "are you on a hunger strike? Your arms are, like, petite."

Brandon Hancock's arms are simian and rippling, actually, but he doesn't need to hear that. Hancock, you'll recall, is the senior fullback who tore up his knee in August. He told me earlier in the season that there was a slim chance he might suit up for the bowl game, but that idea has come and gone. After undergoing two ACL reconstructions to the same knee—doctors used cadaver tissue in the most recent procedure—he's got no meniscus left, so "the joint is close to being bone on bone." If he stays with football, he'll be a candidate for a full knee replacement before he's 30. He is an NFL-calibre talent who will never take a snap in the League.

He is 23, and has had seven orthopedic operations. He's had two serious ankle injuries. He dislocated his wrist while performing a power clean in 2004. "That was actually fairly serious," he says. And then there was the exploding pectoral. Ask Shaun Cody about that one.

Cody, a former Trojans defensive tackle, was Hancock's spotter a few years back for a set of bench presses. Lying supine, Hancock "felt a little tingle" as he lifted the weight off the rack. "As I lowered it, it was actually audible, like someone tearing cardboard, louder and louder and then a pop, like a gunshot, when the pectoral tendon tore off the bone. The muscle rolled up like a window shade under my skin. It was like an alien popping up under my shirt. The muscle thought it was still lifting the weight. It was moving and jumping around. I was slapping it to get it to stop. Cody almost threw up."

The surgeon who reattached the pectoral "did a fantastic job," reports Hancock, who may not have a football future, but at least has a symmetrical chest. Concerned that there may be no end to his stories of fractures and fickle connective tissue, I ask him about the Trojans offense.

More particularly, I want his take on how the attrition at fullback—as you'll remember, Hancock's was the first of three season-ending injuries suffered by Trojans at that position—has limited the 'SC attack.

I'll boil his answer down. It hurts three ways. It hurts with pass blocking. "When you have a fullback who's a good pass blocker," says Hancock, a Phi Beta Kappa now working on a master's degree, "you can help out your tackles. You can offset him to the weak side"—the side of the formation away from the tight end—"help him double-team defensive end, or pick up a blitzer."

Obviously, it hurts the running game. In short-yardage situations, you're forced to go one back, double tight end, "which makes it much easier for a defense to understand what you're doing," the Hulk explains. While there was no shortage of studly reserves, "We really didn't have a powerful blocking fullback," he says. While converted linebacker Thomas Williams is a beast, "he didn't really understand how zone blocking works. It takes a long time to learn position; that chemistry's not gonna be there overnight."

It hurts the passing game. "On passing downs it's much easier to disguise plays when you've got a fullback in the game," rather than a fourth or fifth receiver. "I could motion out, create a mismatch—a lot of linebackers didn't have the speed to cover me. It opened up a lot of things."

Deprived of that threat, the Trojans' aerial attack has grown more vanilla than in seasons past. As Walker will later note, "Their offense was predictable in some aspects, especially the passing game. They're very talented but in some respects it's not too complicated."

As Hancock tells me now, "When you have a fullback who is a good lead blocker, but who can also catch a pass out of the backfield, it presents problems for a defense. When you don't have that guy, it's limiting."

We are about to find out how limiting.


Dorrell's "mini-season" is going swimmingly. His guys followed those four straight losses with wins over Oregon State and Arizona State. A fortuitous bye week preceding the 'SC game gave UCLA's staff an extra week to prepare for the Trojans. DeWayne Walker bore down hard.

"What you always want to do," he says, invoking one of the lessons he took from Belichick, "is take away their best weapon and make someone else beat you." The guys UCLA decided to erase were named Jarrett and Smith. The Bruins would sell out to contain 'SC's star wide outs, "and take our chances against the run," Walker tells me after the game. "We've had a pretty good run defense all year, so we'll take a guy out of the box and use him to double Smith or Jarrett."

Meanwhile, he has made preparations to ensure that Booty will have the most miserable outing of his brief career as a starter. He will call a dizzying array of blitzes and stunts. He will mix coverages—from "aggressive cover two" to "doubling Jarrett and Smith with man-to-man on the other guys" to soft zone. The goal: to make Booty wonder what fresh hell lies in store for him on each and every snap.


Booty gets hit in the mouth on the first play from scrimmage by some blitzing linebacker. He gets the ball off, but just barely. Two plays later Kyle Williams jumps before the snap, the first of his three false starts on the day. He is the right tackle; his eagerness to get into his backpedal is a measure of how deeply the Bruins' speed-rushing ends, Bruce Davis and Justin Hickman, have burrowed into his psyche.

He isn't alone. Early in the game, Davis settles into his stance across from Baker, the All-American left tackle. "Sam Baker's eyes were about this big," Davis will say afterward, making a circle with thumb and forefinger. "I just told him, 'You're going to need some help today.' "

That help is not forthcoming. Booty extricates the O from that second-and-19 hole with an 18-yard completion to Fred Davis on a crosser. On the ensuing third-and-one, a blitzer jolts Thomas Williams behind the line of scrimmage. Having started at linebacker last season, Thomas is the latest in a series of at least six conscripts at fullback—guys glumly temping at that spot until Carroll lets them go back to their true positions. Knocked backward, he throws off the rhythm of this play. Washington gets nothing. On fourth-and-one, the fullback whiffs on his block. Washington gets less than nothing. Trojans lose the ball on downs.

USC's second possession: Kyle Williams's second false start in nine plays leads to third-and-long that compounds his anxiety and pumps up Hickman and Davis, who live for this down and distance. Kyle is beaten on the ensuing speed rush; Booty must step up—flee, actually—or risk debilitating personal injury. His rushed throw has no prayer. Bring on the punt team.

The longest touchdown drive against the Trojans this season—84 yards—was mounted by Arizona State. The Bruins now devour 91 yards in 12 plays. Aside from a 17-yard pass to his tailback, Cowan gets most of the yardage with his feet. The kid didn't find out he'd be starting until Wednesday; now he scrambles for 29, 16, 9, and, finally, 2 yards to get his team into the end zone.

With the offense completely confounded, the Trojans steal two points with special teams and defense. Woidneck's punt early in the second quarter is downed on the Bruins one-yard line. Center

Robert Chai is called for holding Sedrick Ellis in the end zone, resulting in a safety.

With the score 7–2, the Trojans get the ball back on a free kick. Now, with Bruce Davis pawing the turf opposite him, it is tight end Fred Davis's turn to false-start. Booty's pass on third-and-11—he's hurried again, unable to set his feet—picks up only eight. Punt team!

It is not until their fifth series that the Trojans find some semblance of a rhythm: taking 12 plays to move 66 yards for a touchdown. The score is 9–7 at the half.

IT WILL BE determined by amateur psychologists in the days and weeks that follow that the Trojans were victims of some unpreventable malaise. The task of "getting up" for four straight huge games on four consecutive Saturdays was judged, in the end, too Herculean. The poor Trojans simply lacked the emotional wherewithal to survive a classic "trap" game.

Booty and others will reject the "emotional letdown" theory out of hand. But there is an intensity gap in this game, and Walker comes closest to identifying its root cause. "We didn't have anything to lose," he later tells me. "No reason to play it safe, no reason not to let it rip."

The Trojans have gotten to the cusp of still another national title game by achieving peak performances the Carroll way. They've been relaxed, having fun, exhibiting their true nature by lighting up opponents.

As the reality has dawned that UCLA's defense has the upper hand, it is the Bruins who are loose, relaxed, and devastatingly effective. And it is the guys in USC's offensive huddle, with everything to lose, who are now playing as if they have everything to lose.

The Trojans' first drive of the second half is gutted by a personal foul, courtesy of right guard Chilo Rachal. Drive No. 2 is stunted by Kyle Williams's third false start. On their third drive—

the Bruins having just taken a 10–9 lead on a short field goal— Gable is stuffed and Hickman deflects a pass. The Trojans, God help them, are looking at another third-and-long.

On a broiling afternoon in Tempe 14 months earlier, the Trojans had found themselves in a similar situation. Trailing in the second half, unable to jump-start the passing game, Leinart came to the line of scrimmage on third down. Still groggy from a first-half shot to the head, he flipped a short pass to fullback David Kirtman on a little wheel route that went for 42 yards.

Here, today, in the Rose Bowl, the Trojans come out empty (no one in the backfield). The pressure, as it has been all day, is intense. Flustered by the proximity of 17 and 44, Hickman and Davis, Booty somehow loses his footing and sacks himself.

It was Sedrick Ellis who stood on the field at the Coliseum a week ago and warned against looking past UCLA, Ellis who drew the hold that resulted in the safety. And it is Ellis, 6'1", 295 pounds of distilled mayhem, who recovers a fumble at the Bruins 44-yard line. The Trojans need 15 yards to get in field goal range. Here is USC's best chance to reclaim the lead, gift-wrapped with a nice bow.

Thus begins the Trojans' resolute march . . . backward. Kyle Williams will catch immense flak after the game for his false-start hat trick, but no one on the offensive line is making 'SC fans forget about Ron Yary and Tony Boselli this afternoon. Rachal's third penalty of the day—his second false start—puts the Trojans in a hole that gets deeper on the next snap, as Gable is tackled from behind by blitzing linebacker Reggie Carter.

It is all leading to a crucial fourth-and-two. First play of the fourth quarter. Ball on the left hash. Kalil snaps the ball on the quick count, 'SC trying vainly to catch the Bruins flatfooted. Booty pitches left to Gable, who looks up to see a powder blue wave crashing over him. Linebacker Christian Taylor is a meteor up the middle: he hits Gable high. Deterred not in the slightest by the attempted cut block of Thomas Williams, freshman cornerback Alterraun Verner slices off the right edge and hits Gable low.

He and Taylor arrive simultaneously, flipping the tailback on his head—ass over teakettle, as the saying goes—for a four-yard loss. Dorrell, whose storied stoicism has led one local columnist to nickname him (a bit cruelly) Karl Dullard, now becomes more animated than anyone can remember, screaming (he has already lost his voice, we will later learn) and pumping his fist like Tiger Woods. This perfect day in Pasadena may also be The Elusive Day.

Six minutes later the Trojans yield a field goal, bringing the score to 13–9. More damaging than the three points is the six minutes UCLA runs off the clock.

Following another sad little three-and-out, the Trojans get the ball back with 5:52 left to play. They have failed to gain so much as a first down in their previous three possessions. After the punt, during a TV timeout, these ancient rivals have a kind of Jets versus Sharks moment. The Trojans, trying to psyche themselves up (and to remind the Bruins which of them is ranked No. 2 in the country and which is unranked), spill out onto the field and commence hopping and woofing at the boys in powder blue.

This infuriates Davis, the defensive end. "You want to jump up and down and pretend you're hyped when you're down with six minutes to go—it doesn't work like that," he will fume after the game. "We were hyped the whole time! They wanta show they're upbeat, that's fine—we'll do it right back."

Having fed left tackle Sam Baker a steady diet of speed, Davis fakes an outside rush, then cuts inside to sack Booty, who'd been looking for Jarrett up the right sideline. On third-and-14, with the pocket collapsing and flames licking at his feet and Jack Nicholson's axe coming through the bathroom door, Booty calmly releases a rope to Steve Smith, who is tackled one yard shy of the first down.

For a change, the Trojans *gain ground* in a short-yardage situation, Booty plowing behind Kalil for enough to move the sticks. He then connects on three short passes. On third-and-three with the clock under two minutes, Booty looks right and sees Smith in single coverage with Verner, the freshman corner. Smith literally turns the kid around, making his cut, then vacuums Booty's low throw for an 18-yard gain. Trojans ball, first-and-10 on the Bruins 24-yard line. Booty looks more comfortable than he has the entire half. Remember, this is the quarterback who grew up in the fourth quarter of that Oregon State game. He knows he can bring these guys back.

After Smith's big pickup, Booty hits McFoy for six. On second down he throws the ball away. With 1:15 left in the game, the Trojans are looking at third-and-four at UCLA's 18-yard line.

HAVING CALLED OFF the dogs late in that loss to Notre Dame, and been crucified for it, Walker will not make the same mistake twice. Even as Booty moves the Trojans inexorably up the field, the Bruins stay aggressive, keep blitzing, slanting, looping. Now, with the Trojans facing third down in the Bruins red zone, the call in the defensive huddle is "Sam Gold," which sounds like a malt liquor, but is in fact a defense that calls on weakside (Will) linebacker Eric McNeal to blitz.

Relegated to a backup role at the Will spot, McNeal had bugged Walker before the season to switch him back to safety. The coordinator told him the secondary was "pretty much set," and that he'd better get comfortable at the Will spot. He got most of his snaps on passing downs. ("The season didn't work out exactly the way I wanted," McNeal would tell me later. He has no complaints with the way it ended.)

On that third-and-four he cheats up to the right side of the line—his right—and allows the tight end a clean release. He takes five choppy steps toward Booty, then goes airborne, and gets his right hand on what was to have been a safe little dink pass to Smith. Pivoting in midair like a cat, he locates the ball, dives for it, plucks it from the warm air inches above the blades of Bermuda Bullseye, the grass favored by Rose Bowl agronomists.

The stadium detonates, the tectonic plates beneath the season undergo a massive shift. Just like that, someone else will play for the national championship. You see Booty, stunned, trying to process what has just happened, turning to leave the field. Carroll sets his jaw, hands on his hips. He looks stricken, the knowledge now irrevocable: *Not this year.* His agony is ambrosia to Bruins fans, who begrudge him his success more than followers of the Cal Bears, of the Fighting Irish, of the Razorbacks whose manhood the Trojans have taken two years running. Because they have to live with the guy.

SPEAKING OF ARKANSAS, the Razorbacks have rebounded handsomely since the Trojans opened that 55-gallon drum of whoopass on them in the season opener. The Hawgs rattled off 10 straight wins, earning the right to play Florida for the SEC championship. That game kicked off in the Georgia Dome an hour and a half after the start of the Silicone Bowl.

The Gators are up 17–7 at halftime, as the Trojans claw their way down the field on their final desperation drive.

Surfing YouTube.com for clips of the Bruins triumph, I spotted one labeled "Gators Men's Bathroom During UCLA USC Upset."

Sure enough, the videographer has captured the scene inside a Georgia Dome men's lavatory in the moments before, during, and after McNeal's interception. Forty or so guys have trained their eyes on a TV monitor, willing to postpone their business until they find out if the Bruins can finish the job. "Knock it down!" shouts one fan as Booty drops back, and then—bedlam in the loo, a din that gives way to a spontaneous rendition of the "It's Great/ To Be/A Florida Gator!" cheer, which a lot of guys keep chanting even as they belly up to the porcelain. You've never seen so many perfect strangers high-fiving and making eye contact in the men's room.

The Gators damn near give the game away in the second half, falling behind 21–17, before Meyer has the nerve to call a fake punt on his own 15-yard line. This after Leak had thrown his weekly grotesque interception, but before freshman Percy Harvin's electrifying 67-yard touchdown run, at the beginning of which he is sprinting to his right but makes a cut to the inside that is so blinding and sudden that it is as if a whole row of Razorbacks are caught in quicksand.

Florida rallies for a 38–28 win. Now the question becomes: Who's No. 2? With 'SC out of the mix, BCS voters must ask themselves: Which team has done more to earn the right to face Ohio State in the BCS title game? Is it the 12-1 Gators, who suffered their only loss at No. 3 Auburn, and who played the toughest schedule in the land? Or is it Michigan, whose only blemish came in the Horseshoe a fortnight earlier? Working against the Wolverines is the fact that few people outside the Big Ten care to see a Michigan–Ohio State rematch.

While Lloyd Carr disdains the very idea of politicking for votes, lobbying pollsters—could you see Bo or Fielding Yost or Fritz Crisler grubbing for favors like Chicago ward heelers?—Florida's Meyer shares no such concern.

"Florida belongs," he declares after the Arkansas game. "The other team had a shot [at the Buckeyes]. We went 12-1, and I think the county wants to see the Southeastern Conference champion against a Big Ten champion. I think that's what this is all about."

Two days later, on December 4, it is made official: The computers and the pollsters agree. Florida will play for the national championship. Michigan will return to Pasadena for its third Rose Bowl in five years. If the Wolverines aren't exactly jacked up to return yet again to Disneyland, to put on the feed bag at Lawry's Beef Bowl in Beverly Hills, they are much too polite to say so. Nor are the Trojans, their opponent, especially thrilled to have backed into this game, which I suggest renaming the Bitter Bowl.

. . . .

THE SAD BEHEMOTH is standing in white cotton briefs at his locker, speaking to no one yet repeating himself. "F___, f___, f___, f___, f___!" says Drew Radovich, the left guard. When his profane incantation is over, I pull up a chair next to him and ask what happened out there. It makes him feel better to talk about it. "They slanted the front, slanted the lines, it seemed like they were blitzing almost every play." It wasn't the blitzes that confounded them, he says, so much as the *delayed* blitzes. Whether Walker was bringing a corner, safety, or linebacker, "They would either send him late, or he would loop the front," Radovich recounts. "It was like they threw a change-up every play."

Carroll stands between a cinder block wall outside the locker room and a semicircle of inquisitors, TV lights picking up the lines around his eyes. This is his third defeat in 13 games. The speculation that bubbled up after the Oregon State loss—the empire is crumbling—will now return in full force.

He speaks of a "very difficult day," salutes the great play of UCLA's defense in general and the great job done by his former assistant, Walker. He laments the Trojans' many penalties, their lack of rhythm, all the third downs left unconverted. "We just kept waiting for it to happen," he reflects, "looking for our chances to make something happen, and it just didn't come around."

In the room, Booty is facing down his own scrum of reporters, talking about McNeal's interception. "The dude jumped up and tipped it to himself. . . . I was just praying, bounce, one way or the other; sure enough it went straight up."

I know the big men in front of him stunk up the joint today, but I was looking for a little more bravura, a little more fire from this gunslinger from Shreveport. "He was rattled" is the charge later leveled by chatty Bruins cornerback Rodney Van. "You could see it in his eyes. Normally a quarterback of his stature is confident and composed, but he was rattled" when he came to the line, "looking for where the blitz was coming from instead of looking for his reads and his check-downs."

Reviewing the video of the game, I will soften my judgment. Booty didn't miss on throws so much as he didn't have time to make them.

DAVIS IS STILL on a roll, 40 minutes after the game. In a tumultuous Bruins locker room, he feels comfortable speculating what USC must have been thinking: "They just kind of figured that we're kinda small, so they're gonna beat these guys up."

Had he crawled into Booty's head? Big smile. "Oh yeah. At one point, they false-started, and we ended up chest to chest. He was like, 'Hey, hey, hey, just calm down.' Well, I'm *never* gonna calm down."

He is a handsome guy who bears more than a passing resemblance to Jason Taylor, the Miami Dolphins Pro Bowler who plays the same position. More remarkable is the fact that, with his uncanny burst off the ball, Davis *plays* like Taylor, too. "I've heard that," he tells me, smiling.

I ask about that tattooed row of glyphs on his right arm, Asian symbols running from his deltoid down to his right biceps. What do they say? He smiles again, and translates: "Fear no man."

# CHAPTER 17

# Bowlnanza

**BCS TOP 10**

*1. Ohio State*
*2. Florida*
*3. Michigan*
*4. LSU*
*5. USC*
*6. Louisville*
*7. Wisconsin*
*8. Boise State*
*9. Auburn*
*10. Oklahoma*

Decmber 31, Los Angeles —The athletes are so fluid and effortless on the field that it is useful to remind ourselves, every so often, how much time and sweat goes into each performance. That is why, on the eve of the Rose Bowl—the first of three BCS games we will attend over the next eight days—I have requested an audience with several USC Song Girls. Because there are other Big Questions out there besides *"Are the Trojans in decline?"* and *"Do the Gators have a prayer against Ohio State?"* and *"How badly did Michigan get screwed by the BCS?"*

I pose one of those questions now to Natalie, Anasheh, and Lauren, seniors on the squad who prefer not to share their last names (stalker issues):

Ladies, let's talk about the sweater. It's chaste—a long-sleeved turtleneck—but offers a glimpse of midriff when you raise your arms. Are you wearing the same sweater in January that you wear in August?

"We do have a halter top," Natalie informs me. "But it has to be 85 degrees or hotter" to doff the sweaters. "So, when it's warm, we're like praying to God that it gets warmer."

"If it's 84," Anasheh adds, "we're still in the sweater. People seem to prefer the sweaters."

Why would that be? I wonder.

"They're so classic and traditional," Natalie notes. "But we're miserable when it's that hot. Song Girls have gone off in stretchers, because of dehydration and heat exhaustion."

"And you're not unionized," I sympathize, "so you can't file a grievance."

The squad's call time for tomorrow's Rose Parade is 4:00 a.m. "At five, they load the buses for the Parade," I am told by Lori Nelson, their director. "So they're thinking they'd better get up at three to start curling their hair."

Natalie attracted unwanted attention a year ago when she was photographed cheering as Vince Young scored a touchdown. (She thought the Trojans defense had stopped him.) All across the blogosphere, wiseacres entered into an unofficial competition to see who could Photoshop her effervescent likeness onto the least appropriate background. There she is, "cheering" the sinking Titanic, the burning Hindenburg, the carnage in Picasso's *Guernica*. How did she cope with the unwanted pub?

By laughing it off, basically. "Hey, it was good media coverage," she says. "I was asked to be on Jay Leno, I was asked to do a spread for *Maxim*." She said "Thanks, but no thanks" to both. "It's funny: I've been going to 'SC games since I was four, I've dated a football player"—she and Trojans linebacker Dallas Sartz were an item for two years—"so I know more football than most people."

SHE HAS A better feel for this team than I do. Natalie thinks the Trojans are going to win. (It turns out she's got a source inside the huddle: Within three months she will be engaged to Ryan Kalil. Bright and and handsome talented as he is, Kalil outkicked his coverage by about 30 yards when he got her to say "Yes.")

From where I stand, this looks like another trap game for the Trojans. No matter what they're saying, the guys have got to be bummed that they had the BCS title game in their hands, and let it slip through their grasp.

Nor do they match up well against the Michigan defense, which bears a disturbing resemblance to the defense that humiliated them on December 2. Special teams coach Sam Anno put it succinctly: "They got, like, some sack gurus and shit."

One particular matchup gives Trojans coaches pause. While no one on the offensive line played well against UCLA, right tackle Kyle Williams had the longest day at the office. He was eviscerated on the message boards, demeaned on sports talk radio. Williams was even verbally accosted on the street after the game, he told the *L.A. Times*, when a quartet of fans in 'SC jerseys chanted, "Nice false starts!"

Compounding his depression was the news that Carroll and Pat Ruel, the offensive line coach, had made the decision to bench him for the Rose Bowl. The plan was to start Matt Spanos, a redshirt junior who'd taken the 2006 season off on account of some academic issues. An attempt was made to get Spanos eligible in time for the Rose Bowl. Even though that attempt fell short—meaning Williams would get the start, after all—it was still a kick in teeth.

Williams will spend much of his afternoon in hand-to-hand combat with LaMarr Woodley. After finishing the season with 11 sacks and 16 tackles for loss, the Wolverine senior had been named the Big Ten defensive player of the year, and, more recently, collected the Lombardi Award, given to the nation's top lineman or linebacker. He knows all about Kyle Williams. "I know who he is," Woodley told the *L.A. Times*. "And he is not just going to be getting me, he's going to be getting all of us. He's going to get worn out. That's what we do."

. . . .

MIKE HART GASHES the Trojans line for 11 yards on Michigan's first play from scrimmage, making me wonder if the Trojans will be susceptible to the Wolverines zone-blocking schemes. After a while I stop wondering. Two snaps later Cushing, the elephant, bursts into the backfield to sack Chad Henne. The Wolverines punt, just as they will punt on three of their four remaining possessions of the first half. On that occasion, Garrett Rivas kicks a 43-yard field goal, tying the game 3–3.

Despite the deadlock, theses offenses are on different trajectories. Paralyzed by pressure from every conceivable angle, Henne barely has time to find the laces on the football before he is besieged by Trojans. On one ridiculous series he is sacked three times. It brings to mind a similar pillaging that took place on this same turf, between these same teams, three years earlier. In that Rose Bowl—fondly remembered by the Trojans as the festival called "Car-Navarre"—Wolverines quarterback John Navarre was sacked nine times in a 28–14 'SC win.

USC's failure to score a touchdown in the first half masks the fact that Booty has looked sharp and—with the exception of one undignified moment in which he fumbles and possibly voids his bladder under a Wolverine onslaught—much more comfortable than he had against UCLA. He's completed 10 of 16 passes. He's had time to settle his feet, time to throw.

The game plan calls for him to take shorter drops and to get rid of the ball more quickly. "The idea," Kiffin explains after the game, "was to get him in a rhythm, get him some completions, get him some confidence."

For this one evening, Booty is also under instructions to give the audibles a rest. By calling plays on a quick count, he cuts down on the amount of time the Wolverines can shift and move before the snap. Through 30 minutes, LaMarr Woodley hasn't been a factor in the game, which is blessed news for Kyle Williams. The fifth-year senior is playing well today. Guess what Carroll-recommended book he's reading?

Not that the Trojans have any sort of ground game to speak of. Feature back C. J. Gable has 17 yards on 10 carries at halftime. The Trojans braintrust is th-i-i-s close to giving up on the running game. Three plays into the second half, the decision is made.

On first down, Booty finds Smith for a nine-yard pickup off a play-action fake. "On second-and-one," Kiffin recalls, "we ran it for nothin'. Third-and-one, we ran it for nothin'. And at that point we said, We're not gonna run the football anymore. We don't care if it's short yardage. We don't care if it's on the goal line. We're not calling another running play."

He is exaggerating. Late in the fourth quarter with the game decided, Booty will hand off three times. But in the interim, he fills the afternoon air with footballs.

Carrying its dominance over to the second half, 'SC's defense takes the ball from Michigan on its first series, Sartz torpedoing in, hurrying Henne into an ugly throw picked off by Lawrence Jackson. Booty comes out firing—SarKiffian having forsaken the run—and connects on four straight passes. On the last of those, he fakes a pitch left—a play the Trojans ran in the first half—then rolls right and throws on the run to yeoman wide out Chris McFoy, who for the last five years has thrown downfield blocks for and toiled in the shadow of NFL-bound receivers like Mike Williams, Keary Colbert, Jarrett, and Smith. But it is McFoy's touchdown catch, the second of his career, that opens the floodgates for 'SC.

The Trojans defense forces a three-and-out—LoJack's heavy pressure on Henne forces the incomplete pass on third down—and 'SC gets right back to work. With the Wolverines freshly conscious of McFoy, Booty looks to Smith on a slant. No. 2 shakes off the arm tackle of Brandon Harrison, a sophomore corner, and is ridden down after a 35-yard gain.

Next play, with Michigan chests still heaving from that exer-

tion, Jarrett does a little jitterbug at the line of scrimmage, gets an
inside release on cornerback Morgan Trent, snags a look-in pass
from Booty, and lopes into the end zone.

THE 'SC OFFENSE and the 'SC defense have arrived in that rarefied zone in which, as players say, "We were feeding off each
other." With Michigan facing a second-and-eight near midfield,
Elephant Man Cushing comes free up the middle. There is left
guard Adam Krauss lunging at his feet, pronate and helpless as
Cushing sacks Henne and strips him, the ball bouncing obediently
toward LoJack, who has his second takeaway in three series.

If the Trojans play to their potential in 2007, they'll finish the
season on a bigger stage than this one. For the 2006 Trojans, this
out-and-out schooling of the No. 3 team in the nation will be as
good as it gets. After keeping a drive alive with a quarterback sneak
on third-and-one, Booty takes a seven-step drop and looks for Jarrett on the left side. While Sam Baker is washing Woodley out of
the play, Jarrett is defeating the bump-and-run coverage of cornerback Leon Hall, who is a step behind the receiver when Booty's
pass hits him in stride at the Michigan 30. He goes untouched the
rest of the way.

The score is 25–11 midway through the final quarter when
Booty trots onto the field for the team's sixth possession of the
half. What follows is a series of plays that will hold its own beside any of the pyrotechnics engineered by Leinart, or Palmer
before him.

Booty solves the problem of lousy field position—the drive
starts at the Trojans 15—by rifling the ball to Smith, who comes
open with a crisp out-cut and makes a 26-yard reception.

Ranging far to his right on the next play, Booty wings it in the
direction of a well-covered Jarrett, who elevates over Trent, the
Wolverine corner, snaring the ball when it is at least 10 feet in the
air. In the aftermath of the play, the receiver and defensive back
find themselves seated on the turf, facing one another. Jarrett, in a

mood to walk the line between ebullience and poor sportsmanship, crosses that line by handing the ball to Trent, as if to say, *You were looking for this?*

Now Booty works the left side of the field, parachuting a pass over the outside shoulder of Davis, his tight end, who is tightly covered by linebacker Shawn Crable. Holding Crable off with his right arm, Davis makes a sensational, one-handed grab to pick up 23 more yards. That circus catch reminds me of the one-handed touchdown snag made by tight end Dominique Byrd against Oklahoma in the 2005 Orange Bowl, a near-miraculous play that sent an ominous message to the Sooners: When we are on our game—and we are—we will not be stopped.

Booty is well into that zone—The Zone—on this possession, which he brings to a close on the next play. Taking a three-step drop, he sets up to pass as two Wolverines draw beads on him. Defensive end Tim Jamison has shaken Baker with an inside move, and is now bearing down on Booty's, well, booty. Woodley, having hurdled the chop block of Kyle Williams, charges hard from the other side. At the last second Booty steps up: the converging Wolverines collide, comically and spectacularly, as the quarterback threads a seven-yard touchdown pass to Smith, who has come open on a devilish double-move that makes another pair of defenders look very silly. Mario Danelo makes the extra point—noteworthy because he's missed two today—and the Trojans lead 32–11 with seven minutes to play. Game over.

THE FINAL SCORE is 32–18. Booty scales a stepladder and "conducts" the Spirit of Troy with a sword borrowed from the guy who dresses up like a Trojan. Whatever stature and confidence he'd lost in this same stadium on December 2, he has seized back on this day. Booty threw for 391 yards, four touchdowns, and no interceptions. All the touchdowns and nearly 300 of those yards came in the Trojans' explosive second half.

"It feels about how you'd think it would," he tells me in a near-deserted locker room 40 minutes later. "For them to trust me enough to put the game in my hands, to tell me, 'We're gonna throw to win, we're calling on you to lead us'—it makes you stand a little taller, throw your shoulders back a little more. It feels good."

When it's over, Dwayne Jarrett has caught 11 balls for 205 yards and two touchdowns. While still on the field, Booty approached him, smiling like a salesman. "One more year, man! We gotta do this again next year!" Jarrett started laughing. Asked if he would enter the NFL draft or stick around for a fourth college season, No. 8 starts talking about "my family"—one's surest indication that the athlete in question has decided it's time to get paid.

When it's over, Kyle Williams stands just a bit taller on the field as reporters gather around. "So much for [his] critics," notes Kalil, the center, who is taking in the scene. "He just spent the last three hours blocking the best defensive end in the country." To a team that posted 41 quarterback sacks in 2006, the Trojans yielded a single one—late in the fourth quarter, with the outcome decided.

When it's over, Michigan has rushed for a net total of 12 yards. Cushing, whose sore left knee gave him pause during warm-ups, played through the pain, racking up two and a half sacks, four tackles for loss, and a forced fumble. The Trojans hadn't done anything Michigan wasn't prepared for. Overmatched by 'SC's athletes, the Wolverines simply couldn't do anything about it.

IT IS BRUTUS who notes on the eve of his death in *Julius Caesar*:

> *The enemy increaseth every day;*
> *We, at the height, are ready to decline.*

The decline is reversed. Today's victory is a rebirth for a program that only a month earlier looked listless and past its prime. So it is appropriate when Carroll is "baptized" by his players on the field with several gallons of sports drink.

"What concerned me most," says Carroll, stuffing the last few items in his garment bag nearly an hour after the game, "was that we not allow ourselves to be defined by that last time we played. 'Cause that was such an outlying statistic. It didn't fit with anything we've done here. It was just a crap game."

"Your father says 'crap game,' " I note to 19-year-old Nathan Carroll, a USC freshman who is sitting nearby, patiently waiting for his father to finish packing his bag and flapping his gums so they can go get something to eat. "I say 'anomaly.' "

In a team meeting the previous night, Carroll had ~~subjected~~ treated the squad to a cavalcade of glorious moments from recent seasons: Carson Palmer eviscerating Iowa in the 2003 Orange Bowl; dominating, spirit-crushing wins in national title games against Michigan, then Oklahoma. They were part of a continuum of excellence that was very much alive. "We've had defining moments," he told them. "Tomorrow is our opportunity to have another one."

"We've been hearing it for a month," Carroll tells me as he steps out of the locker room into the brisk night air. "We're done. It's over. We won't play hard because we're not in the national championship. All the fun is gone."

The fun is back. A golf cart awaits to whisk him to the team party in a huge tent set up on a nearby golf course. But the coach is not quite ready to let go of this game. "Give me a minute," he tells the guy driving the golf cart. Accompanied by his son, Carroll walks back through the tunnel for the sole purpose of standing one more time on the field where the Trojans were so recently reborn.

THE TROJAN FAMILY will have five days to celebrate. Early on the morning of January 6, Mario Danelo, the exuberant placekicker whose 83 extra points in 2005 set an NCAA record, is found dead at the base of a 120-foot cliff near Point Fermin lighthouse in San Pedro, California.

The son of former NFL kicker Joe Danelo, Mario had starred at linebacker at San Pedro High. At 5'10", 200 pounds, though, he wasn't going to be playing that for any Division I team. So the old man taught him to kick. After walking on to the Trojans squad in 2003, Mario earned a scholarship two years later. Asked how he was doing, his stock response was "Living the dream!"

Police ruled out foul play, and Mario's family and friends said it was inconceivable that he would have taken his own life. A coroner later revealed that he was drunk when he fell.

A week later, some 2,000 mourners attended a memorial for Danelo at San Pedro's Mary Star of the Sea church. As Lori Nelson, the Song Girl director, wrote to me in an e-mail, "Mario's father and brother, Joey, had to carry his mother in and out because she did not have enough strength to take one step. Her sobs could be heard throughout the service.

"The entire football team attended, as did the Song Girls and I. At the end of Pete's eulogy he talked about Mario's record-setting season and career accomplishments. He then asked everyone to give a cheer for Mario—loud enough for him to hear in heaven. The applause, cheers, whistles, and chants seemed to last forever."

Two DAYS AFTER the Rose Bowl I'm in New Orleans, standing at the intersection of St. Charles Avenue and Canal Street. A 40-something Notre Dame alum, minding his own business, walks past a quintet of 20-something LSU grads in their cups. He is wearing the widely popular navy tee on which the word TRADITION is spelled out on the back. The LSU guys, incidentally, are all wearing QUINN BLEAUX T-shirts. They are not here to live and let live. The ringleader shouts after the Domer, "Yeah—nice tradition—a tradition of getting blown out by Top 25 teams. Nice bowl history."

The guy my age can only sputter a feeble comeback—"The SEC's totally overrated!"—before they are gone. It is lamentable but a fact that Notre Dame has lost eight straight bowl games. And things aren't looking real good for tonight.

It's sad and surreal to be in this venue, this dome that was a symbol of both the damage wrought by Hurricane Katrina and the government's botched response to it. It's wonderful that they've got the Superdome fixed up and spit-shined—last year's Sugar Bowl had to be moved to Atlanta—but it also just heightens the contrast between the few blocks of this city that have been reclaimed and mile upon square mile of New Orleans that remain, 16 months after the disaster, unreclaimed, postapocalyptic, and dangerous. In tomorrow's predawn darkness I will miss my turn for I-10 and be amazed at how quickly, after one leaves the city center, one is driving through a series of vignettes from hell: boarded-up apartments, with spray-painted signs with messages like DANGER.

Standing on the field before the game, I'm having trouble recognizing any of the Fighting Irish players who have come out for early warm-ups. It's a bunch of short white guys in football pants and sleeveless T-shirts, playing catch, running routes, smiling ear to ear.

"That's the Rudy Patrol," I am told by Brian Hardin, the school's sports information director. "They're walk-ons. That's about as much of the field as they're going to see. They run around, catch a few balls, their parents go nuts."

Some LSU guys are also warming up, doing some midair chest bumps. They do not appear to be walk-ons.

By now JaMarcus Russell has come out, and is tossing the ball around 30 yards from us. Hardin speaks for me when he says, "Wow. That's a big muchacho."

Russell is large—6'5", 257—and in charge. After losing to Florida in The Swamp, the Bayou Bengals have run off six straight wins. Until 'SC did that tap dance on Michigan, I would've called LSU the best two-loss team in the country. Russell, for his part, has probably the strongest arm in college football: He is said to be able to throw the ball the length of the field. Much has been made this week about his ability to throw the ball through the goalposts from the far 40-yard line—while sitting on his butt.

I spot Weis walking up the sideline with—how best to say this—a guy you just wouldn't normally picture Charlie hanging out with. This is a dashing fellow in a leather jacket, his handsome features crowned by a tastefully highlighted mane.

"Who's the hair farmer with Charlie?" I ask Hardin. It's fellow Garden State native Jon Bon Jovi, whose music, according to the *60 Minutes* profile CBS ran on Weis in October, Weis cranks at his desk when he gets to work at four-thirty every morning. They make an odd pair, the head coach at Notre Dame and the guy who belts out songs like "Social Disease" and "Living in Sin."

Maybe not so odd. Up in the press box, I Google Jon Bon Jovi, and learn that in September 2005, he and his three bandmates donated $1 million to Oprah Winfrey's Angel Network to help victims of Katrina. This apparently wasn't a great leap for Bon Jovi, who's long been active in Habitat for Humanity. It made sense that he would have felt at home on the sideline of the school that brought 400 students and alumni this week to help repair this drowned, broken city. I'm willing to give the Irish the moral high ground tonight because it may be the only battle they'll win.

Q<small>UINN IS OBVIOUSLY</small> jacked up for his final game in a gold helmet. It's obvious because he keeps throwing passes eight feet over the heads of his receivers. On third-and-10 he finds Samardzija at the sideline for a 12-yard gain, which forward progress is negated by the 15-yard unsportsmanlike penalty assessed on the Shark after he tosses the ball to the defender he's just beaten. My personal theory: It's Dwayne Jarrett's fault. Jarrett embellished his incredible performance two nights ago with several extracurricular flourishes—the fadeaway jumper with the football in the end zone after a score; handing the rock to the cornerback he'd just burned. How much you want to bet the Big 12 officials working tonight's game were watching that and saying to themselves, *Man, those boys better not try to pull that shit on my watch.*

On fourth down at his own 34, Weis is feeling lucky. He calls a fake punt—a direct snap to the up back, Travis Thomas, who is stuffed for a one-yard gain. Whether or not he intended it, the message Weis sends is: *If we play these guys straight up, we got no chance.*

Russell reinforces that message on the next play, flicking the ball to wide out Early Doucet for a 31-yard gain down to the Irish three-yard line. Two plays later it's 7–0.

Russell makes the score 14–nil with an 11-yard TD pass to Dwayne Bowe on the Tigers' next possession. The Irish awaken on their next series. Quinn hits Grimes, the team's wide out of the future, on a 24-yard flag route for a touchdown. After Travis Leitko recovers a Russell fumble, the offense can't capitalize. Quinn, who has been badly out of sync for so much of the half, throws a perfect pass . . . that doinks off Samardzija's helmet. Carl Gioia butchers the 33-yard field goal attempt, and it's still 14–0.

The defense, God bless it, gets a stop: Ndukwe makes a spectacular pass breakup; Landri tips a pass; Zbikowski rides Russell to the ground when the giant quarterback tries to run for the first.

On their ensuing drive, something strange happens to the Irish. They are enjoying success in the running game against a Top 10 defense. Darius Walker sweeps right for seven; picks up another seven on the same stretch play to the left. The drive dies when Quinn is picked off by cornerback Jonathan Zenon, but the Irish pick up where they left off on their next possession. Intoxicated with its run-blocking success, the Notre Dame offensive line delivers more of the same: Quinn runs for 12 out of the shotgun. Walker tears off a 35-yard gain off right tackle, then gets 15 more around left end, then gives props to Grimes for the crackback block. Quinn finishes the drive with a 10-yard pass to Samardzija, who beats Zenon for the touchdown. Quite improbably, the score is 14–all with 2:25 left in the half. One more courageous stand by the defense, and these guys can get into the locker room with a tie score.

Reality intrudes on the next series. Breaking at least four tackles—did Weis sneak the Rudy Patrol onto the field for a series?—LSU tailback Justin Vincent gets a too-easy 19 yards up the left side. Two plays later there is Russell, literally taking money out of Quinn's pocket tonight, stepping up, moving to his right, then flicking a pass across his body that travels 50 yards in the air. It is caught by Doucet, streaking down the left side. He is tackled at the five-yard line by the late-arriving Ndukwe. Russell scores on a quarterback draw two plays later.

NOTRE DAME IS done scoring for the night. The Tigers get something figured out at halftime, and suddenly Walker, who rushed for 125 first-half yards, can't get out of the backfield. He'll finish with 128. The Irish will be outgained in the final two quarters, 333–30. After settling for field goals on his first two drives of the half, Russell goes deep again on third-and-eight from his own 42. The Irish know what's coming. As against Michigan and 'SC, they're simply powerless to stop it. Abiamiri gets through, and actually gets a paw on Russell, who sidesteps and keeps shuffling right as he flicks another 58-yard pass. This one, to Brandon LaFell, goes for six, jacking LSU's lead up to 34–14.

Russell's decision about whether to return for his senior season—officially, he's undecided—is getting easier all the time. The guy's physical skills are obvious. Earlier in his career he had problems with throwing the ball too hard, breaking his receivers' fingers, that sort of thing. Truly. But he's developed some touch. He recognizes defenses, calls audibles to get out of bad plays, picks coverages apart. And the word is that he's got the strongest arm in football . . . at any level. The question after this game will be: How high did he rise in the draft, and how far, if at all, did Quinn fall.

The answer: very high, and pretty low.

Their numbers tonight present a stark contrast: Russell will complete 21 of his 34 passes for 332 yards, and two touchdowns against a single interception (he ran for another score). Quinn is under 50 percent on the night, connecting on just 15 of his 35 throws for two touchdowns and two picks. The second of those isn't his fault: Flailing after a pass, McKnight deflects it into the air. As he looks around to see where it went—LeRon Landry has picked it off and is sailing for the Irish end zone—you can practically hear the clown music.

The unoriginal "Overrated!" chant cascades onto the field when the Tigers take a 41–14 lead. Tiring of that, the LSU fans begin pleading (vainly) with Russell: "One more year! One more year!"

When the game is over, I see Quinn and Russell go through the motions of embracing. Neither smiles. As the Irish raise their helmets to sing the alma mater, it comes out like a dirge.

It was close for a half, Weis notes afterward. "For the rest of the game they really laid the wood on us."

How were Russell's receivers able to get separation? "I'm not sure," reports Weis, before floating the theory that his defensive backs were "not being physical enough with them."

Russell's receivers were able to get separation, Russell's linemen were able to protect him, because LSU had better athletes *all over the field.* As did USC, as did Michigan, as did Ohio State when it played Notre Dame a year ago.

Quinn is up on the dais beside Weis. Both are so glum, I think of the old joke: "Horse walks into a bar. Bartender says, 'Why the long face?' "

"It's tough," says the Irish quarterback, now the ex–Irish quarterback. "Notre Dame's been a great place, a place I've come to love. The best part about it was the people." He speaks of "bonds that will never be broken," and I think I see Weis's eyes misting over. A little.

But by the time it's Charlie's turn to talk again, he is in control, the hard-ass realist we are most comfortable with. He is making the point that his players "can't be content with being 10-3, going to a bowl, and getting their clock cleaned."

They can't because he won't. Defensive coordinator Rick Minter is already a dead man walking; Weis will fire him shortly after they get back to South Bend. Minter will be replaced by Corwin Brown, an ex–Michigan Wolverine and NFL safety whose previous job was defensive backs coach for the New York Jets. Clearly, Weis hopes to awaken and ignite a moribund unit as Ron English did at Michigan; as DeWayne Walker did at UCLA. It's an inspired hire. But the fact remains, Minter didn't suddenly forget how to coach in 2006. He got axed because Weis can't fire all the slow guys on his two-deep.

Listen to Urban Meyer, explaining his decision to take the Florida job. Nowhere does he utter the words "Notre Dame." But this quote has everything to do with Notre Dame: "I might not act very smart sometimes. But I'm not going to a place that doesn't have players. People say, 'You've got five years to build a program'—no, you don't. You got this many. [He holds up two fingers.] Like I said, I'm not that smart, but I'm smart enough to know that."

Weis doesn't want to hear this, doesn't want his players glomming on to it as an excuse—the title of the man's book is *No Excuses*, after all—but the fact is, the Irish have nowhere near the number of elite athletes that the other BCS teams do. Which brings me to the conclusion reached by my buddy John Walters. "Notre Dame is not a BCS bowl team. . . . Worse, they are no better than their 2005 selves."

Maybe the novelty of Weis's attack wore off in his second year in South Bend. Maybe the guys that left—offensive linemen Mark LeVoir and Dan Stevenson; tight end Anthony Fasano; wide receiver Maurice Stovall—were just that good. Probably some of both. Regardless, it's a compliment to Weis, a measure of the regard in which Domers hold him, that 10-3 is a little disappointing. The 2006 Irish had their moments. But when it was over, it felt like they'd been running in place.

# CHAPTER 18

# TBCSNCG

**D**ecember 9, New York —It is Ohio State's world, and the rest of us are just subletting. That is the takeaway from tonight's festivities at the Nokia Theater in Times Square, where Troy Smith—beyond dapper in charcoal gray suit, accessorized with scarlet and gray cravat and a crimson pocket square—becomes the seventh Ohio State player to win the Heisman Trophy. Some years, this 25-pound doorstop is college football's equivalent of an Irving Thalberg, bestowed on a player for his achievements over the course of a career. Other years it goes to the best player from the season just finished. Smith deserved it either way. In leading the No. 1 team to an undefeated season—during which he threw for 2,507 yards and 30 touchdowns, against just five interceptions, three of which were tipped—he ran his record as the Buckeyes starter to 25-2, including a 10-1 mark against ranked teams. If someone else had

**BCS TOP 10**

1. *Ohio State*
2. *Florida*
3. *Michigan*
4. *LSU*
5. *USC*
6. *Louisville*
7. *Wisconsin*
8. *Boise State*
9. *Auburn*
10. *Oklahoma*

won this trophy, the Justice Department would've had some actual, legitimate voter fraud on its hands.

He has also delivered one of the most gracious and touching Heisman acceptance speeches in memory, expressing gratitude to his Maker; to his mother and sister; to the trio of powerful male influences in his life, none of whom was his biological father. He thanks Tressel, who appears on the verge of tears; Ted Ginn Sr., whom he describes as "my father, my dad, who shaped me into the man I am today"; and, farther down the list—after his receivers and linemen—the Irvin White family, which took him in when he was nine years old while his mother got her life back in order. He thanks Brady Quinn and Darren McFadden, the other finalists, for pushing him.

Empty at last of "I'd-also-like-to-thank"s, he is bustled a block and a half south to the Hard Rock Cafe, where we, the media serfs for whom there was no room at the Nokia Theater, await our audience with the winner.

His journey from the "mean streets of Glenville" to this night proves, in his view, that "any kid in any situation can do anything he puts his mind to." As a member of this elite group, he acknowledges, he is a "role model," and, as such, will be under "the microscope" to a degree even greater than before. Having heard those words come out of his mouth, I find myself highly skeptical of a report in the December 17 *New York Post* alleging that, during his visit to Gotham, Smith paid a call to a high-end strip joint named Scores, whose dancers "hailed Smith as a generous tipper," the *Post* reported.

One Michigan blogger had a field day with this news, posting a picture of a scantily clad pole dancer posing the question, "Is that the Heisman Trophy in your pocket, or are you just glad to see me?" Surely, there's been some mix-up! Scores is a den of iniquity, and Smith had stood before the national media two nights earlier thanking God for his "blessings," talking about how "the decisions you make shape so many people," saying that "with accolades come responsibilities."

(Apparently, there is an impostor roaming lower Manhattan, passing himself off as Troy Smith. The real Troy Smith might want to look into that.)

Back at the Hard Rock, Ivan Maisel of ESPN makes a good point. There is a rich history of Heisman winners going on to lay eggs in national title games. How would Smith be on guard against something like that?

He would sharpen his focus by spending "even more time in prayer. Even more time with my coaches in the film room. Even more time with my teammates, because my hourglass is dwindling down."

These poor guys have nothing but time. Fifty-one days will elapse between the time the Buckeyes dispatch Michigan and the moment they take the field against Florida—another of the absurd consequences of college football's ill-advised marriage to the BCS.

How TO PASS that time? Practice. Study film. Study more film. Study film of practice. The coaches have plenty to do. This is a critical period in the recruiting process. Two days after the Heisman presentation, I am in Gainesville to do some reporting on the BCS title game. Florida sports information director Steve Mc-Clain has arranged for me to interview Meyer during his drive from the football offices to the Gainesville Regional Airport. He's got a home visit with some studfish schoolboy scheduled for this afternoon, but he can't tell me who or where. He can only tell me, when I ask how recruiting is going, that it's going "very well." He is in the shotgun seat of an SUV piloted by a burly, stone-faced, middle-aged man whom I take to be his bodyguard. I am mildly embarrassed upon finding out later that he is Greg Mattison, Florida's defensive coordinator.

Traffic is stop-and-go on 39th Avenue, the main artery to the airport, but Meyer isn't in a huge hurry. Which is actually too bad, because McClain has been known to hop out of the car and direct traffic if the coach is running behind.

We've all heard about superfrosh Percy and Tebow, the guys who will form the nucleus of this team for the next few years. But Florida wouldn't be 12-1 and Glendale-bound if Meyer and his staff had not transformed the group they inherited from Zook after the 2004 season—a collection of highly talented, self-centered underachievers who wanted for discipline, cohesion, and, on occasion, lawyers.

That culture was replaced by Meyer's family-style tough love. Displeased with the posture of his players at their first meeting with him, he quietly ordered them to "sit up when I'm talking to you."

He forbade them to wear shorts or shirts with Florida logos while working out, his point being, according to center Steve Rissler, "we hadn't won anything. We hadn't won an SEC championship. We had to earn that stuff."

He ratcheted up off-season conditioning to the point that there was kvetching and retching. He made the guys learn the fight song, and to sing it with him in front of the marching band after each game. These, frankly, are the garden-variety measures of coaches' engineering turnarounds, as was Meyer's emphasis on molding these individuals into a family. Where he enters terra incognita is in the lengths to which he and his staff go to make that happen. The Gators soon understood that no matter how ill at ease it made them at first, they would become closer to one another.

ON THE WAY to the airport Meyer reiterates his three preferred forms of motivation: love, fear, and hate. "We try to use all three," he tells me. "At times, when you're on 'em relentlessly, fear comes into play. At times you challenge 'em to the point where they wanna prove you wrong and they hate you."

And probably the best one—he is talking about love again, but cannot bring himself to speak the word a second time in such a brief interval—"Where you get so deep in their lives that they feel committed to you, like your children. That's the strongest form of motivation—getting extremely close with your players."

Plenty of guys in this program—in Division I athletics, in fact—are not coming from two-parent households in Westport, Connecticut. The breakdown of the family is so significant, says Meyer, that "teaching a kid how to run a curl route is not the number one priority. You're teaching him how to live right, go to class, become accountable, and be unselfish."

It's cool that the Gators are accountable to each other: Those bonds kept them from splintering after that toxic loss at Auburn. But can brotherhood keep them in the game against the Buck-eyes? We saw what happened to the Wolverines, who came into their game in the Horseshoe with a stifling defense, but could not get enough pressure on Smith. Loaded though they are at other positions, Florida's cornerbacks are nice players but not elite. Expect receivers Ted Ginn and Anthony Gonzalez to attack them. There's a reason Vegas has installed the Buckeyes as 7½-point favorites.

Ohio State has taken on a sheen of invincibility as we in the media spent the season seeking new adjectives and superlatives with which to describe Ginn's speed, Smith's field generalship, the vulpine savvy of the man in the red sweater-vest. Remember, before Tressel beat Miami for the 2002 national title, before he ran his record against Michigan to 5-1, he'd clinched four national titles with the Youngstown State Penguins. He is the best big-game coach in the country, and he's had a month and a half to poke around looking for weaknesses.

Then again, so has Meyer. It is Friday, January 5, three days before the Tostitos Bowl Championship Series National Championship Game. Cruising south on an artery called the Agua Fria Highway en route to the Gators practice facility, Meyer exudes cool confidence.

Somewhat sluggish when they first arrived in Arizona four days ago, the Gators are finding that razor's edge.

"Yesterday's practice was one of the best we've had all year," Meyer says, and I ask him what stood out about it.

"Chris Leak's command," he replies without hesitation. "Sometimes, if he's thinking too much, he's not in command, and the offense doesn't run smoothly. He's gotta call plays real crisp, make his checks, check the protection, do whatever we're doing. If he's sharp, everyone else is sharp."

When I mention Quinn Pitcock, the Buckeyes' credenza-shaped All-American defensive tackle, Meyer tips his hand ever so slightly, acknowledging that Florida's offensive line versus Ohio State's vaunted front four was not a matchup favoring the Gators. "That's their strength," he allows. "Just running right at 'em—I don't think we can do that."

He seems not the least bit bothered by the prospect of not establishing an inside running game. He reminds me that he's never been all that beholden to the conventional methods for gaining yards. "We're fairly fast and deep at receiver, so we're going to try to get our athletes the ball in space."

And they don't just do it with passes from Leak. Says Meyer, "We hand it, we flip it, we pitch it, we direct-snap it." They run options, reverses off the option, bubble screens, and shovel passes.

I recall talking with Arizona head coach Mike Stoops about defending USC. It was 2004, his first season as head coach at Arizona. "You do everything right," he lamented, "you disguise your coverage, take away Bush, take away Jarrett—and Leinart finds some other creature running open down the middle of the field."

He used the word "creature" as a supreme compliment: It connoted a player with freakish, five-star abilities—the kind of guy 'SC's been attracting under Carroll. The offense Florida fields in Glendale can fairly be called a Creature Feature.

Harvin you've heard of. You've also got Dallas Baker, whom Meyer describes as his best "overall receiver—best blocker, best route-runner." Bubba Caldwell is a blazer with a knack for beating people deep; he's also "very good on that bubble screen," having most recently taken one 66 yards to the house against Florida State.

Jemalle Cornelius "is probably our most consistent receiver; he does a lot of things very well." Ex-quarterback Cornelius (CI) Ingram, a 6'4", 230-pound wide out/tight end hybrid, is too swift for most linebackers to cover. The way Meyer perks up when talking about him makes me underline his name in my notebook. Oh yeah, they've got plans for this guy.

WILL IT MATTER? Finally, in the Phoenix suburb of Glendale, in the bulbous and barrel cactus–shaped University of Phoenix Stadium, Senator John McCain flips the coin. Florida wins the toss, defers, then regrets. Ginn fields the ball at his seven, cuts sharply right at the 25—Gator Kyle Jackson goes pinwheeling past—then engages his afterburners up the right sideline. Ginn is the fastest guy on the field. No one's running him down from behind. Buckeyes lead 7–0 sixteen seconds into the game.

Momentum immediately swings the other way. And I mean immediately. In the dog pile celebration following the score, teammate Roy Hall fractures a bone in Ginn's left foot. While Ginn will take a few more snaps the rest of the way, his TBCSNCG is over.

Buckeyes kicker Aaron Pettrey facemasks Brandon James at the end of a nice return, giving Florida great field position. Three quick passes, three completions. DeShawn Wynn rushes for four. Fullback and all-around-useful engine Billy Latsko takes a short pass 11 yards. Changeup. Now it's Tebow time. With Leak split out wide, the better to short-circuit the brains of an already baffled defense, Tebow takes a direct snap up the gut for seven. Thanks, Tim, take a break. Leak back in. Tailback motions to the right, giving Florida four receivers on that side of the field. The Buckeyes are hopping around before the snap, looking at each other, discombobulated. With the Buckeye defense leaning to the four-receiver side, Leak throws left to Baker, who easily defeats the jam of cornerback Malcolm Jenkins, then spins around Brandon Mitchell for a 14-yard touchdown.

I made it a point in the days before the game to seek out Gonzalez, the Ohio State wide out and philosophy major who was hands down the brightest football player I met all season. When I asked him what he'd been reading lately, he mentioned a book called *Victims of Groupthink*, by Irving Janis. The author, a research psychologist, describes the systematic errors made by groups arriving at collective decisions. The first mistake: an illusion of invulnerability, shared by most or all members.

I doubted that many of the Buckeyes in the crowd of 75,000 were overly concerned about the apparent ease with which the Gators had just skipped down the field. All that misdirection and deception, the two-headed quarterback—it might work in the short term. But the Buckeyes would make adjustments. And besides, it was their year. They'd been No. 1 all season. They were favored by a touchdown. They had Troy Smith.

But Smith has problems. Dropping back to pass on third-and-six, he doesn't even have time to set up before defensive end Derrick Harvey, having whooshed past tight end Rory Nicol, plants the qb in the sod. Ohio State commits a personal foul on the ensuing punt, giving Florida another short field.

The Gators score five plays later. On the touchdown, Florida comes out empty (no backs) with three wide receivers left. Here comes Harvin in motion from the right, behind Leak, who takes the snap, rolls left, then pitches to Harvin on the option. The freshman torpedoes under Laurinaitis for the touchdown.

As soon as the Gators exhaust their store of trickeration, Ohio State will be poised for a comeback. If they can just get a first down.

Now they're on the move, picking up 13 yards on three running plays. But here is Harvey on first-and-10, bull-rushing right tackle Kirk Barton five yards into the backfield, where he comes face-to-face with the Heisman Trophy winner, who can run but cannot hide. Harvey's second sack is good for minus-10 yards. It is strange—nearly as odd as contesting a college football game in this hermetically sealed, anodyne environment—to see Troy

Smith on the ground with the ball. Carving up Michigan 51 days ago, he seemed shielded by a force field. After the win, Barton broke the rules by firing up a Cuban cigar in the locker room.

Now he's getting smoked. He and left tackle Alex Boone haven't seen the likes of this speed-rushing duo of Harvey and Jarvis Moss, from whom we shall soon be hearing. On second-and-25, following a Boone false start, Florida sends the house. Rather than eat the ball and take his third sack of the quarter, Smith flings a desperation pass that is easily picked off by safety Reggie Lewis.

To better empathize with the Buckeyes, let's review the formations and deceptions employed by the Gators on this next drive:

- They open with a four–wide receiver set (Leak hits Ingram for 19).
- Three guys go in motion (not at the same time); pitch right to Harvin for six.
- Mass substitutions, option action to the right, reverse left to Caldwell. Picks up 11.
- Five wide receivers. Leak throws it away, his first incomplete pass of the night. He is now nine of 10 for 99 yards and a touchdown. (Your Heisman winner is one-for-three for 11 yards, an interception, and minus-seven yards.)
- Tebow batters for five yards.
- And finally, for old times' sake, this retro flourish: Wynn lines up in the "I" formation and follows Latsko into the end zone. Based on what Florida has shown so far, that passes for exotic. We are four seconds into the second quarter. Gators lead 21–7.

It's definitely still a game. Now the Buckeyes bow their necks, moving 64 yards on four plays (with an invaluable assist from Siler, who is flagged 15 yards for roughing Smith). The Gators cool off a little, settling for two field goals on their next three drives. The second of those is a gift from Tressel, who is so unnerved by this Gator attack that he decides he has to go for it on fourth-and-one at his own 29. Beanie Wells is stuffed, and Chris

Hetland, Florida's much-maligned kicker, drills the 40-yarder to make it 27–14. It looks like Florida will take a 13-point lead into intermission.

But no! While Smith takes a seven-step drop, Jarvis Moss is beating Boone so badly to the outside that the tackle *tries* to grab some jersey—*tries* to commit a holding penalty. But he can't. Moss is already out of reach. Smith takes another sack from the blind side, but this time Moss chops the ball out of his hands. Harvey recovers on the five.

Tebow rushes for two.

Tebow rushes for two.

Tebow rushes—no, Tebow *starts* to run the ball, then retreats two steps and tosses a one-yard touchdown pass to Bubba Caldwell.

So IT's 34–14 at halftime, and the many thousands of members of Buckeye Nation who booked trips out here in September, after the Texas game, are stricken and silent, as if they've ingested some bad kielbasa. One gets the impression that even if they had 151 days to get ready for these guys, Ohio State still wouldn't have any idea how to defense them. (After the game, Gators offensive coordinator Dan Mullen will tell me that his job was made easier by the Buckeyes' reluctance to come out of their base defense. "We wanted to see if they'd substitute with us," he said, meaning, when Florida put five wide receivers in the game, would the Buckeyes put extra defensive backs in the game? If they didn't, they were going to have linebackers trying to cover some very fleet young men. There were going to be mismatches.)

I'd asked Meyer, the native Ohioan and ex–Buckeye grad assistant, if he thought this Ohio State team might be the fastest Big Ten squad ever. "That's an interesting question," he'd replied—unwilling to voice the belief that regardless of whether or not these Buckeyes were the fastest team in the history of their conference, there were, according to many Gators, a half-dozen SEC teams that Ohio State wouldn't be able to keep up with. The Big Ten champs had great speed at the skill positions. What they lacked was speed all over the field.

No score in the third, the Gators content to devour clock, the Buckeyes basket cases on offense. Florida will score once more, an eight-play drive on which Leak and Tebow split the work, with the freshman bulling in for his second touchdown of this stunning night.

Harvey comes marauding in for one more sack of Smith after the game has been decided. Ohio State has been so overmatched it almost seems unsporting. In the end, the favorites cannot get the underdogs off the field: Florida bleeds the last eight minutes off the clock with a 12-play drive. What was it Smith had said? *My time is dwindling down.*

The game ends with Leak hurling the ball toward the hole in the roof. His euphoria is irresistible. You can't look away. Here was a guy with great individual statistics whose biggest flaw—and a lot of Florida fans couldn't get past it—was that he couldn't win a big game. I doubt he'll ever win a bigger one.


LEAK IS AN introvert whom Meyer worked to bring out of his shell. Now, in his moment of greatest triumph, the quarterback holds himself at a certain remove. With his teammates celebrating on the field, he's taken refuge on a stage where, in short order, he will accept the trophy awarded the MVP of this game.

While Leak waits for those formalities, he leans over the railing, smiling at the fright-wigged, face-painted, blue-and-orange-clad mob beyond the south end zone among whom there are surely some who've booed him in the past. Even though he finished his career with 11,213 passing yards and 88 touchdown passes, he never fully captured the heart of a Gator Nation infatuated with the potential of Tebow.

He captured it tonight, with a flawless, nervy performance on the biggest stage. Leak completed 25 of his 36 passes for a touchdown and no interceptions in a 41–14 win. He completed passes to six different receivers; handed off, flipped, pitched, and otherwise conveyed the ball to four rushers.

More stunning than the Buckeyes' failure to stop (or even slow) Florida was the woeful performance of Smith, who might as well have had the Heisman tucked under his game jersey for all the success he had eluding Moss and Harvey, who combined for five sacks. "Derrick, check this out!" shouts Meyer to Harvey as they exit the postgame press conference. He is pointing to a number on a stat sheet: "*Eighty-two!*" he proclaims. "They had 82 yards of total offense."

How could this happen? How could a squad that looked so gleaming and bulletproof for an entire season be made to look so pedestrian and mortal on its last day?

Linebacker Brian Crum shouts the answer on the field: "We've been doing this all year, man. This is a FAST . . . ASS . . . TEAM!"

I follow Leak, the erstwhile hermit, from his press conference down a raucous corridor to the Gators locker room. He is mobbed the moment he opens the door. Coaches, teammates, Meyer—everyone wants a piece of him. And Leak, who lingers in each embrace, wants a piece of them.

"I can't tell you how proud I am of him," Meyer says amid the din. "I love a fighter, and he's a fighter."

Back at his stall at long last, Leak places his helmet on a shelf, and as he does a small shower of confetti comes streaming down. For a moment it is like Chris Leak's private party.


I file that story around 1:00 a.m., hit the media hospitality room for an hour, crash hard, and head for the airport late the next morning. The college football season is over, but I'm not finished covering college football. Six days later I board a United Airlines Bombardier CRJ-200 regional jet to Boise, where the small businesses along Broadway have spelled out such messages on their marquees as Boise State, True Champions; Hey OU, Welcome to Wild, Wild Wac; and Our Pre-Soak Eats Road Salt.

The same night the Trojans waxed Michigan, in the same stadium Florida schooled Ohio State, fans girded themselves for what was shaping up to be one of the more lopsided games of the postseason. Possibly college football's most resilient team in 2006, the Oklahoma Sooners withstood serial misfortunes to win the Big 12 title. With Adrian Peterson's collarbone mended, the Sooners were looking to finish the season with an exclamation point.

The Boise State Broncos would serve nicely as their personal crash test dummies. Yes, the Broncos were champions, but of what? The Western Athletic Conference is a cobbled-together confederacy of such unlikely bedfellows as Louisiana Tech, Utah State, Hawaii, San Jose State, and others, including the Broncos. The WAC had nearly expired seven years earlier, when half its teams bolted to form another league. Heck, Boise State's football budget for 2006, $2.5 million, was less than the amount Oklahoma head coach Bob Stoops made in the same year. Of all the BCS bowls, this one had the most potential for a blowout.

And so it came to pass. The Broncos hit Oklahoma in the mouth the instant the Big 12 champs set foot on the field. Boise State led 28–10 with just over five minutes to play in the third quarter. That's when a Sooner punt took an improbable bounce, caroming off the calf of a Bronco and turning the tide in the game.

For almost 20 minutes it was all Oklahoma. With 17 seconds left in regulation, the Sooners led 35–28. That's when head coach Chris Petersen sent in the play called "Circus."

Thus began the most outrageous, implausible conclusion to a college football game since Cal's kickoff return team lateraled its way through the Stanford band 24 years earlier.

. . . .

I cannot recall a Division I head coach's office more modest than that of Petersen, who went 13-0 in his first season leading the Broncos. He has just returned to Boise after receiving his Paul (Bear) Bryant Coach of the Year award. Quietly intense, slightly ascetic in appearance—he looks like a marathoner—he smiles at the irony of his situation. "It's interesting that everybody's talking about our trick plays, because our whole mission in life around here is to be a tough, hard-nosed blue-collar outfit. We always say, 'When you can run the ball, it becomes an easy game.' "

Much of that toughness is born of resentment. "As good a place as this is," he says, motioning out the window to the famed blue turf of Bronco Stadium and the foothills beyond, "we get a lot of kids who believe they should be playing for the Pittsburgh Steelers, and they want to prove it to the world. And we like that mentality."

Lords of WAC, the Broncos turned into Team Ugly Betty the moment they arrived in Glendale. At his first press conference, star running back Ian Johnson was informed that Adrian Peterson had not heard of him. How did he feel about that?

Johnson, whose 24 touchdowns this season led the nation, responded tactfully. ("Maybe he's not a huge sports fan.") But for him and his teammates, the cataloging of slights had begun. Two weeks after the game, they ticked off the sins of the Sooners, who on at least two occasions mistook the WAC—gasp!—for the MAC. "Walking around the mall when we first got there," recalled Ryan Clady, the Broncos' starting left tackle, "they were kind of looking down on us." While Clady, a 6'6", 319-pound sophomore, spoke figuratively, the offense taken by him and his teammates was real. SI.com's Arash Markazi was given behind-the-scenes access to the Broncos all week, and chronicled this scene in Boise State's locker room in the moments before the game: "Take those f____g chips on your shoulder when you walk out there tonight," commanded Jeff Choate, who coaches running backs and special teams.

"Everybody doubted us," shouted Jared Zabransky. "No one gives us any respect. We're going to take it tonight!"

They did take it. They took this game with unheard of chutzpah and sterling execution—but only after Zabransky damn near gave it away.


BOISE STATE SEEMED destined to lose this game two ways: gradually, then suddenly. One play after Oklahoma tied the score at 28–all, Zabransky was picked off by Sooners cornerback Marcus Walker, who returned the ball 33 yards for a touchdown. Walker's pick-six gave his team its first lead of the game. Zabransky's first thoughts, in the wake of that disaster, were despairing. "He was pretty down," recalls backup quarterback Taylor Tharp. "He was thinking about how he was going to feel, being responsible" for the loss. "When he saw he still had some time, he kind of changed."

"Some time" amounted to 54 seconds—all that remained on the clock after Quinton Jones brought the kickoff out to the Boise State 22. Stepping up in the pocket on first down, Z—as he is identified by the tattoo on his right biceps—completed a 36-yard pass to tight end Derek Schouman, a senior from Eagle, Idaho, who, like more than a few Broncos on this night, is playing the best game of his career.

Slanting inside on the next play, Sooners defensive end Larry Birdine basically jumped over Johnson's block for a catastrophic, eight-yard sack of Zabransky. (Z tore cartilage in his ribs on the play, but pushed the pain out of his mind.) One timeout and two incomplete passes left the Broncos in a fourth-and-18, 50 yards from the end zone. That's when Tharp started juggling those imaginary balls. No one in the stands at the University of Phoenix Stadium knew it, but the Circus had come to town.

How much confidence did the guys have in Circus? The question is posed to seven Broncos sitting around a table at Boise's Smoky Mountain Pizza and Pasta two weeks after the Fiesta Bowl. They respond by cracking up.

"To be honest," says reserve quarterback Bush Hamdan, when the laughter dies down, "we run it once a week. On Friday. During the walk-through. It's like a basketball team practicing a half-court shot once in a while. It's a screw-around play. Half the time, we don't even complete the first pass. Our attitude was, basically, We're never going to use this. It's a desperation play."

"And now," adds flanker Vinny Perretta, "we need a new one."

Clady, the man-child left tackle twirling pasta to my right, hasn't said much. So I ask him, "What were you thinking when they called the play?"

"Me?" he replies. "I was thinking 92 just got a sack, and sometimes when I play NCAA"—a college football video game—"you see impact players get hot and just start going off. That's what I was thinking."

Circus calls for three receivers to line up wide to the right, one of whom is speedy senior Jerard Rabb. A fourth—Drisan James, who'd already caught a pair of touchdown passes against the Sooners—splits out to the left. He runs a 15-yard square-in and looks for the ball. After making the catch, he tucks it and turns upfield for a step or two—drawing all defenders in the area to him, ideally—before turning and pitching to Rabb, who by this time should be crossing the field beneath him, going in the opposite direction. It's harder to execute than it sounds.

One of the reasons the play seldom works in practice, it turns out, is because Drisan and Rabb like to sneak in some Harlem Globetrotter sleight-of-hand when they hear it called. As if a simple hook-and-lateral is insufficiently baroque.

"Drisan will try to flip it behind his back," says Hamdan. "When Rabb gets it, he'll go with a through-the-legs pitch to Ian."

Oh yes—it is Johnson and Zabransky's responsibility to pursue the play, in case further laterals become necessary.

Against Oklahoma, they weren't, thanks to James's gifts as a thespian. He reeled in Z's pass just shy of the first down, tucked the ball, and took a step upfield. On the replay, you see Sooners converging, then gouging out chunks of the turf trying to change direction as Rabb takes James's navel-high pitch going the other way. "They set it up perfect," sighs Oklahoma linebacker Rufus Alexander. Of course, he added, "It didn't help that I slipped when he threw the ball."

"When Jerard catches the pitch and sees all that green in front of him," Broncos offensive coordinator Brian Harsin tells me, "his body language is like, 'Holy crap, I can't believe it!' And then he finds another gear." Sooners corner Lendy Holmes was closing, but not fast enough to catch Rabb, who dove into the end zone with seven seconds left.

Congratulated on the composure he showed under intense pressure, James shrugs it off. "To be honest," he says, "I didn't realize it was fourth down."

THERE WAS CONSIDERABLE sentiment on the Broncos sideline to end the game on the next play. Petersen decided to kick the point and take his chances in OT. "I felt like we had the momentum back," he explains. "Then we won the coin toss, so I'm thinking, Okay, this thing's going our way."

Umm, not exactly. Oklahoma's first play in OT proved to be Adrian Peterson's final carry as a Sooner. The NFL-bound junior bounced a stretch play to the outside, ran through two tackles like a man pushing through a turnstile, and scored on a 25-yard run. To that point the Boise State defense had stood toe to toe with the Sooners, forcing four turnovers and holding Peterson to 52 yards rushing. Marty Tadman, a prodigiously tattooed, 5'10", 178-pound free safety—the guy looks like a refugee from the Ultimate Frisbee team—had picked off two passes, returning one for a touchdown. By now, however, the Broncos were running on fumes. "Our dee was gassed," allows senior linebacker Korey Hall, the WAC defensive player of the year. "I know I was hurting."

By scoring with such ease, Peterson made Petersen's life less complicated. "I decided then and there that if we scored again, we were going for two," the coach recalls.

Easier said than done. It took the Broncos eight plays to grind out the same 25 yards Peterson devoured in five seconds. The key players were a pair of undersized receivers.

Schouman you've met. Similar in appearance to a lumberjack, the softspoken four-year starter is smallish for a tight end—6'2", 233—but smart, and blessed with soft hands. If he couldn't catch, Harsin wouldn't have called his number three times in OT. Three plays after "Shoe" moved the chains with a 10-yard reception, Johnson lost the ball on the five-yard line. Officials ruled, correctly, that his knee was down. While the play was reviewed Zabransky and Petersen had a bit of a tiff on the sideline.

Facing fourth-and-two from the five, Petersen wanted to run a halfback pass. I can't really blame Z for griping a little. He's the general, and here Coach Pete wants to take the ball out of his hands on what might be the last play of his college career. Rather, he would serve as a decoy, motioning away from the play while former walk-on Vinny Perretta, who had yet to throw a forward pass this season, would decide the game.

"I really didn't want to run it," recalls Z. "I told Pete, 'Let's go with something else.' He said, 'They know we're gonna pass it. We might as well throw 'em off a little.' "

It seemed like a vast amount of trust to put in a 5'9" utility player—Perretta alternates between running back and receiver—who didn't even rate a scholarship when he came out La Costa Canyon High in Encinatas, California. (Perretta earned one after his redshirt-freshman season in 2004.) But Perretta is a quintessential Bronco: tough, smart, and still just a little perturbed that he was so lightly regarded coming out of high school.

And he can act. On "Shop to Bunch Right, Q-Out, 18 Crack Halfback Pass," he took a direct snap and swept right—action identical to a running play the Broncos have run all season. He tucked the ball away, put his head down, then lifted it back up, cocking his arm while looking toward the back of the end zone.

Key to the success of the play, says Harsin, is how convincingly everyone, Perretta included, sold the run. As he made a show trying (and failing) to get a piece of Alexander, the Sooners linebacker, Schouman's body language said, *Ooops! Oh well. I guess that's why I'm at Boise State and you're at Oklahoma!* Then he burst toward the right corner of the end zone. Perretta did not have a passing lane: he had to put some air under the ball to get it over weakside 'backer Zach Latimore, who recovered quickly and was only a step behind. It might have helped if he'd removed his receiving gloves.

The pass was perfect: a spiral Schouman snatched from the air an instant before Latimore wiped him out, to no avail.

To HEAR THE guys around the table at the pizzeria tell it, playcalling at Boise is a more democratic exercise than at most other programs. The backup quarterbacks all wear headphones, and are free to chime in with suggestions. "The whole fourth quarter," says Tharp, "we kept agitating for Statue." The Broncos had it called with 5:35 left in the fourth quarter, but Oklahoma called time-out, and Harsin slid it back into his quiver.

The Broncos' version of the Statue of Liberty features a funky twist, the brainchild of reserve sophomore quarterback Nick Lomax (yes, ex–NFL qb Neil is his father). During an idle moment in practice earlier in the season—such moments are plentiful, Lomax explains, for fourth-string quarterbacks—"this idea popped into my head that we should run this play a different way. You make the same throwing motion, but all the while the ball's in your left hand. I thought it would be even more confusing to defenses."

Harsin remembers that day. "I look over at the quarterbacks, and they're sticking the ball behind their backs with their left hand. I just said, 'You gotta be kidding me.' But they were all fired up on it, like it was the coolest thing ever." He relented. Lomax's empty-handed fake carried the day.

When Zabransky called "Statue Left" in the huddle for the two-point conversion, wide out Legedu Nanee declared, "We just scored, guys. We just won this game."

Dispensing with the usual array of shifts and motions, Zabransky broke the huddle intending to use hurry-up cadence, hoping to catch Oklahoma flatfooted. But the Sooners called a time-out. Petersen never considered changing the play. "We're givin' it to Ian," he pointed out. "We're running over Schouman and Clady, two of our best blockers. And there's great deception on it."

The Broncos had run Statue once earlier in the season. It went for 10 yards against Idaho. Alexander, the Sooners linebacker, remembers seeing that play during film study. "We watched it five or six times," he recalls. "We just said, 'Man, that's *nice*.' Everyone is so patient—it's almost like it happens in slow motion. But when it's happening on the field . . ."

On the field, Zabransky's barehanded fake freezes the defense for a full one-Mississippi. It is Johnson's job, during this pregnant pause, to appear idle. Detached. With intimations of resentment. Check out the replay: You see him put his hands on his hips, "like I'm just futzing around," he recalls. "I'm looking over at the receivers" as if to say, "How could they not call my number on this play?"

That moment ends. Now Johnson pivots left, takes the ball from Zabransky's outstretched hand, and motors for the goal line. His recollection of that instant? "I'm just thinking, Don't drop the ball or trip."

Left guard Tad Miller earns a stalemate with defensive tackle Carl Pendleton. Schouman puts Birdine on the ground with a cut block. Clady loops wide, hinges to his right, and takes Holmes, the corner, out of the play. "I was going downhill, but I was a gap away," Alexander laments. He can only watch as Johnson runs through the side of the end zone and toward the 54 members of his family, now beside themselves in the nearby stands, and flings the ball in the direction of his father.

"I overthrew him by 20 rows," he will later admit. "That's why they didn't have me try the halfback pass on the play before."


JOHNSON, MEANWHILE, HAD some misdirection going in his personal life. His girlfriend is the Broncos' head cheerleader, Chrissy Popadics. They'd been dating for over a year; things were getting serious. A month or so before the game they'd visited a jeweler. After the Fiesta Bowl, the plan was to hang out at Johnson's house in San Dimas, California, until the start of the spring semester.

Before leaving for Arizona, they visited the jeweler, who said the ring should be ready by the time they returned from California. "And my heart sank a little bit," Chrissy admits, " 'cause I thought maybe it would happen in California, or even at the Fiesta Bowl—a Christmas engagement.

"He led me completely off track," she says, smiling at him.

"That's right," he says. "I had my own little Statue of Liberty going."

While it may rank near the bottom of all states in categories like money spent on public school education, give Arizona this: it gets the big things right. The important things. Like keeping celebrating fans off the field after the Fiesta Bowl. After whooping it up with his family in the stands, Johnson actually had to talk, then push his way through police to get back on the field. Amidst the bedlam, he found Chrissy. Soon after, Fox Sports found him. Could they do a quick postgame interview?

Earlier in the week, a Fiesta Bowl official had suggested to Johnson, Why not propose to Chrissy on national TV, after the game? He considered the idea, then dismissed it. "I never planned to [propose] on the field," Johnson told me, "but then she found me, and the TV guys found me, and I thought, This is working out perfectly."

And so, at the end of a quick Q&A with Chris Myers, Johnson dropped to one knee and proposed to Chrissy, who was stunned, and said yes.

The sight of the star running back on bended knee before the head cheerleader further delighted a national TV audience convinced that the spectacle it had just witnessed could not possibly contain an another dramatic turn, could not pack—unless your team was Oklahoma—another iota of joy.

Eighteen hours later, Chrissy and Ian found themselves on a flight from Phoenix to Newark, courtesy of *Good Morning America*, on which they appeared the next day. They were recognized when they got off the plane, in Times Square, in the lobby of the Millennium Hotel, where *GMA* put them up.

"They gave us a suite," says Chrissy.

"Two bathrooms!" adds Ian.

"Two flat-screen TVs."

"LCD TVs," he corrects.

When they went out shopping, "people were asking to have their pictures taken with us," says Chrissy. "One of those guys in Times Square who takes your picture and sells it to you—he asked to have his picture taken with us."

A fortnight after the Fiesta Bowl, her wonderment has yet to wear off. A New Jersey native who moved to Boise when she was nine, Chrissy had longed to visit the Garden State during the Christmas season, to be with extended family members she hadn't seen in years. "Then, in the snap of a finger, we were there."

"It was so surreal, it went by in such a blur," she goes on, unaware that she is speaking for millions of people when she admits, "I catch myself thinking, Did that really happen?"

# Epilogue

April 28, Kauai, Hawaii —In exchange for a killer room rate, the nice lady behind the Starwood desk asks that we consider purchasing a time-share. After carefully weighing the matter for up to 2.5 seconds, my wife and I respond in unison—"No, thank you!"—and are free to enjoy our five-day vacation at the Princeville Resort at the rugged northern tip of this island. Our room opens onto a beach lined with coconut palms, where one can snorkel, surf, or recline on chaises longues among bridesmaids in bikinis (there are at least six wedding parties in the hotel).

On this brilliant Saturday morning in paradise, I am doing none of the above. I am in our room, gripped by an unfolding TV drama: ESPN is airing a four-hour special called *The Incredible Plunging Domer.*

Actually, the program's proper title is *The NFL Draft,* but it has quickly morphed into the saga of Brady Quinn, who, like Sherman McCoy in *Bonfire of the Vanities,* is *hemorrhaging* money, as team after team turns up its nose at him.

It had been Quinn's stated ambition to be the first pick in the draft. We've known for a while that wouldn't happen (the Raiders, as expected, took JaMarcus Russell). Up second, not in the market for a quarterback, the Detroit Lions plucked Calvin Johnson, the outrageously gifted Georgia Tech wide receiver. The Cleveland Browns, at No. 3, had evinced great interest in Quinn. But when their turn came, they chose Joe Thomas, the sun-eclipsing tackle out of Wisconsin.

Oh well. At least Quinn had the Dolphins, picking at No. 9, in his back pocket. Miami had studied Quinn, interviewed him, and had good things to say about him. The Fish had been in negotiations with Kansas City to trade for Chiefs quarterback Trent Green, but that deal hadn't happened, and now Quinn was falling into their laps.

"With the ninth pick in the 2007 NFL draft," intones NFL commissioner Roger Goodell, "the Miami Dolphins select . . . Ted Ginn."

"Whoa, Nellie!" says one of ESPN's talking heads. Suddenly the program becomes a deathwatch. Quinn's biggest problem is that none of the next 20 or so teams selecting really *needs* a quarterback. His other biggest problem is that he's the last guy left in ESPN's green room. He's flanked by his mother—I'm not sure how much longer Robin can keep forcing that smile—and his girlfriend, Lindy Slinger, a midfielder on the soccer team at Miami of Ohio.

It's one thing to be deeply disappointed. It's quite another to have five ESPN cameras in your mug while you try to cope with it. As the Niners, Rams, Jets, and Steelers fill defensive needs, Quinn is left twisting in the wind, putting on a brave face for the cameras while he dies a thousand deaths. Finally, Goodell puts an end to the nationwide rubbernecking, inviting the quarterback and his family into his private suite.

Green Bay has the 16th pick. While the Packers are on the clock, Quinn graciously agrees to an interview with ESPN's Suzy Kolbert. He strives mightily to sound philosophical. "It's draft day," he says. "Anything can happen. Some teams don't need quarterbacks."

How is everyone coping with his epic slide? "I've been trying to calm my family down," he says. "They're a little more affected by this than I am."

Green Bay has Brett Favre, a future Hall of Famer who is long in the tooth, and qb of the future Aaron Rogers. Still, there's talk the Pack might take Quinn, which would put him on the same team with his brother-in-law. Brady's older sister, Laura, is married to Packers linebacker A. J. Hawk.

But the Packers go with Tennessee defensive tackle Justin Harrell. My 10-year-old son, less interested than I in Quinn's destiny, begs me to change the channel back to the movie he was watching before I tuned into the draft. It is the Kurt Russell vehicle *Breakdown*, in which the hero's SUV craps out in the desert, resulting in his wife's being kidnapped by murderous rednecks. Devin and I spend the next hour switching between the movie *Breakdown* and the looming breakdown of Robin Quinn.

With the 17th pick, the Broncos take Jarvis Moss, last seen swabbing the turf at the University of Phoenix Stadium with poor Troy Smith, who won't be picked until tomorrow, in the fifth round, by the Baltimore Ravens.

Kurt almost gets his ass kicked in a diner, then strikes up a conversation with the village idiot, who tells him, yeah, his wife was in the café not long before. This is getting sinister.

It isn't looking so hot for Quinn, either. Every time Goodell reads someone else's name, I will later calculate, Quinn is out another $925K. The question of the day becomes: Will Quinn be drafted before Kurt Russell finds his wife?

The Titans take Michael Griffin with the 19th pick: he is the dreadlocked Texas safety we met at the beginning of chapter 4. Incredibly, the New York Giants take Aaron Ross, the Longhorns corner, with the very next selection. A third Texas defensive back, Tarell Brown—the guy from chapter 4 with the gun in his lap in the backseat—will be taken in the fifth round, begging the question: How the hell did Texas end up with the nation's 99th-ranked pass defense?

This isn't good: Russell just got ambushed by a bad man in a beefy pickup who is now in high-speed pursuit of our protagonist, who has no choice but to drive his Grand Cherokee into a river. While the pickup driver tries to shoot him, Russell floats downstream, out of harm's way . . . for now.

The Jaguars take Reggie Nelson, the Gators safety, with the 21st pick. In all, nine Florida players will be drafted. Not among their number: Chris Leak, who will sign a free agent contract with the Chicago Bears. Seven other Gators sign free agent deals, which means 17 players from the 2006 national champs will be in NFL camps this summer. Helluva job, Ron Zook.

Oh, great. Kurt Russell is spying on the bad guys from behind when the village idiot sneaks up on him and knocks him out with a wrench. I hate when that happens.

We've got some action in New York. With only a minute left to make up their minds, the Cowboys have traded the 22nd pick to the Cleveland Browns, who use it—*finally*—to select Quinn. Our long national nightmare is over.

Striding into camera range, pulling a Browns cap onto his head, then posing for pictures with Goodell, he looks pissed, relieved, excited. It's reported afterward that his freefall from the Top 5 to No. 22 cost him an estimated $17 million in guaranteed money. At No. 22, he's likely to sign a six-year deal in the neighborhood of $30 million, with $10 million guaranteed.

Kurt Russell locates his wife (Kathleen Quinlan, in a small but meaty role), and, like his namesake JaMarcus Russell, proceeds to California.

MY LAST CONVERSATION with Brady Quinn took place two months earlier, at the NFL Combine—so named, I suspect, because it combines elements of a beauty pageant, livestock auction, and Guantanamo-style interrogation session. NFL wannabes dressed in NFL-issue gray sweatshirts bearing their league-assigned four-character code—Buckeyes wide out Anthony Gonzalez, for instance, is W016—are put through a series of physical and "psychological" tests. Grim-faced security personnel pepper them with such probing questions as "Have you ever smoked marijuana?"

The appropriate answer is something along the lines of "Very rarely. Probably fewer times than you've had sex without having to pay for it." But the guys don't want to screw up their draft prospects. And the gumshoes tell them, "If you lie to us, we'll find out." So, a lot of them spill.

The interrogations are videotaped and available to any team that cares to review them. The players are assured their answers will remain confidential. It's bullshit. Three players who admitted having experimented with marijuana were identified in *Pro Football Weekly* shortly before the draft. Goodell later apologized to the players. As he should have.

The squeaky-clean Quinn is not among the admitted dopers. After acing a Q&A with reporters on the afternoon of February 23, he was led out of a pressroom that is too small to contain the Combine's 300-plus accredited journalists. "We've outgrown this room," noted Nancy Gay, who covers the league for the *SF Chronicle*. "They're letting everyone but ham radio operators in here."

When I caught up with Quinn, he was standing in one of the Indianapolis Convention Center's many auxiliary rooms, peeling off a Reebok jersey. (Eat your heart out, Boi from Troy.) He'd been deposed in the NFL Network's *Total Access* room.

There, with the Network cameras rolling, a freelance producer named T-L Fiedler (that's how she spells it) peppered athletes with a battery of questions: "Who are you off the field?" and "Where do you find your strength?"

Toward the end of the session, players were invited to express themselves however they chose—by speaking to the camera, cracking jokes, dancing.

"I'm not dancing," Quinn firmly declared.

He told me he'd been up since four-forty that morning. He wanted to be one of the first guys to submit his urine sample. On the advice of his agent, he would perform none of the physical tests. (He would put on a show at Notre Dame's "pro day," on

March 4.) Except one. What the hell was the point of lifting as many weights as he has over the last four years if he wasn't going to do the Combine bench press? So Quinn walked in and put up 225 pounds 24 times, a record for quarterbacks, and—read into this what you will—more than Ryan Harris and Dan Santucci, two of his offensive linemen.

I attempted once again to draw him out on the subject of the talent around him. It seemed to me that Notre Dame had fewer elite athletes than Michigan, USC, or LSU.

"You'll never hear me saying something like that," he assured me. "I mean, there's no question we were up and down the whole season. But somehow we *just* managed to find a way to get into a BCS game."

They got there, and got spanked, which meant that he'd finished his college career without beating USC or winning a bowl game. When you set goals and fall short of them, I asked, what then?

"You gotta be tough about it," he told me while pulling on his mandatory gray sweatshirt. "Use it as motivation. You take that loss, put a chip on your shoulder, and you run with it." He'd have one more disappointment to use as fuel before it was time to play football again.

I shook his hand, thanked him for his time, told him it was a pleasure covering him.

"No," he said. "Thank *you*."

Too bad they don't test for manners at the Combine.


NOT THAT HE'S perfect. Quinn reportedly dropped an uncharacteristic F-bomb on the bench press, after failing to put up his 25th repetition. That paled in comparison to the strong language to which I was subjected at a USC team meeting a fortnight earlier.

The Trojans had been summoned to Heritage Hall to have a fire lit under them. Once a year, shortly after National Letter of Intent day, Carroll subjects the squad to a reel of highlights—the epic feats of the incoming freshmen. While relatively small—the Trojans signed 17 players—USC's 2007 recruiting class is unmatched in quality. The Trojans reeled in the nation's top-ranked defensive end, wide receiver, linebacker, and, in running back Joe McKnight, its top player, period. As it is every year, the message at this meeting was crystalline: *Take a good look, because these are the guys who are coming in here to try and take your jobs.*

Before giving that speech this year, Carroll lectured the squad about schoolwork. "I wanna make sure we're diggin' in and getting this stuff done. We can't have guys slapdick around and fall out of the program because you're not taking care of business.

"We have all the help we can possibly gather for you, so let's not screw this thing up. We need everybody. Every single guy needs to be there. All of you.

"You must do well academically, or you don't get to play. You *don't get to f____g play.*" He called out a junior whose classroom woes forced him to miss the 2006 season. "He missed the whole season because he couldn't pass six frikkin' units in a semester. And he's still fighting his ass off to get back." Looking directly at the squirming subject of his rant, Carroll commanded him to "Get your ass back on this football team, man. You need to be here, and do your work."

Implicit in his words: If you can't hack it, we won't need to look far for someone who can. Depending on the recruiting service one consults, this latest Trojans bumper crop could be said to be the school's fifth straight top-ranked class. Carroll offered a nuanced explanation for that success. "We got a program that's frikkin' rippin', we got a university that's rippin', and people love to come here."

Time to check out the new guys. Carroll turned it over to Holt, who formally introduced the squad to Everson Griffen. Remember the name.

Griffen, a.k.a. Super Freak, a.k.a. Big E., a.k.a. E Train, hails from Avondale, Arizona. A source inside the program tells me Carroll's staff has never seen a more impressive highlight tape from a defensive end. Here was Nick Holt, describing him to his future teammates: "He is a great defensive end, a prospect at running back also. He's 6'3½", 262 pounds. At our camp, he ran 4.56." This is a lineman, ladies and gentleman. "He already benches 410, power cleans 360," concluded Holt, finally losing the battle to keep the excitement out of his voice. "The guy is a FRIKKIN' BEAST!"

Griffen's video highlights are a literal hit parade of mismatches. He is a helmeted Godzilla wreaking havoc on innocent teenagers. Now here he is on offense, taking a handoff, repelling would-be tacklers, a man among boys. "What's going to happen," Holt confided, "is that he's gonna play a little defense end, and then, when we need to get a first down, we're gonna put him at tailback."

A collective "OOOOooooh" filled the room.

A bit later, linebackers coach Ken Norton provided a play-by-play as Servite (California) High linebacker Chris Galippo brutalized a series of overmatched adolescents. "This is Linebacker University, right?" Norton asked. (It's actually Tailback U. Norton's point is that they're now so loaded at his position that a nickname change is in order.) "Every year we get a number one linebacker, and this year no different. Watch number nine right there. Can he run?" Galippo closes like a cheetah on a running back. "Can he hit?" Several clips answer the question definitively. "Get his ass down," Norton muttered to himself, savoring a punishing Galippo sack. "Can he shoot a gap?" He can.

Could he get on the field at USC, already loaded with future NFL players at linebacker?

As Galippo saw it, that was someone else's problem. Carroll's staff is drawn to athletes so supremely confident in their abilities that they don't really care who is already playing their position.

Consider the case of Broderick Green, the pride of Pulaski (Arkansas) Academy, and one of the nation's top-rated running backs. Trojans coaches told him they saw him as another LenDale White. To which Green replied, "I don't really want to hear that. I want to be *better* than LenDale White."

Narrating the cavalcade of Green highlights was running backs coach Todd McNair. "Linebackers, defensive backs, I hate to do this to you"—it's clear he delighted in it—"but this guy's 6'1", 230. We're talking *physical mismatch*." Onscreen Green annihilates a would-be tackler, eliciting another OOOOooooh from the crowd. "He is the reincarnation of LenDale. These are my type of guys."

When Green disappeared from the screen, the Trojans got an eyeful of five-star tailback Marc Tyler, son of ex-NFLer (and former UCLA Bruin) Wendell Tyler, who had also cast his lot to be a Trojan. Scintillating though both are, neither Tyler nor Green was the best high school back in the nation in 2006. That honor went to Joe McKnight, a 6'1", 200-pound package of dynamite snatched by 'SC from under the nose of LSU. McKnight, who runs a 4.3 forty, was recruited out of John Curtis High, just outside New Orleans, by Norton, who described "Sweet Joe" as "silky smooth, fast, and he can catch. He had 70-some touches [this season], and 30 of 'em went for touchdowns. I'll say that again." He did, and the information seemed no more credible the second time around.

"He compares favorably to—dare I say it?" Norton thought better of it. "I won't say it."

Then allow me. McKnight looked like the second coming of Reggie Bush. Which is precisely what USC will need to counteract the sanctions this program could incur, should any of the principals in the Bush scandal ever decide to testify before the NCAA.

The possibility of such a shit storm has lent momentum to rumors that Carroll might choose this off-season to return to the pro game and slay his NFL demons. After the Rose Bowl, he'd headed to Costa Rica for some body surfing and R and R. Hot on his trail was Dolphins owner Wayne Huizenga, who needed a head coach.

Sitting on the tarmac in Huizenga's jet, Carroll listened as the movie rental magnate made his pitch. Upon his return from Central America, Carroll was less resolute than he'd been in the past when called upon to deny his NFL interest. Even his vow to stay put—"I absolutely expect to be here"—left a smidgen of wiggle room.

In the end, the flirtation led to nothing. Carroll will be back at least one more season. Yes, the 2007 schedule is a bear, with dangerous road games at Nebraska, Notre Dame, Oregon, and Cal. But with the nation's deepest, most talented defense, with a seasoned, second-year quarterback handing off to the most ridiculously gifted group of tailbacks in the college game, the Trojans will be favored to win their third national title in five seasons.

If they can keep the fullback healthy.

WHO'S NO. 2 going into the 2007 season? Tim Tebow tore it up at Florida during spring football. Having said goodbye to Leak, the Freak is ready for his closeup. Bearing in mind the insane recruiting class Meyer summoned to Gainesville, it seems inevitable that Tebow will take a team to a national championship game. But with 17 players off last year's team now in NFL camps, common sense says it won't be this season.

Michigan's got Henne, Hart, and Mario Manningham coming back, and Jake Long, the Big Ten's best offensive linemen, to block for them. I wonder about Ron English's once-terrifying defense, which gave up 74 points and damn near a thousand yards in its last two games. It then bid adieu to four players—Leon Hall, Alan Branch, David Harris, and LaMarr Woodley—in the first 50 picks of the draft. Then again, this is Michigan. The Wolverines have stars we don't yet know about. And they've got the Buckeyes at home in 2007.

What of last year's No. 2 team? With a dozen starters departed, six from each side of the ball, Ohio State will take a step back. After three years of the electrifying Troy Smith at quarterback, the Buckeyes offense will become more conventional behind Todd Boeckman, a dropback quarterback in the Craig Krenzel mold. With Texas off the schedule, Ohio State has a much better chance of getting to its conference schedule undefeated. The Buckeyes' first two opponents? Youngstown State and Akron.

See you at the game, Bebe?

With its top teams getting punked in BCS bowls, the Big Ten found itself in a defensive posture in the off-season, answering charges that it is plodding, overrated, decreasingly relevant. Unable to resist joining the battle was none other Big Ten commissioner Jim Delany, who in February composed a splendidly passive-aggressive memo "to Fans of the Big 10 and College Football." In it, he heaped disingenuous praise on the SEC, all the while implying, as the wickedly funny Orson Swindle remarked in EveryDayShouldBeSaturday.com, that its players "can't read, and have to be told not to eat their mouthpieces, which are not in fact tasty gelatin candies."

Here is Delany, waxing insincere: "I love speed and the SEC has great speed, especially on the defensive line, but there are appropriate balances when mixing academics and athletics. . . . Not every athlete fits athletically, academically or socially at every university."

Before the commissioner pulls a muscle patting himself on the back, he may want to check out the Academic Progress Rating data released by the NCAA in May 2007. The APR is a tool for determining which of its member programs are lagging in graduation rates. As pointed out on sauriansagacity.blogspot.com, SEC football teams scored out higher than Big Ten teams.

As Swindle put it, for "the pope of the Big Ten Network to cry foul on a university's overcommitment to football in the name of Mammon stinks of eau d'hypocrite."

This sublime vitriol is nothing less than college football's staff of life. Midway through the 2006 season, I had lunch with Chris Huston, lord of the definitive HeismanPundit.com. (He does a masterful job of handicapping each year's race by applying his painstakingly researched "10 Heismandments." His preseason favorite going into 2007: John David Booty.)

In arguing against a playoff system, the Pundit made a provocative point. It's only appropriate that, alone among major sports, college football would employ an inexact and deeply flawed method of choosing its champion. "It's all mythological anyway," he said. "You finish number two and argue that you're actually No. 1.

"In all these debates about who's the best team, which is the fastest conference, the deepest conference, the toughest conference"—or, in Delany's case, the *dumbest* conference—"one thing remains constant. *Nothing is ever resolved.* It's like a never-ending constitutional convention.

"You can boil it all down to one word: arguing. It's the feeling of being screwed—that's what makes the college football world go round."

He is half-right. We are also sustained by the faith that better days await—that this gleaming batch of recruits signals a new dawn for the program; that the breaks, at long last, will stop beating the boys. There is always next year.

**FINAL AP RANKINGS:**
*1. Florida*
*2. Ohio State*
*3. LSU*
*4. USC*
*5. Boise State*
*6. Louisville*
*7. Wisconsin*
*8. Michigan*
*9. Auburn*
*10. West Virginia*

# 2007 Revisited: Upsets, Upstarts, and an Untidy Conclusion

This was the season in which "confusion"—if I may borrow from *Macbeth*—"made his masterpiece." And like *Macbeth*, it grabbed you from the get-go.

Thanks to Julian Rauch, who nailed the game-winning field goal, and to quarterback Armanti Edwards, a 19-year-old field general for whom Goliath had no answer. Merci beaucoup to you, Dexter Jackson, for the two touchdowns that landed you on the cover of *SI*, and to Corey Lynch, the four-year starter at free safety whose last-second heroics sealed the deal in Ann Arbor.

Thanks to all the giant-slaying Mountaineers from Appalachian State for bolstering the main argument of this book: that college football is our nation's most unpredictable, sublime pastime.

Early in the afternoon of September 1, 2007, I was driving up University Avenue in Berkeley. As I closed in on Memorial Stadium I began to notice them: orange-clad tourists who seemed out of place in this ultra-liberal enclave known as Berserkley. The Tennessee Volunteers were in town to take on the Cal Bears. This tasty intersectional showdown was to be my first *SI* assignment of the new season.

My phone went off before I found parking. My editor, Mark Godich, said, simply, "Have you heard?" I had not heard. He told me to drive home and start working the phones.

App State had taken down the No. 5 Wolverines of Michigan, 34–32. It's difficult to capture the magnitude of that upset. The Mountaineers play in Division I-AA, where teams are allowed to give out 55 scholarships. Michigan, like all other D-I squads, fields 85 scholarship players—many of them four- and five-star recruits who could not have told you, going into the game, where Appalachian State was. (Neither, in fairness, could I have: It's in Boone, North Carolina.) The Mountaineers play in picturesque Kidd Brewer Stadium. The Rock, as it is known, seats 16,000 fans, less than a sixth of the number of souls who would stream into the Big House to see the Wolverines dispatch this overmatched, sacrificial lamb from the Southern Conference.

Sure, the Mountaineers were the defending I-AA national champs. But they'd be lining up against Michigan: tenants of the Big House, descendants of Bo, standard-bearers of the most distinctive design in sports: that bad-ass maize wing on their helmets. Since the AP expanded its rankings to 25 teams in 1989, no I-AA team had ever beaten a ranked I-A squad—let alone a Top 5 team and the winningest program in the history of the game.

"It's not like we haven't played in big games," head coach Jerry Moore told the Mountaineers on the eve of their trip to Ann Arbor, where they would be four-touchdown underdogs. "We just haven't played 'em in that type of arena. The only difference is, there's gonna be a lot more concrete."

To THE SURPRISE of exactly no one, Michigan marched crisply down the field on its opening drive, taking a 7–0 lead before the game was three minutes old. But Big Blue partisans where disquieted by what happened next. On the visitors' third play from scrimmage, App State came out with five wide receivers and an empty backfield. Jackson, the SoCon's reigning 200-meter sprint champion, took two steps, cut hard to his right, snared the pass from Edwards, and outran the Wolverines' secondary to the end zone. It was a 68-yard touchdown that the Wolverines found perplexing: How could one of their guys be faster than our guys?

Long a proponent of the Power-I, Moore junked that leather-bound attack in 2004, hitching his wagon to what he saw as football's future. He installed a spread offense and won the I-AA national title in 2005 and '06. Michigan defended the spread exactly how App State hoped it would. "They brought two safeties down, one on the right slot receiver, one on the left," recalled quarterbacks coach Scott Satterfield. When those receivers cleared out, "it left the middle wide open." Armanti Edwards's second touchdown pass, to Hans Batichon, exploited the same tendency.

A sophomore in his second season as a starter, Edwards had already earned a reputation for imperturbability. "Ice water in his veins," said Satterfield. Edwards was singularly unintimidated by the Wolverines. "We had nothing to be scared of," he told me late that night. "We had nothing to lose, they had everything to lose."

On second-and-eight from Michigan's 20-yard-line on his team's next possession, Edwards read the Wolverines' all-out blitz and calmly fired his third touchdown pass of the day. By this time it was obvious to everyone in the Big House—and to the hundred or so people following the game on the newly minted Big Ten Network—that the Wolverines had no answer for the spread. The visitors from Boone were pushing the No. 5 team in the nation all over the field.

The halftime score: 28–17. Satterfield described the intermission as "kind of surreal. Because, you know, they hadn't really slowed us down. We put up 28 points in the first half, *in the Big House*. I was thinking, how are we going to finish this up?"

With high drama, is how. Michigan awakened with a vengeance. Heisman candidate Mike Hart put his teammates on his shoulders, rushing for a pair of touchdowns: a prosaic four-yarder, followed by a mind-blowing 54-yard, against-the-grain masterpiece that put Michigan up, 32–31, with four and a half minutes to play.

Edwards was promptly intercepted, and the Big House crowd unclenched. Michigan would prevail, the plucky visitors would settle for a moral victory—along with a $400,000 check from the UM athletic department, App State's fee (such, at least, was the implicit understanding) for serving as an opening-week éclair. The college football universe would remain on its axis.

But Wolverine kicker Jason Gingell missed a 43-yard field goal.

Working with no timeouts, Edwards drove the Mountaineers 69 yards, to the Michigan six. Rauch made his kick, a 24-yarder with just under a minute left, putting App State back on top.

Mario Manningham, our old friend from chapter 6, manufactured more heroics, pulling down a desperate, 46-yard heave from Chad Henne with six seconds left. Gingell would have a shot at redemption.

Enter Lynch, the senior safety whose skills as a ballhawk—24 takeaways in 41 career games—carried over to special teams. It was Lynch who came slicing off the edge, blocking Gingell's kick, scooping it up without breaking stride, and returning it to the far 16 yard line, where he was dog-piled by ecstatic teammates. While a vast, mute crowd looked on, the Mountaineers posed for pictures on the block *M* at midfield. They carried Moore off the field on their shoulders. Junior cornerback Jerome Touchstone joined a conga line with the cheerleaders. Lynch stayed on his back "for a couple of minutes," partly because he wanted to bask in the moment and partly because his teammates had knocked the wind out of him. "When we get home tonight," the coach predicted, accurately, "it'll be like a volcano erupting in Boone."

The Mountaineers would enjoy the fuss for a day or so, he said, then buckle down: "We've got Lenoir-Rhyne coming into our place."

THUS DID APP State extinguish Michigan's national title hopes and hasten the end of an era: Head Coach Lloyd Carr announced his retirement after the regular season. Even as it set the tone for the wildest, least plausible, most upset-intensive season in memory, it set the table for a chaotic, messy, and ultimately unfulfilling resolution.

The Miracle at Michigan Stadium was followed by the Thrilla in Louisvilla: godawful Syracuse, a 36½-point underdog on the road against the 18th-ranked Louisville Cardinals, punked the home team, 38–35. It was Orangemen's first victory over a ranked team in four years.

Those unlikely outcomes proved a mere appetizer for the season's most unhinged weekend. On the 29th of September, five Top 10 teams went down in flames. Coming off a 2–10 season, trailing No. 3 Oklahoma by 17 in the fourth quarter, the Colorado Buffaloes ran off 20 unanswered points, stunning the Sooners. No. 4 Florida bowed to Auburn for the second straight season. No. 7 Texas was exposed by Kansas State, 41–21. Rude, buzz-killing Maryland brought tenth-ranked Rutgers, the darling of '06, back to earth—the second Big East upset in as many days. On Friday night, fifth-ranked West Virginia turned the ball over six times in an ugly, 21–13 loss to South Florida.

There was no great mystery behind the rash of giant-slayings. As Texas head coach Mack Brown told me before the K-State debacle, "We've been talking about parity for a long time"—since 1994, in fact, when the NCAA cut scholarship limits to 85, preventing football factories from bogarting all the talent—"and it's finally here."

Further "democratizing the region"—to borrow from our friends the neocons—was the spread offense, which allows teams rich in fleet skill guys to do just that: spread the field. If the favored team has a single weak link—a plodding linebacker, a gimpy corner, a coach slow on the uptake—that liability can be exploited. Ask Michigan. Jawdropping though it may have been, App State's win over the Wolverines was less outrageous than what went down in the L.A. Coliseum on October 6. Going into its game against second-ranked USC, the Stanford Cardinal looked like a team in extremis. It had lost three straight Pac-10 games by a score of 141–51. Six days before the 'SC game, Cardinal quarterback T. C. Ostrander suffered a seizure. He would be replaced by Tavita Pritchard, a sophomore better known for his family tree—he is the nephew of ex–Washington State star qb Jack "The Throwin' Samoan" Thompson—than his feats on the field. He'd completed one pass in his college career.

Feeding off the swagger and confidence of first-year head man Jim Harbaugh, the overmatched Cardinal hung tough against the

Trojans, trailing just 9–0 at halftime, despite being outgained 222 yards to 74. When Pritchard struggled, the defense picked him up. Strong safety Austin Yancy took a pick to the house, bringing the Cardinal within two. Stanford's dee sacked John David Booty four times. The senior suffered a broken middle finger late in the first half, after which he had no idea where the ball was going: He was intercepted four times on the day. Stanford held the Trojans to 95 rushing yards. (They'd come into the game averaging 223).

Pritchard came alive in the fourth quarter, leading the team to scores on its final three possessions. On fourth and forever with under two minutes left in the game, he looked to the sideline, where Harbaugh was shouting the play at him. Unable to hear the coach, "I called my own play," he recounted, and then found wide out Richard Sherman for a gain of 20 yards . . . and one inch. First down, Cardinal.

On fourth-and-goal from the 10, he looped a pass toward Mark Bradford, a senior from L.A. who'd missed significant practice time over the previous two weeks on account of the death of his father. Now, with a sweet outside move and a *teensy* push off the back of signed corner Mozique McCurtis, Bradford elevated to make the twisting, leaping catch that snapped the Trojans' 35-game Coliseum winning streak.

The result of all these upsets, of course, was a Top 25 that had the appearance of being composed by the late Timothy Leary. It was a brave new world of arrivistes (No. 5 South Florida, No. 15 Cincinnati, No. 16 Hawaii, No. 20 Kansas) and Rip Van Winkles—long-dormant programs that had not breathed this rarefied air in years, if not decades (No. 4 Boston College, No. 7 South Carolina, No. 11 Missouri, No. 18 Illinois).

As the Great Leveling went on, and midseason came and went, those paeans to the unpredictable charms of the college game gave way to fretful predictions from fans all over the country that their team would end up getting hosed. The ride only got bumpier over the season's final month:

Week 11: The Buckeyes, who'd taken over the top spot in a

quiet coup, are humbled in the Horseshoe by unranked Illinois. Juice Williams throws four TD passes, and the proud Buckeye defense can't get a stop to save its life. Williams, workhorse rusher Rashard Mendenhall & Co. compound the insult by holding the ball for the final 8:09 of the game, putting an exclamation point on a 28–21 victory.

Week 12: And now for something completely different: Undefeated Kansas dispatches pesky Iowa State, while Missouri holds off Kansas State in Manhattan, setting up that rarest of occurrences, a meaningful Border War. That's the nickname for the annual blood grudge between KU and Mizzou. In a fitting climax to a surreal regular season, Kansas enters the game ranked No. 2 in the BCS, Missouri No. 4.

Week 13: Fold that Tiger! LSU loses its second triple-overtime game of the season, this time at home to Arkansas. Darren McFadden gashes the Tigers for 206 yards and three touchdowns— D-Mac also threw a 24-yard scoring pass to Peyton Hillis. Arkansas's 50–48 victory, its first over a No. 1 team in 26 years, dashes the Tigers chances of returning to the national title game.

Doesn't it? I mean, it is LSU's second loss. No way they could make it now to the game known as the 'Ship. Right?

Week 14: No great surprise here. After dispatching the Jayhawks in the Border War and spending a heady week at No. 1, Mizzou loses to Oklahoma in the Big 12 title game. Rather more startling are the goings-on at the Backyard Brawl, as the ancient Pitt–West Virginia rivalry is known. The Mountaineers need only to dispatch the bumbling, 4–7 Panthers to advance to their first national title game in two decades. This being the '07 season, that proves too tall an order. Playing the spoiler with a vengeance, the Panthers hold Pat White, Steve Slaton, et al, to 183 yards—292 below their average. Standing at a lectern in the wake of that crippling, 13–9 loss, WVU head coach Rich Rodriguez appears ashen, shocked, *Spitzeresque* as he recounts the evening just passed: "A nightmare. Just a nightmare."

(Seeing an opportunity in the wake of West Virginia's crippling loss, Michigan athletic director Bill Martin swoops in, snagging Rodriquez to fill the vacancy left by Lloyd Carr.)

At which point, as we all know, resilient LSU righted its ship, knocking off Tennessee in the SEC title game. That win, coupled with the dual swoons of Mizzou and the Mountaineers, launched LSU's Bob Beamonesque leap from No. 7 to 1500 Poydras Street, a.k.a. the New Orleans Superdome, site of the BCS title game.

I've spent 300 pages celebrating this sport. Now, let me take it behind the woodshed.

FELICITATIONS TO THE Tigers, who, as we all know by now, steamrolled the Buffalo Bills—excuse me, Ohio State—38–24 in the BCS championship game, becoming the first two-loss team to win a national title. Salute head coach Les Miles for holding the team together during a tumultuous season (and a tense fortnight during which he was rumored to be Michigan-bound). Tip your cap to offensive MVP Matt Flynn, the blue-collar quarterback who tossed four touchdown passes, and whose final game as a Bayou Bengal was his finest.

But let's not pretend the process that got LSU to that game was rational or fair or anything other than a glorified game of rock, paper, scissors. Because in college football in the early part of the 21st century, that's how we roll.

Vying for the No. 2 slot, and the right to face the Buckeyes, were no fewer than seven squads with bona fide arguments. LSU, Oklahoma, and Virginia Tech had clinched their conference championship games. Georgia and USC were on fire. Kansas had but a single defeat; Hawaii none at all. The truth is, the 60 coaches in the *USA Today* poll and the 114 Harris poll voters who slotted LSU into the title game (with help from the system's six computers), were all asked to do the same thing: take a wild guess.

If ever a season screamed for the BCS to be blown up, it was this one. Yes, there have been plenty of deeply unfulfilling resolutions in the decade-long history of this Rube Goldberg contraption, none more absurd than the Gong Show that was 2007.

As I wrote in the wake of that train wreck, there is a way to determine a champion with a scaled-down playoff that doesn't devalue the regular season or kill off any of the 32 bowls filling the postseason landscape.

Standing in the way of progress, as one frustrated AD told me recently, holding an entire sport hostage, "is the Rose Bowl parade."

The guy is right. I talked to BCS coordinator Mike Slive, who didn't rule out the possibility of a "Plus-One"—a kind of modified, miniature compromise playoff—somewhere down the road. I talked to Ed Goren, president of Fox Sports. While describing himself as "thrilled" with Fox's deal to broadcast BCS bowl games through 2010, he didn't pretend there wouldn't be interest on his end if the BCS started talking about a "Plus-One."

Even such a modest tweak as a "Plus-One"—the top two ranked teams knocking heads after the conclusion of the five BCS bowls—is too radical and disturbing for the conferences I call the Axis of Obstruction. In separate interviews, Pac-10 commissioner Tom Hansen and his Big Ten counterpart, Jim Delany, told me basically not to hold my breath. Pointing out that their conferences already compromised once, back in 1998, when they joined the Bowl Alliance—later christened the BCS—Delany says, "We gave up a lot. I don't feel like we're takers. I feel like we're givers."

It is the rest of college football's problem that they are no longer in a giving mood. That nine-year-old decision to play ball with the Bowl Alliance "was not a first step toward a playoff," Delany emphasized, "but a last step."

Besides, Hansen points out, a Plus-One would require teams to be seeded, resulting in "conference champions being seeded out of their traditional bowls. And that would be very injurious to all those games."

So tied to tradition is the Rose Bowl that, having lost Ohio State to the title game, it invited 13th-ranked Illinois, the only three-loss team to get a BCS bid, to face USC. The result: an anti-climactic, 49–17 ass-whupping.

Surely the "granddaddy" of bowls can evolve, can join the 21st century, without doing itself irreparable harm? And there is much worth saving. Only an irredeemable cynic could dislike the 118-year-old Tournament of Roses Parade, with its bands, its floats, and its Rose Queen and her Royal Court. This pageant has held a special place in my heart since the 2002 Rose Bowl. A few nights before Miami met Nebraska for the national title, the Queen and her Court joined the Hurricanes at a restaurant called Lawry's The Prime Rib. I sat at a table where several "Princesses" were dining with most of Miami's offensive line. During the salad course, center Joel Rodriguez introduced Princess Rachel to one of his teammates. "He's 305 pounds, 22 years old, and a virgin," said Rodriguez. Things went downhill from there. Fellow center Brett Romberg pointed out, for the Princesses' benefit, Rodriguez's "brutal teeth." Tackle Bryant McKinnie seemed unsure of how to defend himself when teammates made sport of his colossal skull, which, though beach-ball-sized, did seem to be in proportion with his 6'9", 336-pound body.

Returning to the subject of our FUBAR BCS system, Nebraska had no business in that game, having had its clock cleaned by Colorado, 62–36, the day after Thanksgiving.

I'd just returned from Lincoln, having reported a cover story on quarterback Eric Crouch, who won the Heisman that season. On account of the holiday, most *SI* subscribers got their issue on Friday. The cover posed this question: "Who Is Eric Crouch?"

For millions of ABC-viewing Americans the day after Thanksgiving, that was an easy one: Eric Crouch was the kid getting his head handed to him on national TV—the kid whose mother was crying in the stands. (Whoever was producing the game for ABC couldn't get enough of poor Susan.) Despite that embarrassment—the 14th-ranked Buffs piled up 582 yards of total offense!—the Cornhuskers backed into the title game (thanks, BCS computers!), where Miami spanked them early and often, cruising to a drama-free 37–14 victory. BCS apologists like to pretend their machine can be counted on, most years, to deliver a clean, uncontroversial 1 vs. 2 matchup. The system we have, truth be told, is a blind pig that sometimes finds an acorn.

Speaking of hogs, my boys McKinnie, Romberg, Rodriguez, et al, played lights out in that Rose Bowl. And the Rose Queen and her court looked beautiful in the parade. Despite its many short-comings, college football will always bewitch us. Even as we second-guess and ridicule and bellyache, we cannot look away.

# Top-Ten Lists

## GREATEST RIVALRIES

10   Kansas–Missouri

9   Army–Navy

8   Cal–Stanford

7   Harvard–Yale

6   Miami–Florida State

5   Florida–Georgia

4   Auburn–Alabama

3   Notre Dame–USC

2   Oklahoma–Texas

1   Michigan–Ohio State

## BEST TRADITIONS

10   Georgia Tech's Ramblin' Wreck: a restored 1930 Ford Cabriolet Sport Coupe that leads the team onto the field.

9   Ohio State's custom of allowing a senior sousaphonist to dot the *i* in the band's "script" Ohio before each home game.

8   Wisconsin fans rock out to House of Pain's "Jump Around" before the fourth quarter. The song was briefly banned by the athletic department—some older spectators were unnerved by the swaying of the bleachers—but quickly reinstated when students threatened to revolt

7   Touching Howard's Rock, Clemson: Before each game, Tigers rub the "rock," then run down the hill to the east end zone while the crowd goes bananas.

6   Painting helmets, Notre Dame: Student volunteers apply a fresh coat of gold paint (containing flakes of real gold) to Domer helmets.

5   Tailgating at The Grove, Ole Miss: Southern belles in cock-

tail dresses, gentlemen in coats and ties, sipping adult beverages, partaking of food served on fine china. If there were AP rankings for pregame festivities, the Rebels would never leave the Top 5.

4    March of the Cadets/Midshipmen: The sight of Navy's Brigade of Midshipmen and Army's Corps of Cadets filing into the stadium before the Army–Navy game remains one of the most inspiring in sports.

3    Flight of the eagle, Auburn: "Nova" (a.k.a. War Eagle VII) circles the stadium as the crowd intones "Wa-a-a-a-a-r," then, as the raptor pounces at midfield, "EAGLE!" In a word: awesome.

2    LSU's Tiger: On game days at LSU, opposing players must pass an actual caged tiger (these days it's a Bengal–Siberian mix named Mike VI) to reach the visitors' locker room.

1    Midnight Yell Practice at Texas A&M: Just what it sounds like. On the eve of home games, uniformed yell leaders tell some fables and coach the crowd on what to shout and when. When the lights go off, Aggies "mug down"—that is, enjoy a prolonged clinch with their dates.

### BEST MASCOTS (HUMAN DIVISION)

5    Masked Rider, Texas Tech

4    Chief Osceola (the guy who hurls a flaming spear into the turf before Florida State home games)

3    Sebastian the Ibis, Miami (Rates mention for once attempting to extinguish Chief Osceola's spear with a fire extinguisher. He was instead roughed up by Florida state troopers.)

2    Bucky Badger, Wisconsin (While being cited for crowd surfing, he was asked by the booking officer to spell his name. "Badger," he began. "B-A-D-G . . .")

1    The Leprechaun, Notre Dame. (Detained by police at Michigan State after a crowd-surfing session, Leprechaun Kevin

Braun could not produce an ID. "My knickers don't have any pockets," he explained.)

## BEST MASCOTS (ANIMAL DIVISION)

5    Bevo the longhorn (Texas)
4    Traveler the white stallion (USC)
3    Smokey (Tennessee's bluetick hound)
2    Uga the bulldog (Georgia)
1    Ralphie the buffalo (Colorado)

## TOP PLAYS

10   **Honest Mistake:** Roy "Wrong Way" Riegels of Cal scoops up a Georgia Tech fumble in the 1929 Rose Bowl—so far, so good—but loses his bearings, returning it 69 yards in the wrong direction. A teammate runs him down at his own three yard line. Tech scores on an ensuing safety and wins 8–7.

9    **The Bush Push:** Disobeying his head coach, USC Matt Leinart sneaks two yards for the winning touchdown on the final play against Notre Dame in 2005. Replays show that Leinart was aided by a well-timed (if illegal) shove from tailback Reggie Bush.

8    **The Exclamation Point:** Nebraska quarterback Tommie Frazier's 75-yard touchdown run on a qb draw against Florida in the '96 Fiesta Bowl epitomizes the dominance of one of the best teams, ever.

7    **The Return:** LSU's 18-game winning streak is in danger until Billy Cannon takes an Ole Miss punt up the sideline, in the process sewing up the 1959 Heisman Trophy.

6    **The Coup de Grâce:** Against USC in the 2006 Rose Bowl, on his final play as a collegian, Vince Young breaks a tackle and high-steps eight yards for the touchdown that clinches Texas's first national title in 35 years.

5    **The Play, 2007:** Division III Trinity beats Millsaps as Riley Curry scores on a 15-lateral play with no time left on the

clock. (Tigers coach Steve Mohr confesses afterward, "We couldn't do that against air if we tried.")

4    **Statue of Liberty:** Going for two in OT against Oklahoma in the 2007 Fiesta Bowl, Boise State quarterback Jared Zabransky fakes a throw to the right while slipping the ball with his left hand to running back Ian Johnson, whose dash through the left corner of the end zone clinches the upset of the season.

3    **Hail Mary I:** Kordell Stewart's 64-yard desperation heave to Michael Westbrook (with a helpful tip from Blake Anderson) delivers Colorado a stunning, 27–26 win over No. 4 Michigan in 1994.

2    **Hail Mary II:** In the final seconds against defending national champion Miami in 1984, Boston College quarterback Doug Flutie eludes a sack, scrambles right, and uncorks a pass that travels 70 yards in the air, over a trio of defenders, and into the arms of Eagles wide out Gerard Phelan. BC 47, Miami, 45.

1    **The Play, 1982:** In a surreal ending to the Big Game, Cal completes five laterals and Kevin Moen weaves through the Stanford Band to score the winning touchdown (pretzeling, in the process, one perfectly good trombone, which now rests in the College Football Hall of Fame.)

## BEST GAMES

10    **USC 34, Notre Dame 31, 2005:** The Bush Push was preceded by a pair of similarly incredible plays. Earlier in the drive, Leinart audibled on fourth-and-nine, dropping back and feathering a pass to receiver Dwayne Jarrett for a 61-yard gain. Three plays later Leinart kept the ball and got his bell rung, fumbling out of bounds in the process. Time ran down, Notre Dame students rushed the field . . . only to be told there were still seven seconds to play—time enough for the Bush Push.

9    **Appalachian State 34, Michigan 32, 2007:** Who put the wasabi in the Wolverines' cupcake? For long stretches, the

team with 55 scholarship players ran circles around the guys representing the winningest program in the history of college football. Flummoxed by sophomore quarterback Armanti Edwards and App State's spread offense, Michigan yielded 21 unanswered points to trail at halftime, 28–17. Three App State turnovers gave the Wolverines a late fourth quarter lead, but the nation's No. 5 team couldn't hold it. The game ended with a blocked Michigan field goal and a very quiet Big House.

8   **Ohio State 31, Miami 24, 2003 BCS Title Game:** Craig Krenzel's fourth down pass to Chris Gamble fell incomplete, ending the game and triggering a spectacular display of fireworks . . . and one yellow flag. Pass interference on Miami. Game back on. The Buckeyes won, 31–24, the winning TD scored by star-crossed freshman running back Maurice Clarett.

7   **Boise State 43, Oklahoma 42, 2007 Fiesta Bowl:** After dominating early, the Broncos watched the Sooners storm back. Trailing 35–28 with 17 seconds left, facing fourth-and-18 at midfield, Boise State executed a hook-and-lateral play that went for touchdown. They scored in overtime on a half-back pass (from Vinny Perretta, who hadn't thrown a pass all season), then won the game with that Statue of Liberty.

6   **Alabama 14, Penn State 7, 1979 Sugar Bowl:** On fourth-and-goal from the one-foot line, Nittany Lions running back Mike Guman went airborne—and was met head-on by Alabama linebacker Barry Krauss, who knocked himself unconscious with the hit. Guman lost ground, the top-ranked Nittany Lions lost for the first time in 20 games, and Bear Bryant won his fifth national championship.

5   **Penn State 10, Miami 14, 1987 Fiesta Bowl:** The 'Canes came into the game with a Heisman-winning quarterback, Vinny Testaverde, and roughly half of an NFL roster. They were that good—but not on this night. In a game in which the Nittany Lions' most valuable offensive player was, arguably, punter John Bruno, Testaverde was brutal, throwing

five interceptions, the last of those to Penn State linebacker Pete Giftopoulos, whose pick sealed the upset.

4 **Miami 31, Nebraska, 30, 1984 Orange Bowl:** A last-minute Cornhusker touchdown whittled Miami's lead to a single point. Turning his nose up at the tie, Cornhuskers coach Tom Osborne called for a two-point conversion. Turner Gill's pass was tipped away by safety Ken Calhoun. Osborne would not win a national title for another 11 years . . . in the Orange Bowl, against Miami.

3 **Notre Dame 24, Alabama 23, 1973 Sugar Bowl:** After no fewer than six lead changes, the top-ranked Crimson Tide were trailing No. 3 Notre Dame by a point but had the Irish bottled up on their own one yard line. On third-and-nine, with 2:12 to play, Tom Clements dropped deep into his own end zone and completed a 36-yard pass to back up tight end Robin Weber, who made just his second catch of the season. The Irish hung on and won 24–23, their first national title in seven years. Bryant, who would go 0–4 against Notre Dame, offered to play them the next day.

2 **Texas 15, Arkansas 14, 1969:** With Richard Nixon in the house at Razorback Stadium for the century's first (but not last) Game of the Century, Texas head coach Darrell Royal gambled twice, going for a two-point conversion after the 'Horns first TD, then calling a pass on fourth-and-three late in the game. James Street's perfect throw to tight end Randy Peschel picked up 46 yards. Texas scored the game-winning touchdown two plays later. The Longhorns waited 35 years for their next national title.

1 **Texas 41, USC 38, 2006 BCS Championship Game:** Fielding one of the best college offenses ever was not enough for the Trojans, who had no answer to Vince Young. The long-limbed Longhorn qb threw for 267 yards and rushed for 200 yards and three TDs, including the game-winner, with 19 seconds left. Thus were Leinart, Bush & Co. prevented from winning a third straight national title.

# Acknowledgments

First of all, thanks to my strong spouse, Laura Hilgers, who picked up all that domestic slack I left during the writing of this book. Let's reinstate Date Night. Thanks to Jennifer Barth, a patient, virtuoso editor with whom it was my privilege to work. (Keeping it in the family, I am grateful to her son, Simon Panitz, a hawkeyed twelve-year-old college football fiend who snagged more mistakes than I care to admit.) And I am indebted, as ever, to David Black: gentleman, scholar, mentor, bulldog.

To Terry McDonell, David Bauer, Mark Godich, and Mark Beech at *Sports Illustrated*, thanks for the time off, the support, and—Beecher—the crack reporting.

Likewise, thanks to Pete Carroll, who always made time; to Lane Kiffin, Steve Sarkisian, and everyone else on the Trojans staff, particularly Dennis Slutak, logistician extraordinaire; and the redoubtable Sam Anno (When are we going to have that root beer?).

Tim Tessalone, Paul Goldberg, and Jason Pommier in the USC sports information office, thank you for all the interviews arranged and background provided; and for never cringing at the sight of me, at least not to my face. Thanks to all the Trojans beat writers, especially Dan Weber, who was as generous as he was insightful.

Huge thanks to Steve McClain and Zack Higbee at Florida, who go much further beyond the call of duty than I ever have; as do John Bianco, Scott McConnell, and Jeremy Sharpe at Texas; Marc Dellins at UCLA; and Kirk Sampson at Auburn. I owe you all adult beverages.

To Brian Hardin and John Heisler at Notre Dame, thank you for enduring me throughout the course of the season. Chapeau, also, to Tim Prister, Vaughn McClure, Michael Rothstein, and everyone on the Irish beat who made me feel welcomed in South

Bend. Special thanks to my old friend John Walters, whose V02 max and wit leave me gasping.

To South Bend mayor Steve Luecke and double Domer Dick Nussbaum: let's do it again sometime. After we've all had lessons.

To Gordon Wright, teammate and self-esteem cop, let's hit the mountain, soon. And a shout-out to Kaitlin Shorrock, Notre Dame '07, ex–Sleepy Hollow Sea Lion star and mayorlike residential adviser of Pasquerilla East, for turning me on to Drum Circle, and helping me get to know your awesome family a little better.

Thanks to Dave Widell and Jeff Novak, who spin yarns as well as (better than?) they patrolled the line in Jax. Thanks to the luminous Lori Nelson; to Chester Caddas, a wise man who speaks in anecdote; and to Dr. Glen Albaugh. Salutations also to Sam Farmer of the *L.A. Times*, an all-time great guy with bottomless supply of funny stories (ask him about pickup hoops with O.J.).

I am indebted to the Reverend Angela Kaufman at TCU, where I was fortunate to meet Scott Kull and Rudy Klancnik. Men, it was my privilege to roll with you. (Thanks also to the waitress who hooked us up, even though it was past last call.)

HeismanPundit, I salute you.

To the giant and giant-hearted David Baker; to Robin and Ty Quinn, and to Lou Holtz: thanks for your time, and your superb senses of humor.

To Lou Masucci, my Westerly, Rhode Island–based Notre Dame stringer, thanks for your efforts. Feel free to invoice my father.

To Ryan Powdrell, good luck with the Packers, my friend. May you have a long, prosperous NFL career. And to his fellow fullback Brandon Hancock: for your patient explanations, of both the fullback's role in the offense and your sundry medical procedures. If you've got any leftover Vicodins, send them to me and I'll see that they're properly disposed of.

And a big thank-you to the crew at the Red Hill Peet's in San Anselmo, for not judging me when my hygiene suffered as the deadline for this book approached. Keep up the excellent work— Austin (medium cappuccino, low-fat, semi-dry).